Gunnerkrigg Court

Research

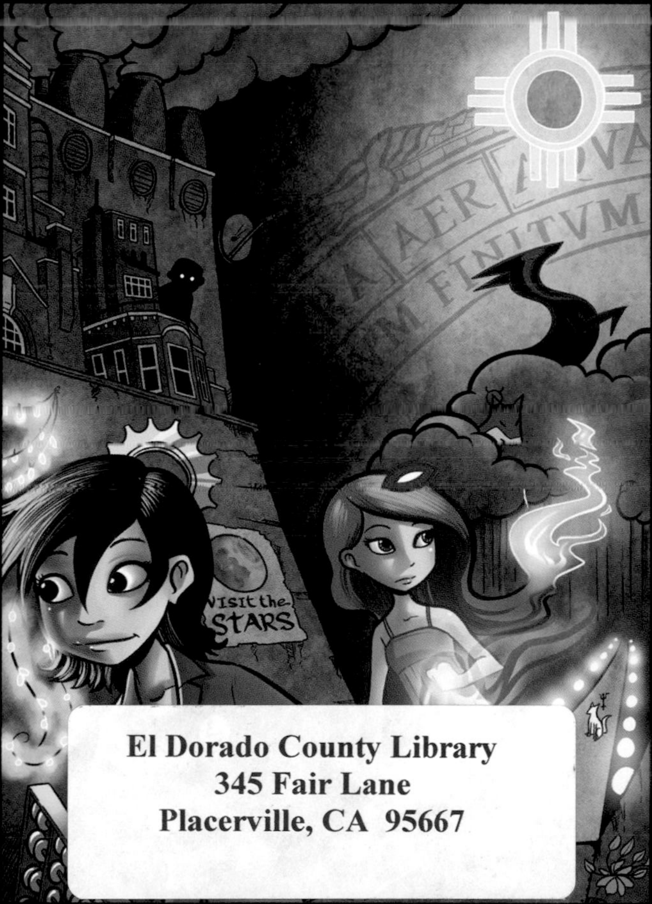
AER
FINITVM
VISIT the
STARS

by Tom Siddell

ARCHAIA™

Gunnerkrigg Court: Research Vol. 2

Written & Illustrated by
Tom Siddell

For this edition
Book Design & Layout by Tom Siddell & Scott Newman

Published by Archaia

PJ Bickett, *President*
Mark Smylie, *Publisher*
Stephen Christy III, *Director of Development*
Kraig Thompson, *Director of Sales*
Paul Morrissey, *Editor*
Mel Caylo, *Marketing Manager*
Scott Newman, *Production Manager*
Danielle Bonadona, Munika S. Lay, Loren Morgenstern
& Jeff Prezenkowski, *Interns*

Archaia Entertainment, LLC
1680 Vine Street, Suite 912
Los Angeles, California, 90028, USA
www.Archaia.com

GUNNERKRIGG COURT: RESEARCH VOL. 2
December 2009
FIRST PRINTING
10 9 8 7 6 5 4 3 2 1
ISBN: 978-1-932386-77-6

Printed in China.

Gunnerkrigg Court

Research

Gunnerkrigg Court

Chapter 15:

Red Returns

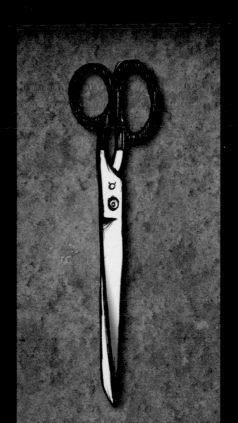

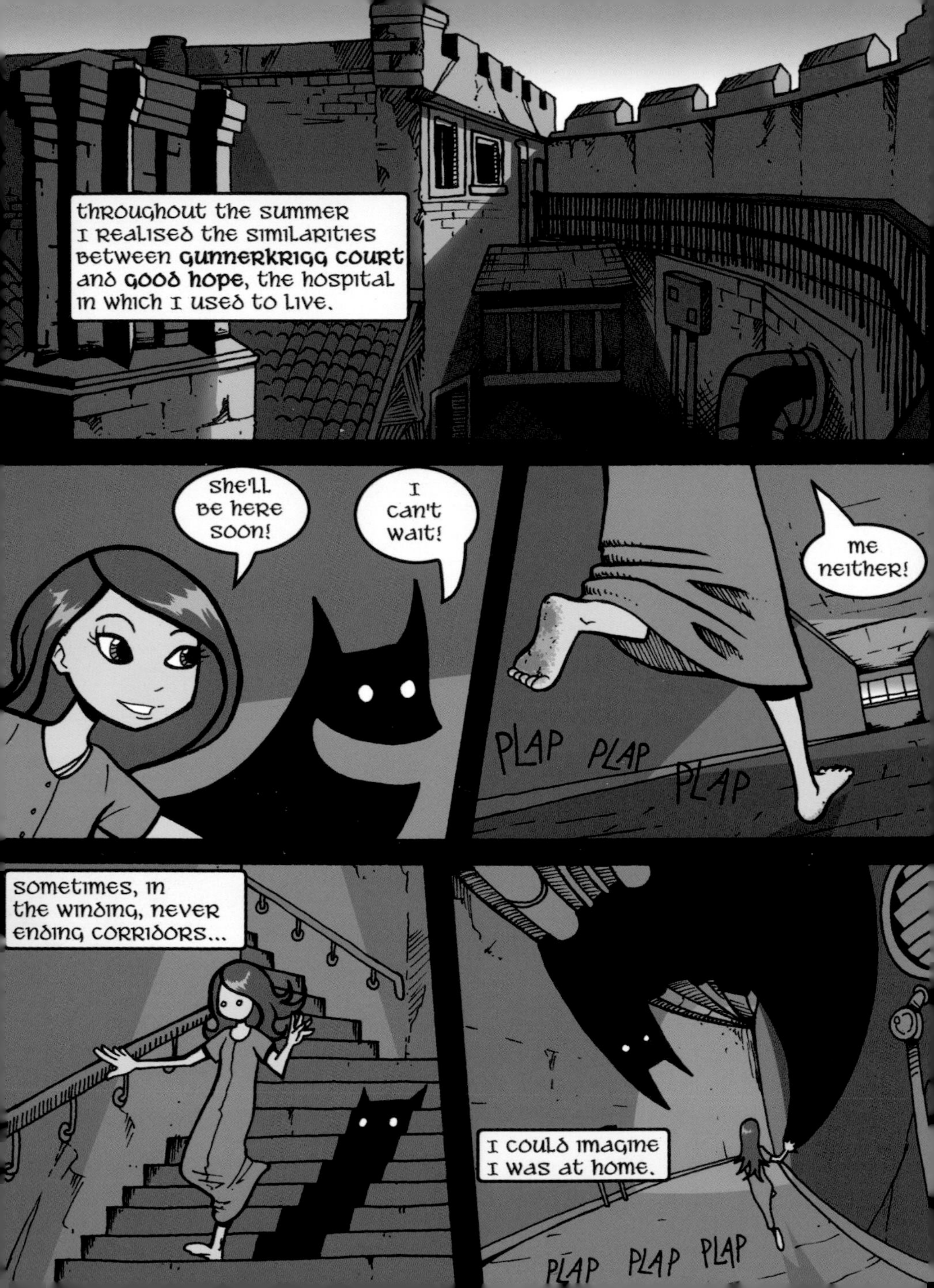
throughout the summer I realised the similarities between **gunnerkrigg court** and **good hope**, the hospital in which I used to live.
she'll be here soon!
I can't wait!
me neither!
PLAP PLAP PLAP
sometimes, in the winding, never ending corridors...
I could imagine I was at home.
PLAP PLAP PLAP

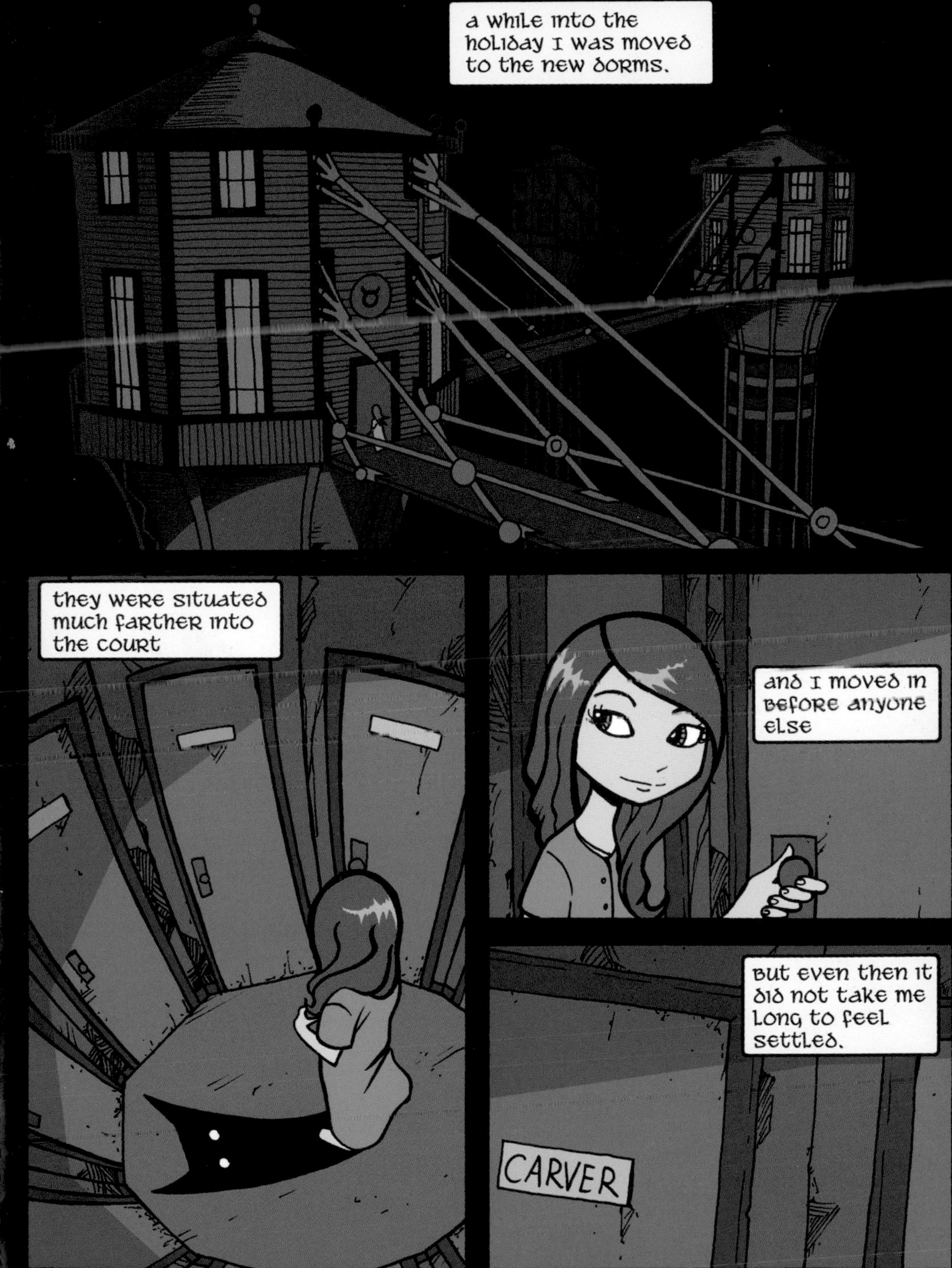
a while into the holiday I was moved to the new dorms.
they were situated much farther into the court
and I moved in before anyone else
but even then it did not take me long to feel settled.
CARVER

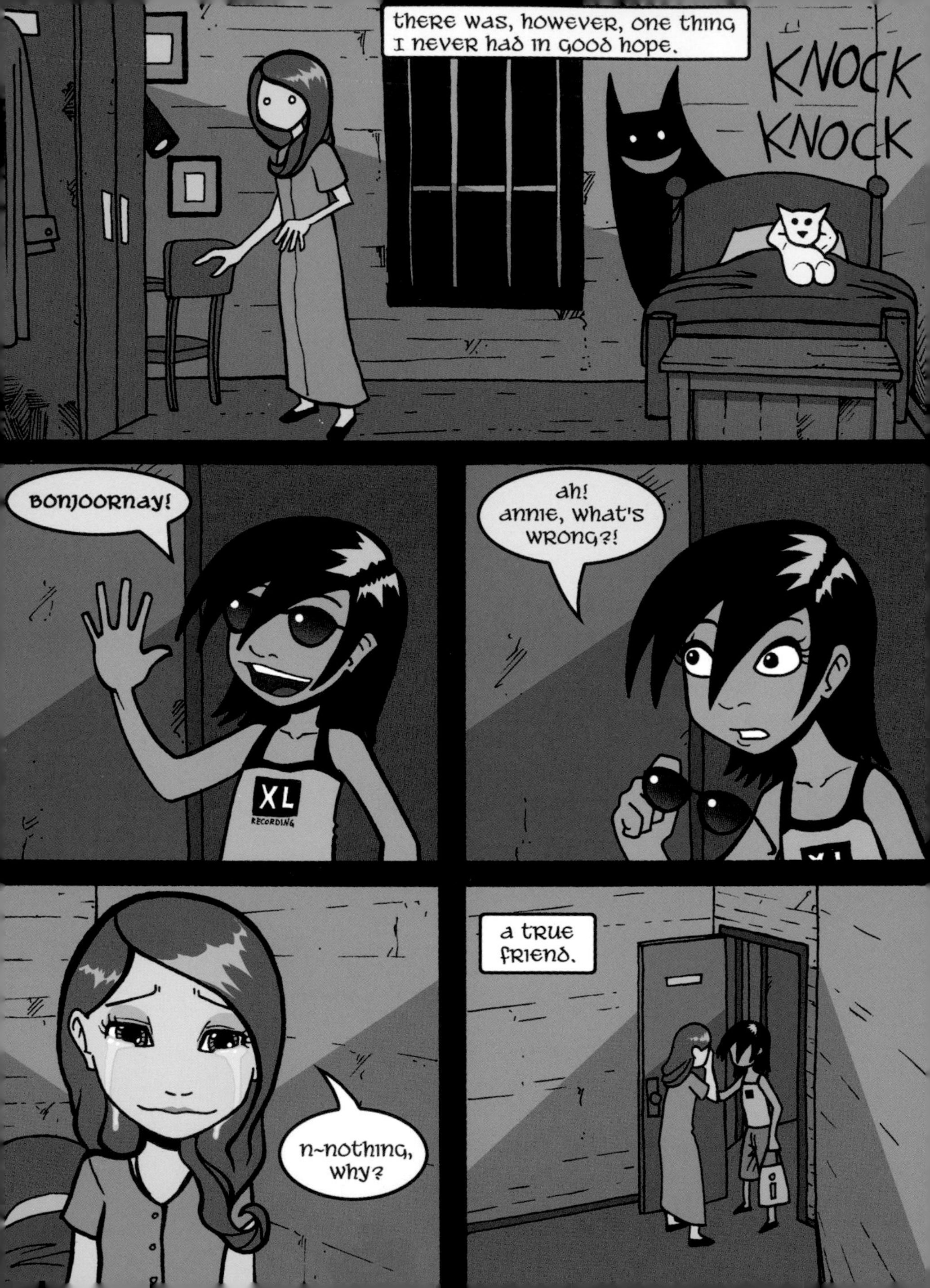
there was, however, one thing I never had in good hope.
KNOCK KNOCK
BONJOORNAY!
ah! annie, what's wrong?!
XL RECORDING
n~nothing, why?
a true friend.

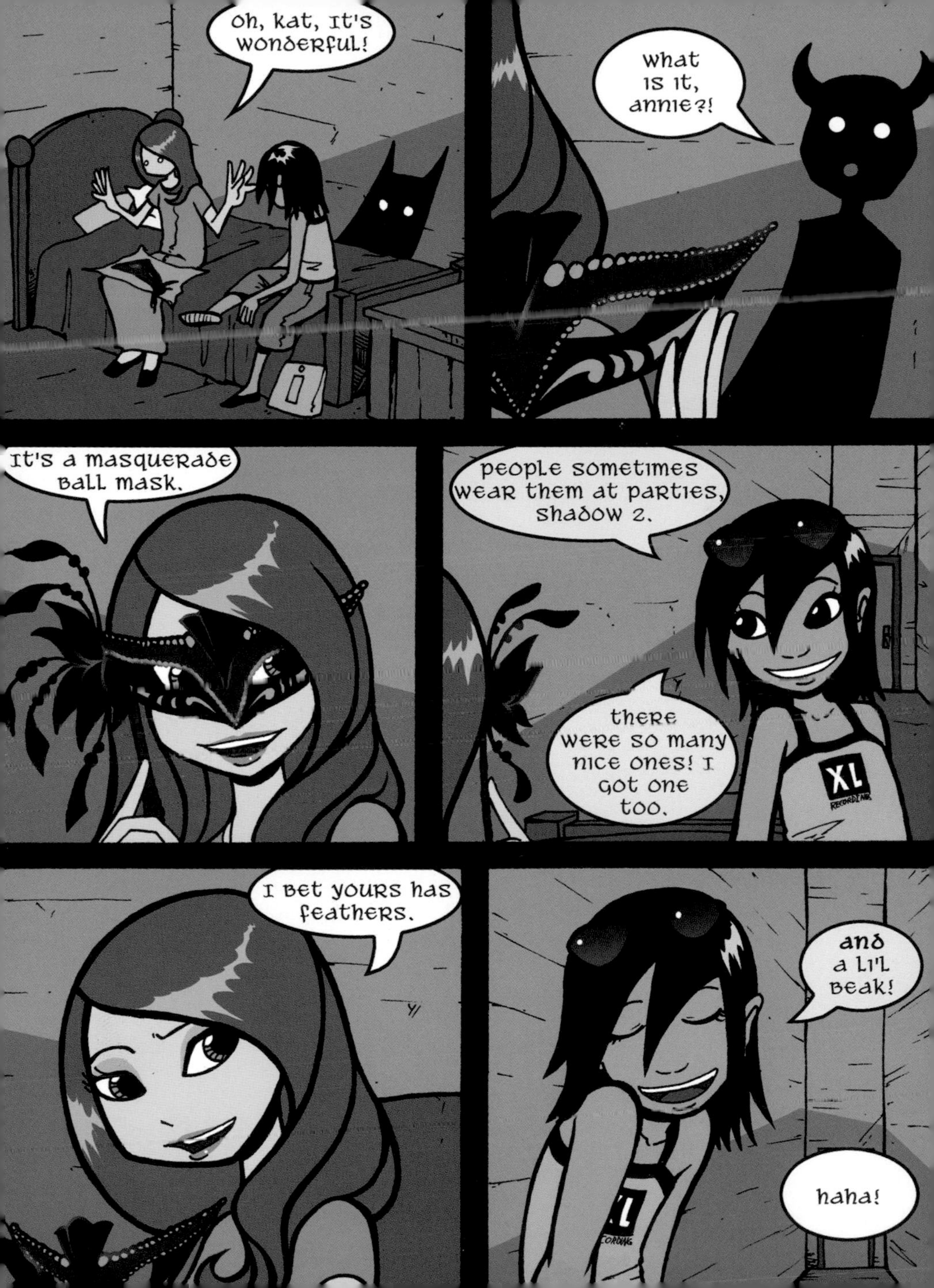
Oh, Kat, It's wonderful!
What is it, Annie?!
It's a masquerade ball mask.
People sometimes wear them at parties, Shadow 2.
There were so many nice ones! I got one too.
XL
I bet yours has feathers.
And a li'l beak!
haha!
XL

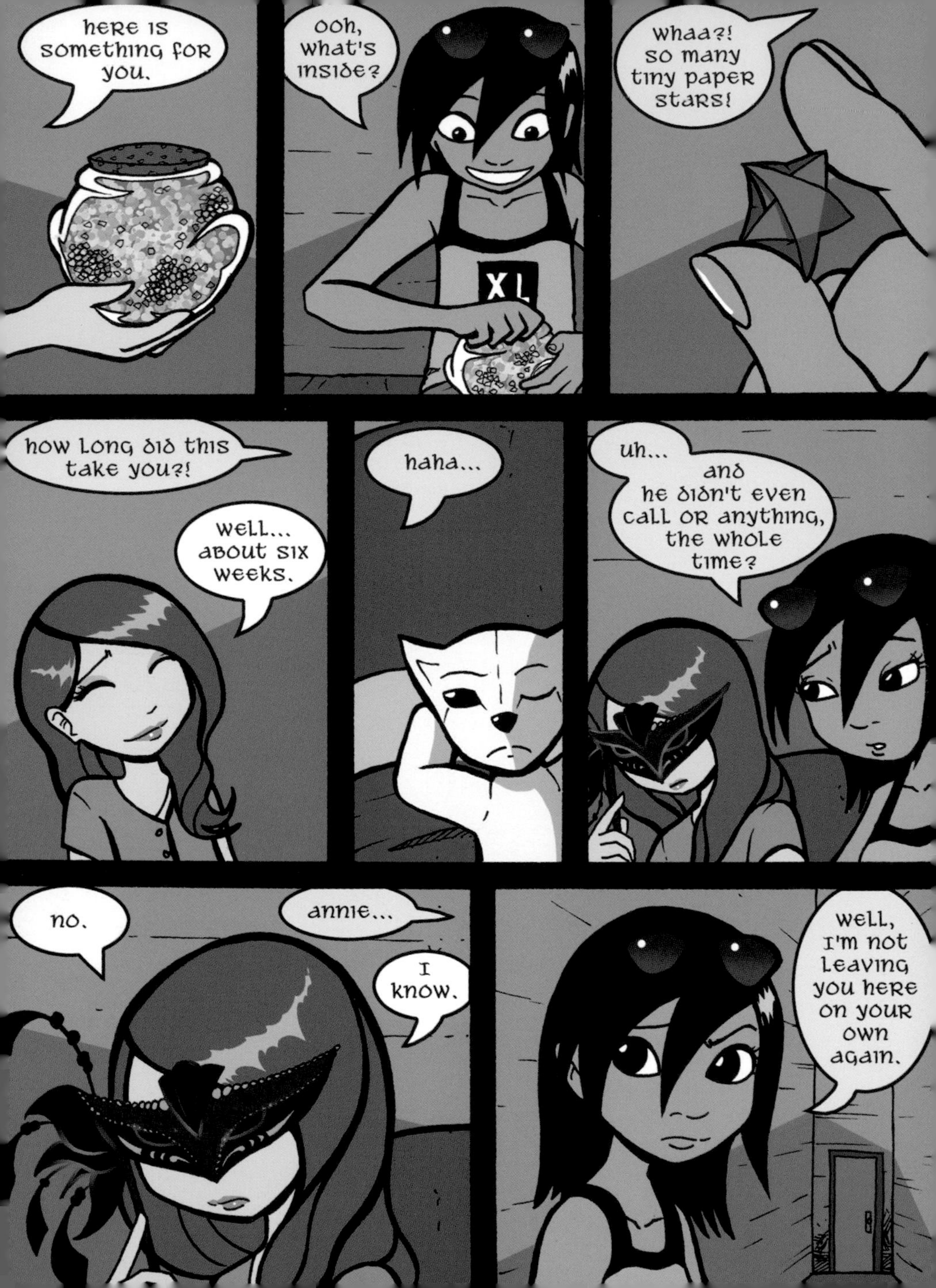
here is something for you.
ooh, what's inside?
Whaa?! so many tiny paper stars!
how long did this take you?!
well... about six weeks.
haha...
uh...
and he didn't even call or anything, the whole time?
no.
annie...
I know.
well, I'm not leaving you here on your own again.

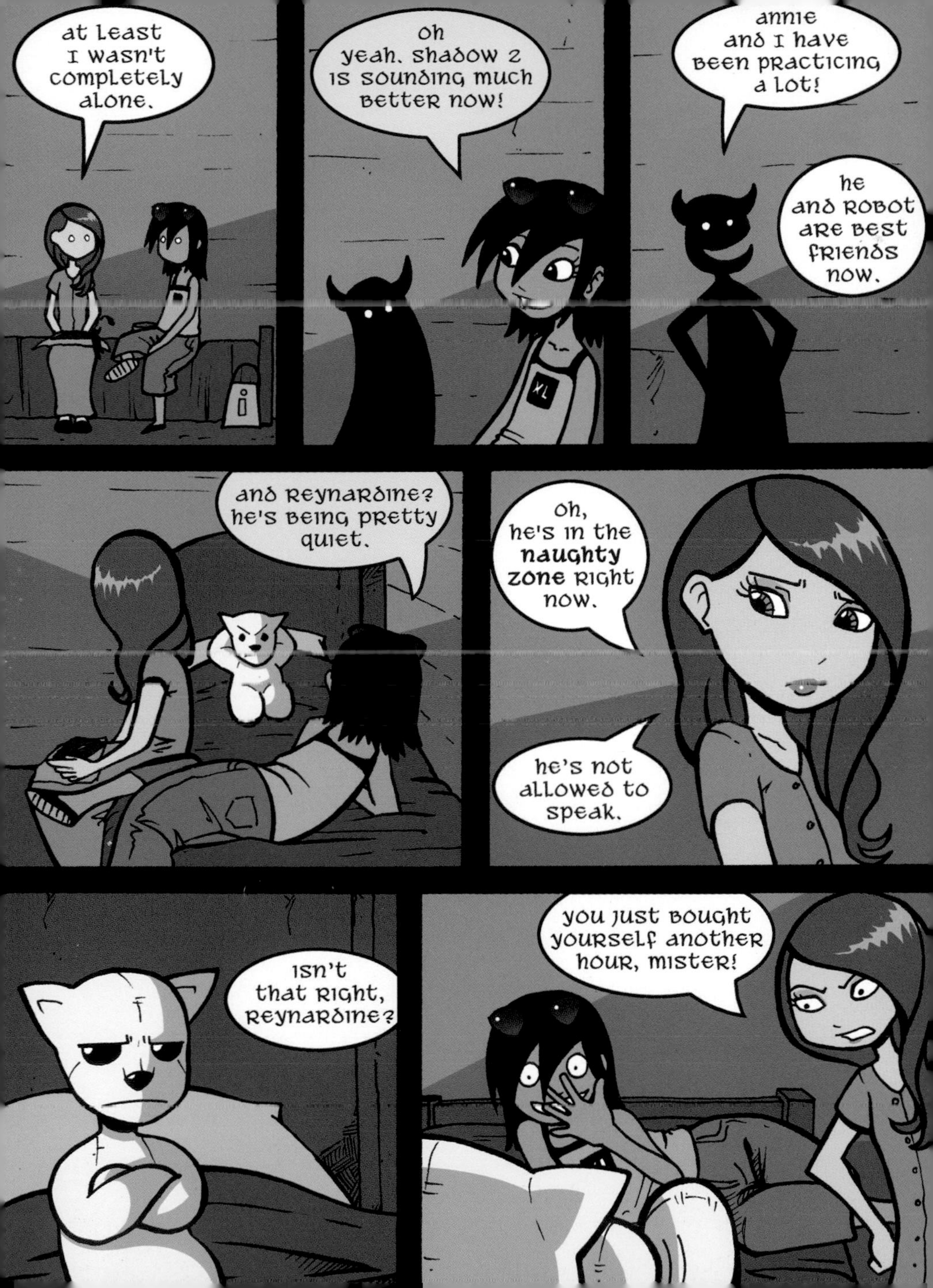
at least I wasn't completely alone.
oh yeah. shadow 2 is sounding much better now!
annie and I have been practicing a lot!
he and robot are best friends now.
and reynardine? he's being pretty quiet.
oh, he's in the **naughty zone** right now.
he's not allowed to speak.
isn't that right, reynardine?
you just bought yourself another hour, mister!

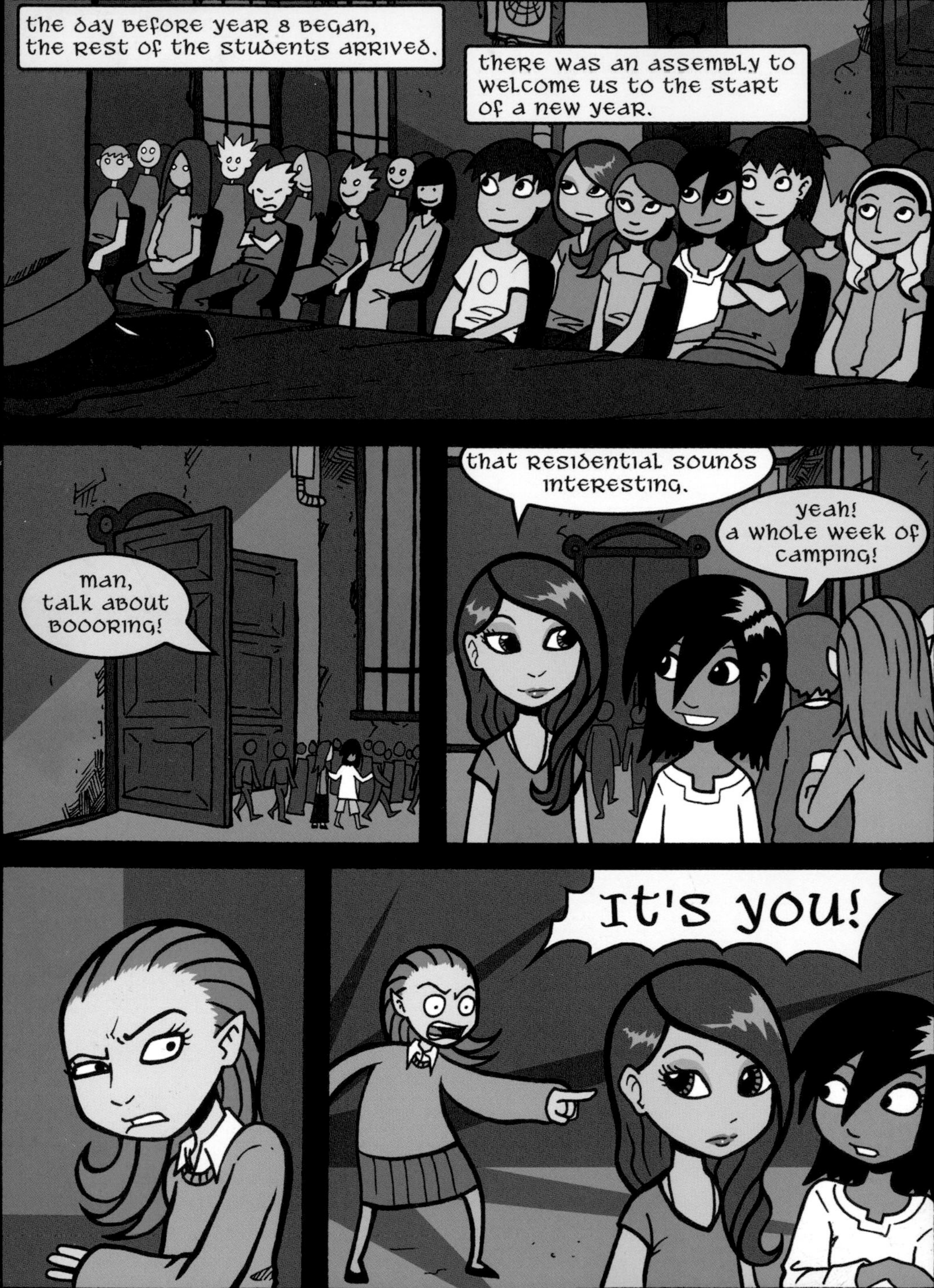
the day before year 8 began, the rest of the students arrived.
there was an assembly to welcome us to the start of a new year.
man, talk about BOOORING!
that residential sounds interesting.
yeah! a whole week of camping!
It's you!

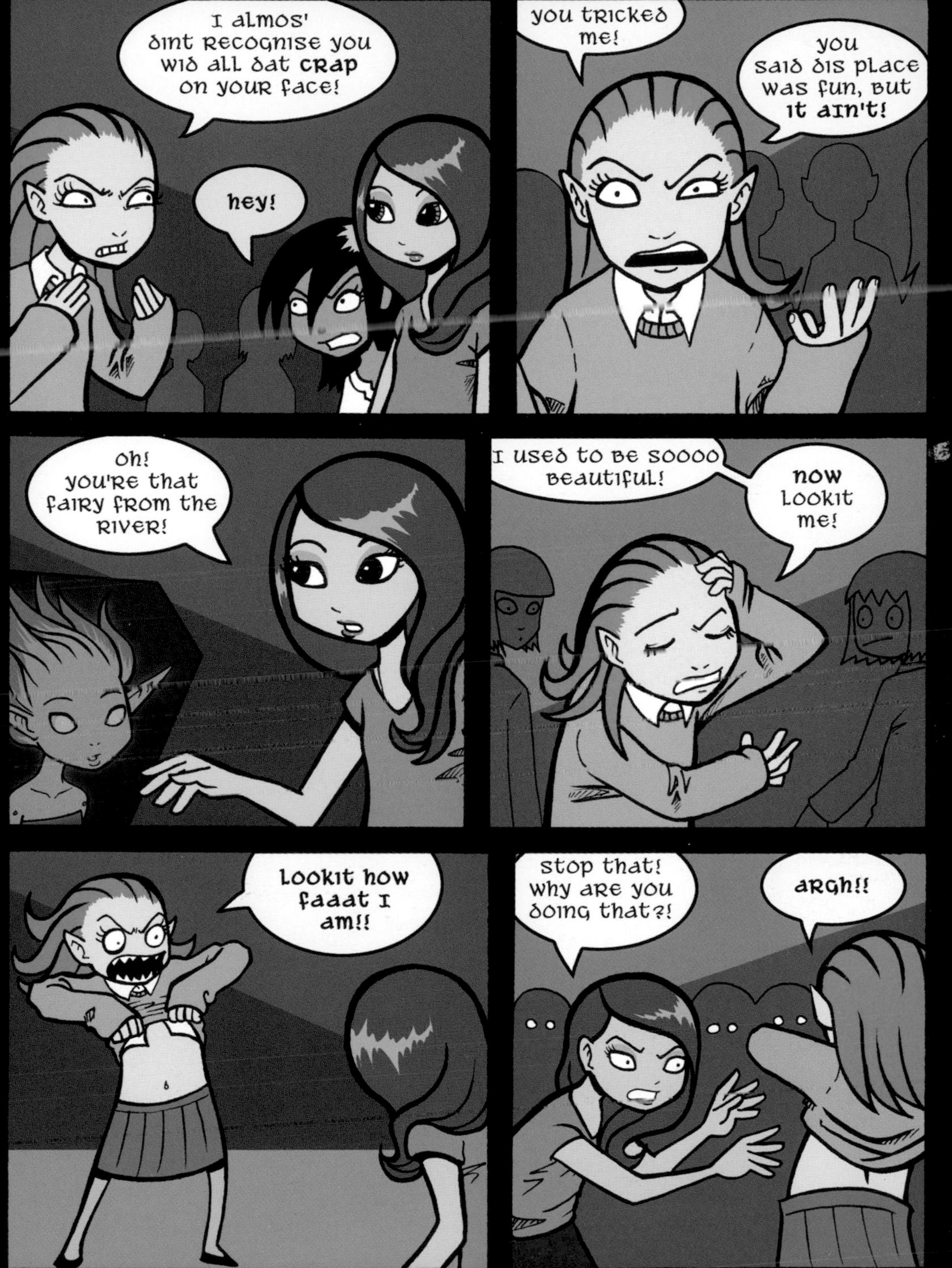
I almos' dint recognise you wid all dat crap on your face!
hey!
you tricked me!
you said dis place was fun, but it ain't!
oh! you're that fairy from the river!
I used to be soooo beautiful!
now lookit me!
lookit how faaat I am!!
stop that! why are you doing that?!
argh!!

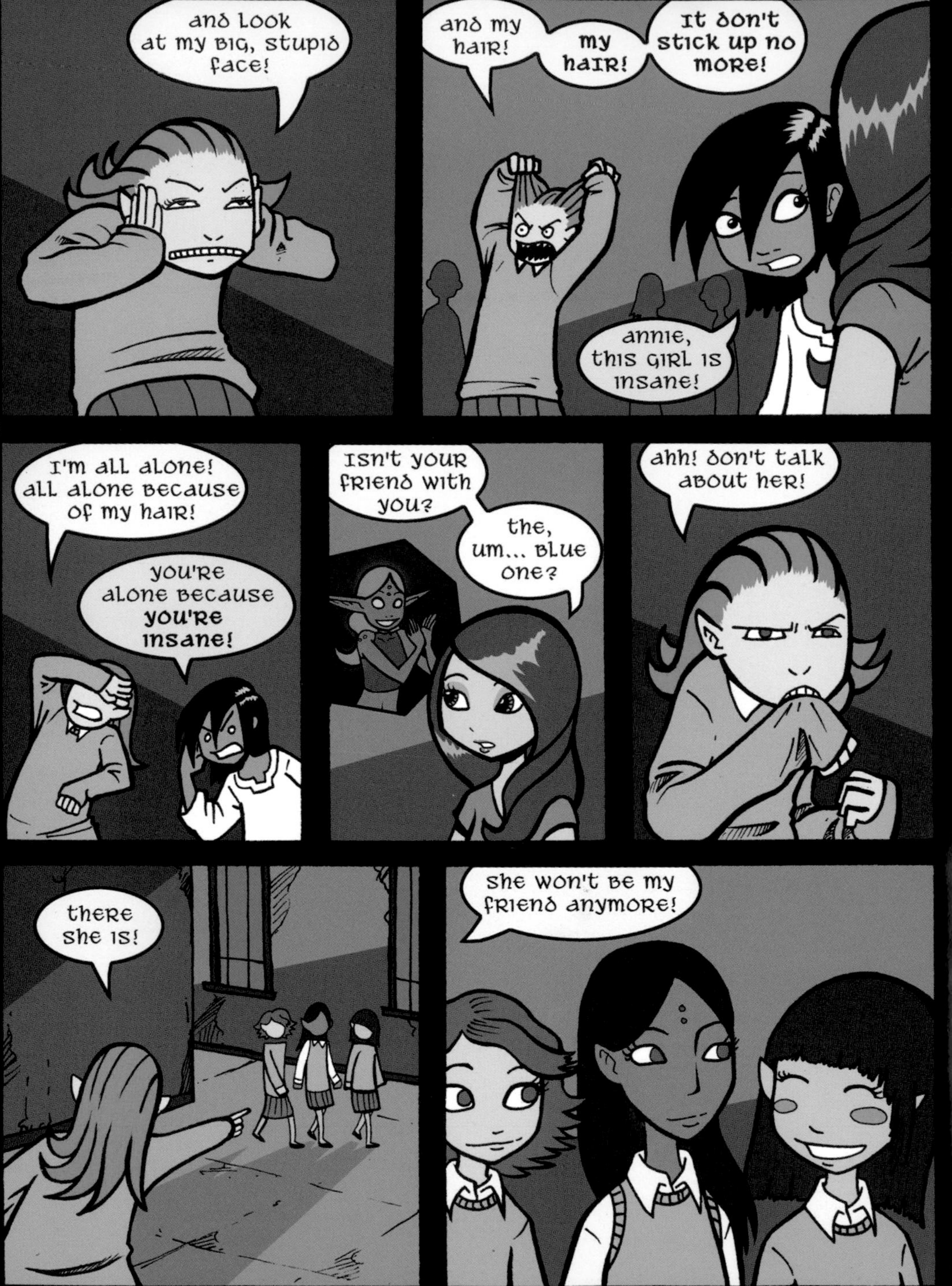

and look at my big, stupid face!
and my hair!
my hair!
It don't stick up no more!
annie, this girl is insane!
I'm all alone! all alone because of my hair!
you're alone because **you're insane!**
Isn't your friend with you?
the, um... blue one?
ahh! don't talk about her!
there she is!
she won't be my friend anymore!

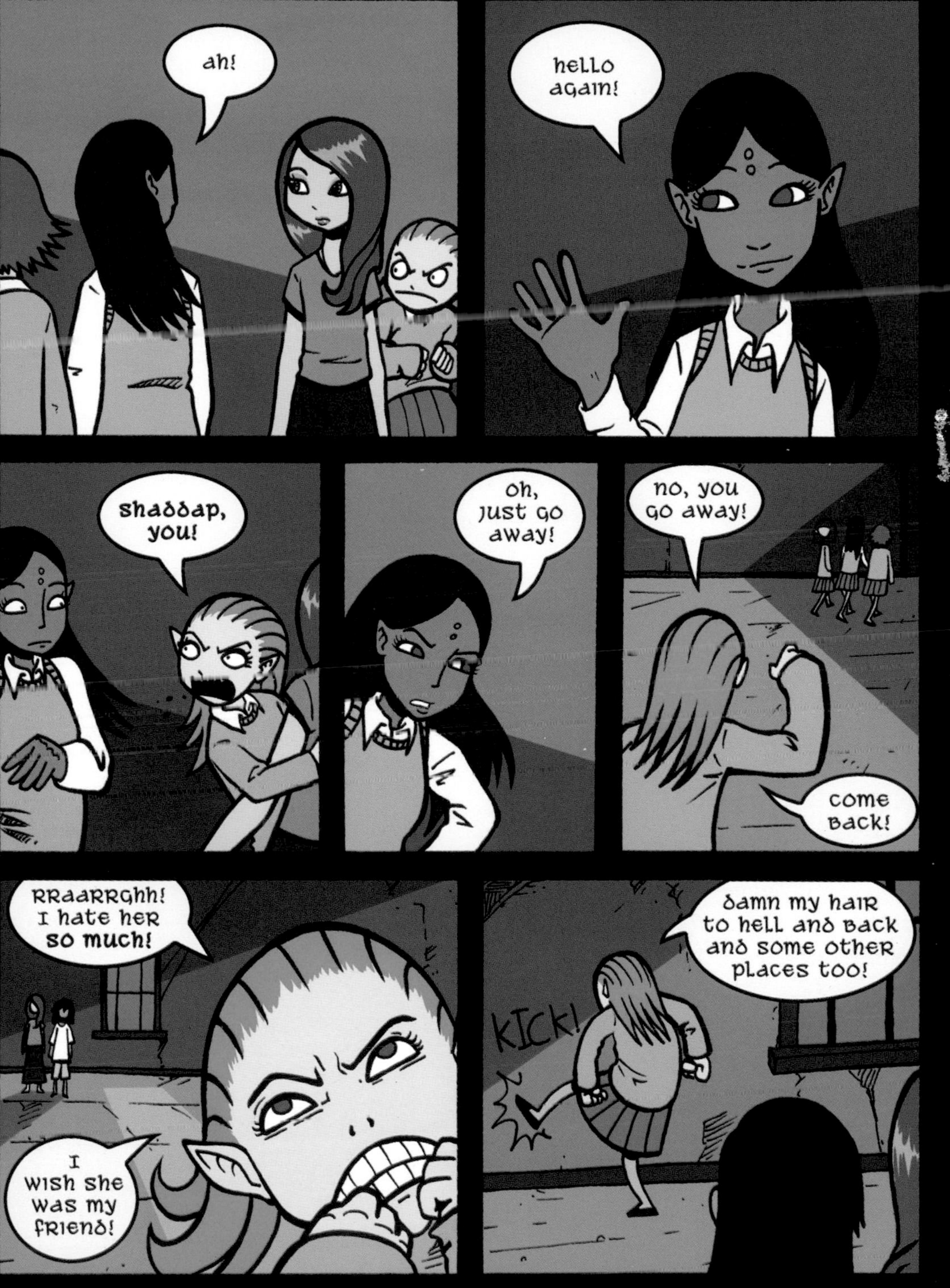
ah!
hello again!
shaddap, you!
oh, just go away!
no, you go away!
come back!
RRaaRRghh! I hate her so much!
I wish she was my friend!
damn my hair to hell and back and some other places too!
KICK!

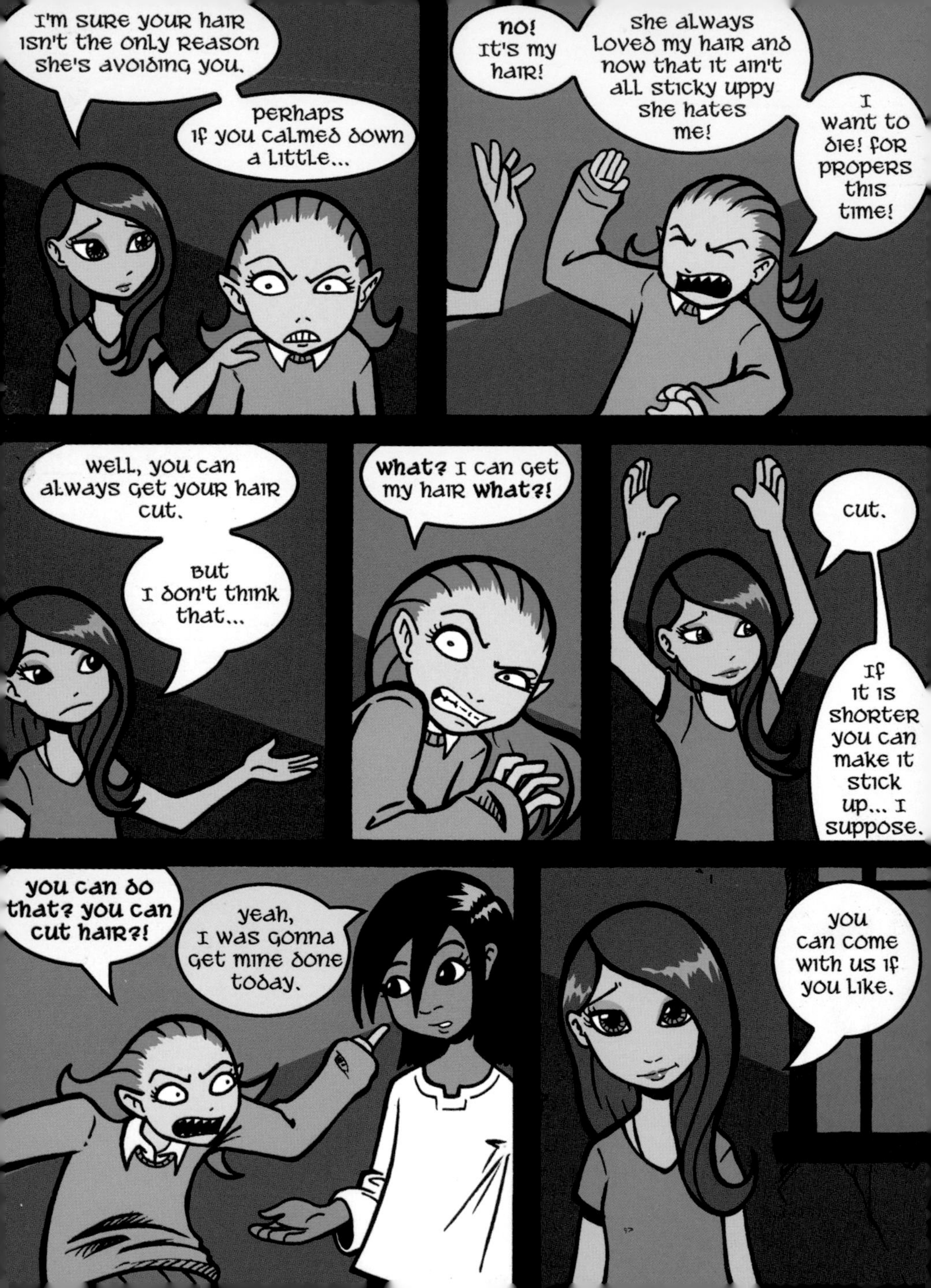
I'm sure your hair isn't the only reason she's avoiding you.
perhaps if you calmed down a little...
no! It's my hair!
she always loved my hair and now that it ain't all sticky uppy she hates me!
I want to die! for propers this time!
well, you can always get your hair cut.
But I don't think that...
what? I can get my hair what?!
cut.
If it is shorter you can make it stick up... I suppose.
you can do that? you can cut hair?!
yeah, I was gonna get mine done today.
you can come with us if you like.

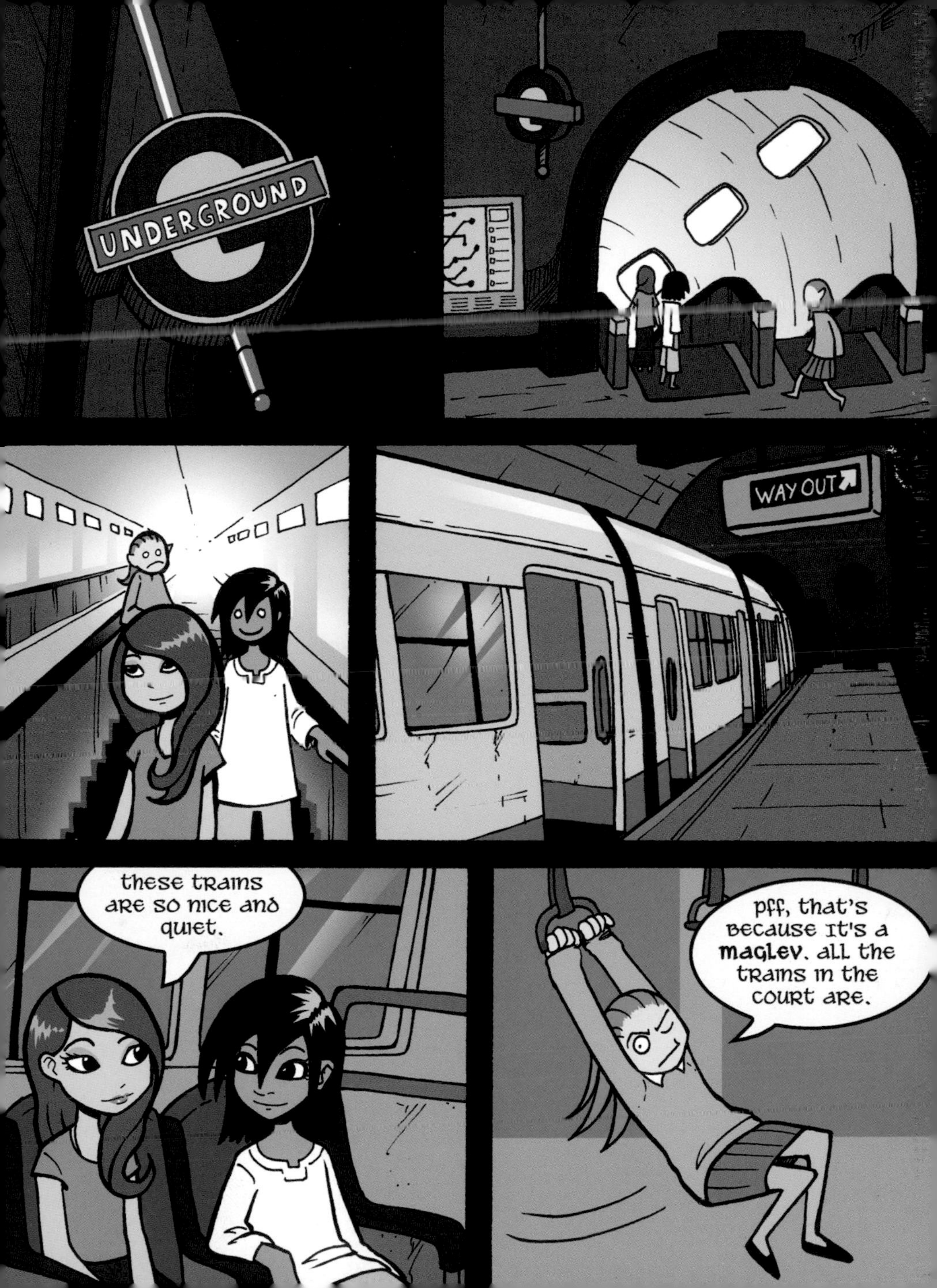
UNDERGROUND
WAY OUT
these trains are so nice and quiet.
pff, that's because it's a maglev. all the trains in the court are.

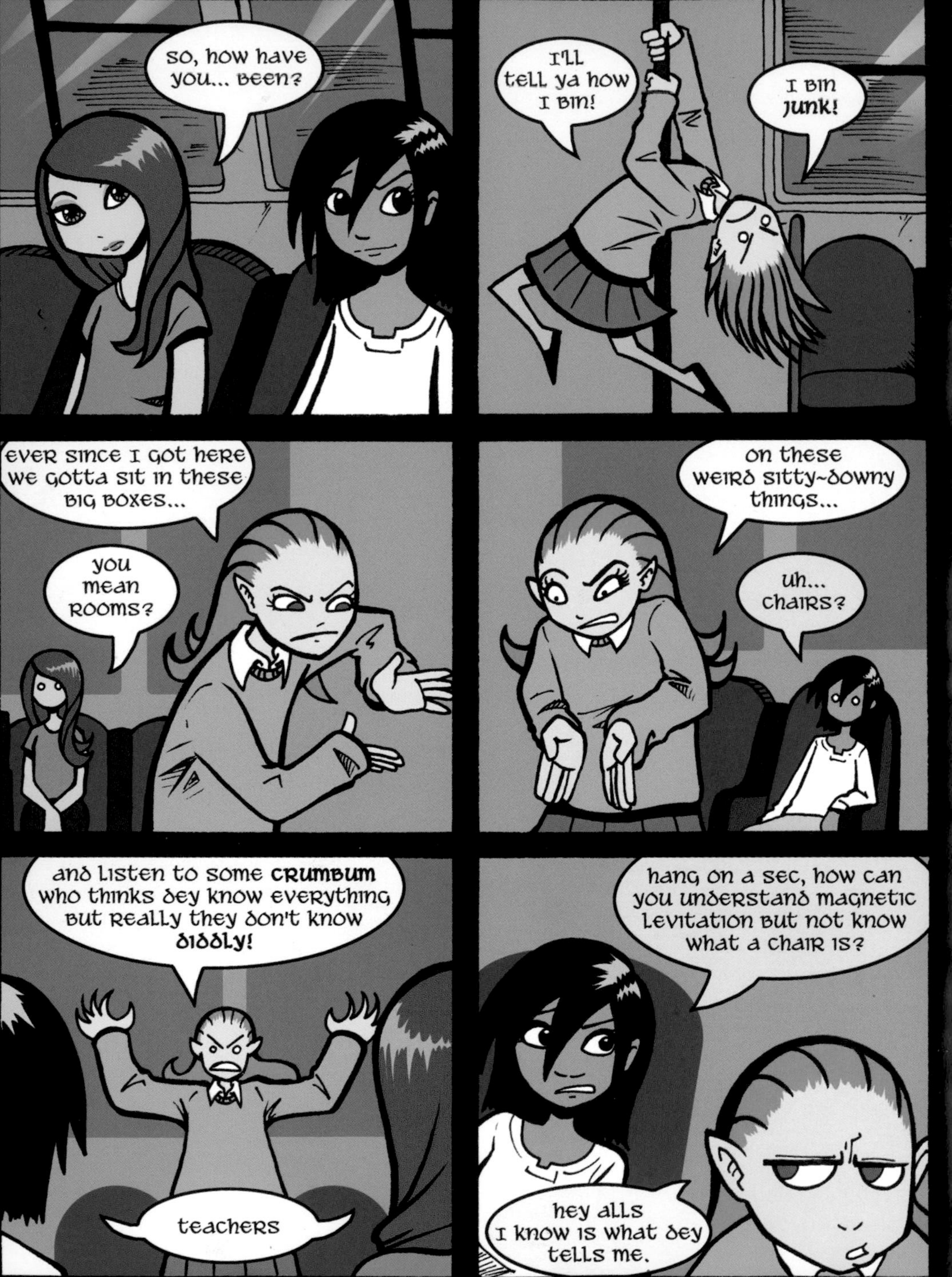
so, how have you... been?
I'll tell ya how I bin!
I bin junk!
ever since I got here we gotta sit in these big boxes...
you mean rooms?
on these weird sitty~downy things...
uh... chairs?
and listen to some crumbum who thinks dey know everything but really they don't know diddly!
teachers
hang on a sec, how can you understand magnetic levitation but not know what a chair is?
hey alls I know is what dey tells me.

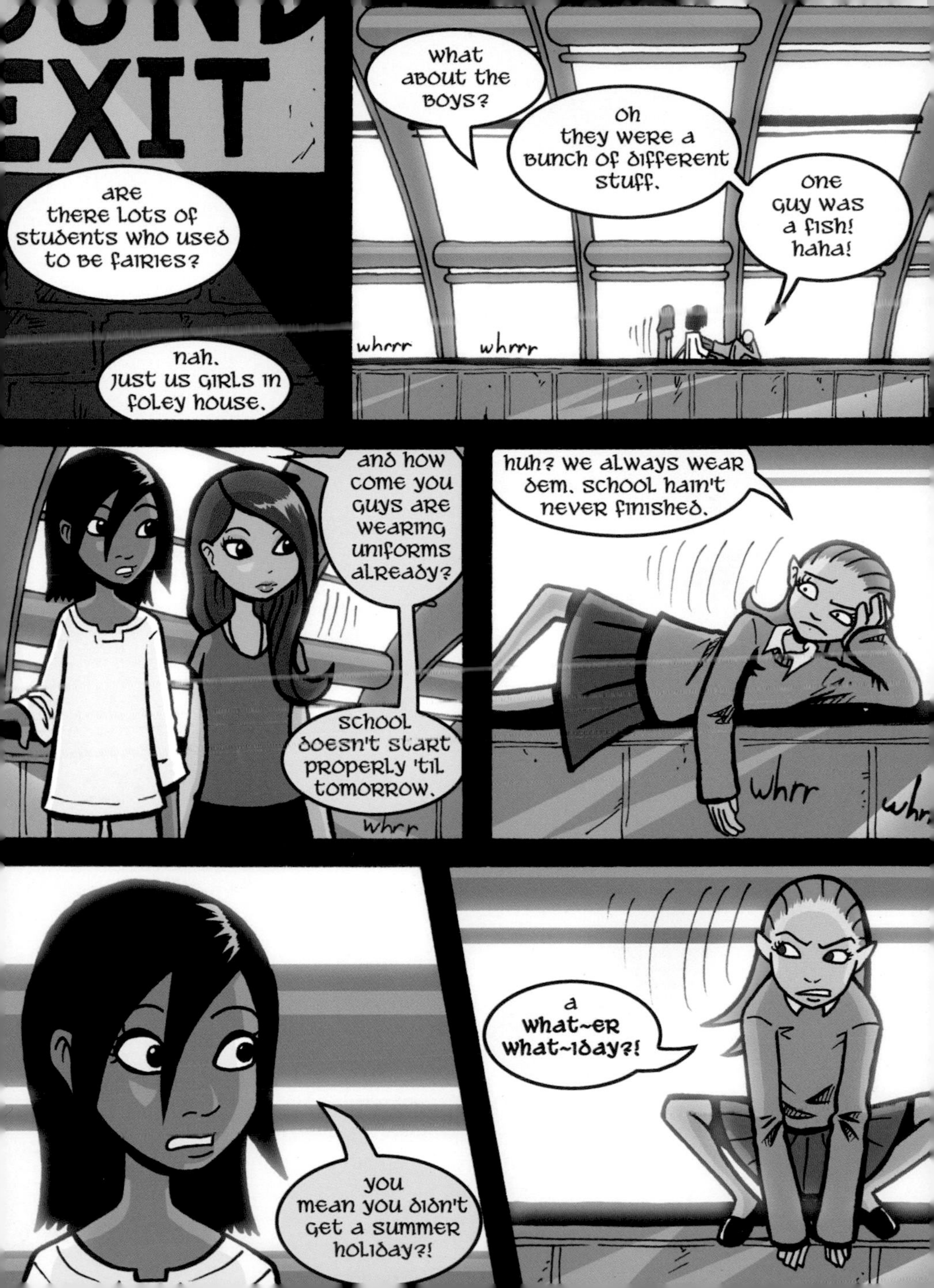
EXIT
are there lots of students who used to be fairies?
nah. just us girls in foley house.
What about the boys?
Oh they were a bunch of different stuff.
One guy was a fish! haha!
whrrr
whrrr
and how come you guys are wearing uniforms already?
school doesn't start properly 'til tomorrow.
whrr
huh? we always wear dem. school hain't never finished.
whrr
a what-er what-iday?!
you mean you didn't get a summer holiday?!

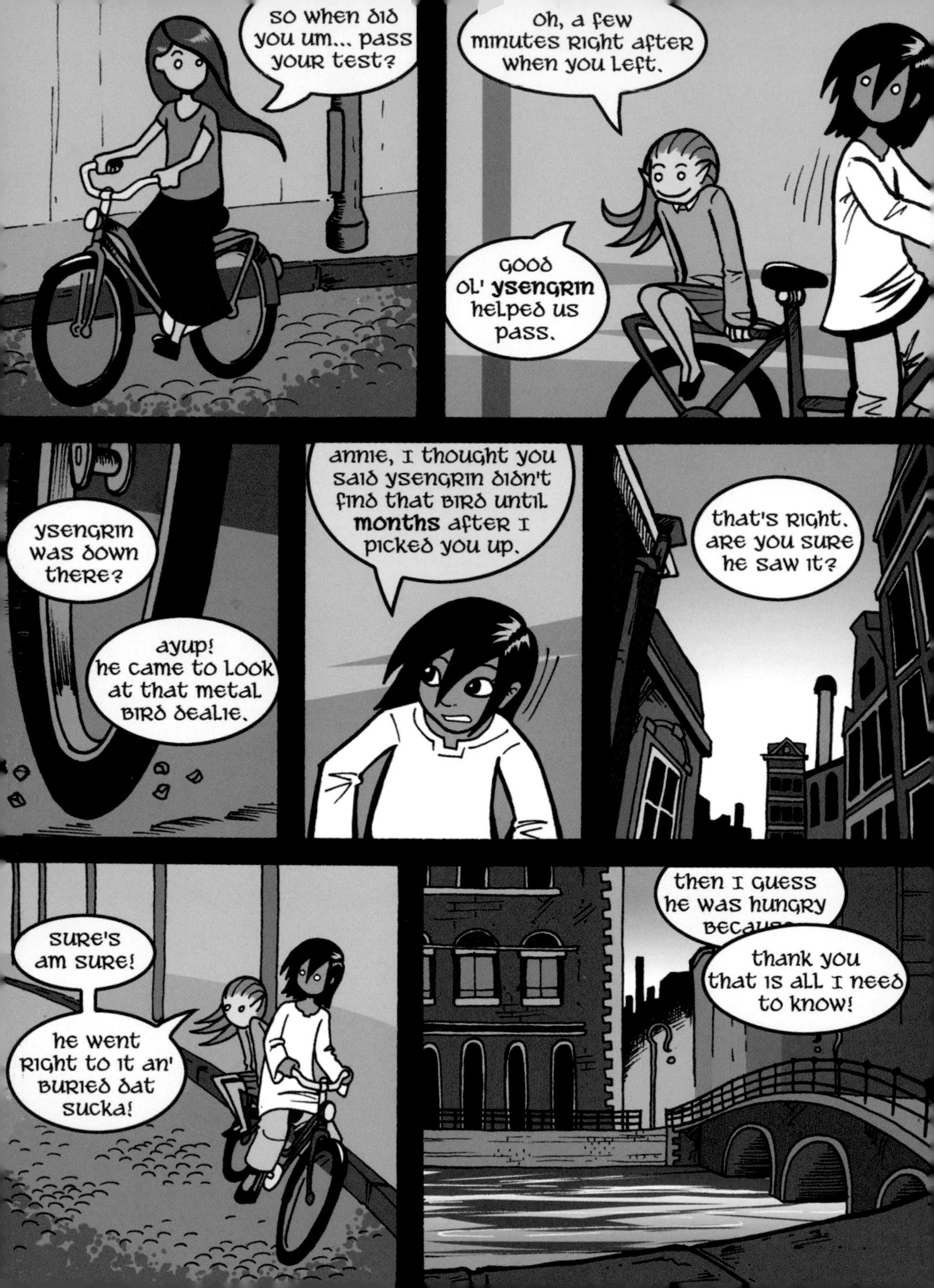
so when did you um... pass your test?
Oh, a few minutes right after when you left.
Good ol' ysengrin helped us pass.
ysengrin was down there?
ayup! he came to look at that metal bird dealie.
annie, I thought you said ysengrin didn't find that bird until months after I picked you up.
that's right. are you sure he saw it?
sure's am sure!
he went right to it an' buried dat sucka!
then I guess he was hungry becau–
thank you that is all I need to know!

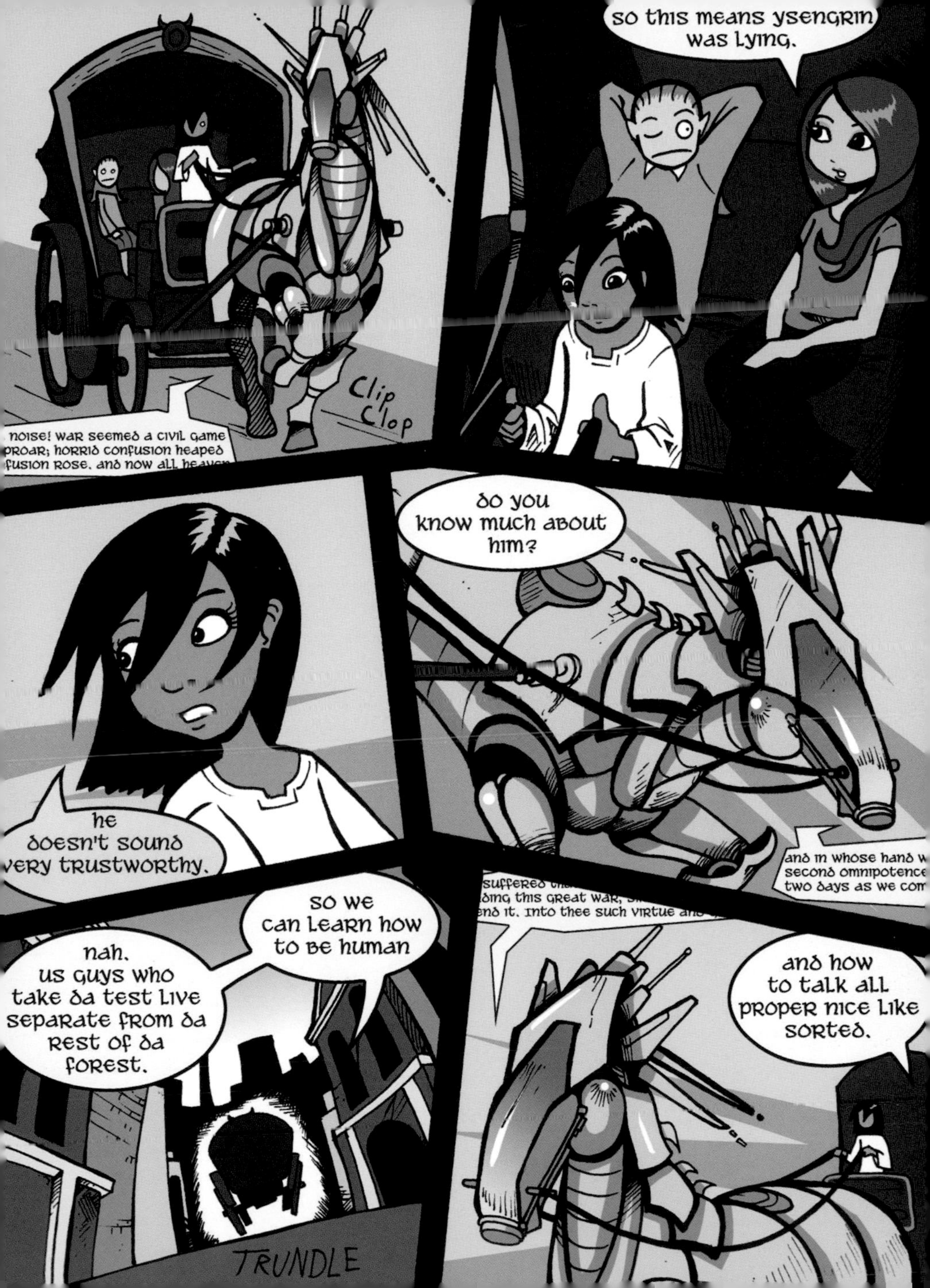

noise! war seemed a civil game
proar; horrid confusion heaped
fusion rose, and now all
Clip Clop
so this means ysengrin was lying.
he doesn't sound very trustworthy.
do you know much about him?
and in whose hand
second omnipotence
two days as we
ding this great war,
end it. into thee such virtue and
nah. us guys who take da test live separate from da rest of da forest.
so we can learn how to be human
TRUNDLE
and how to talk all proper nice like sorted.

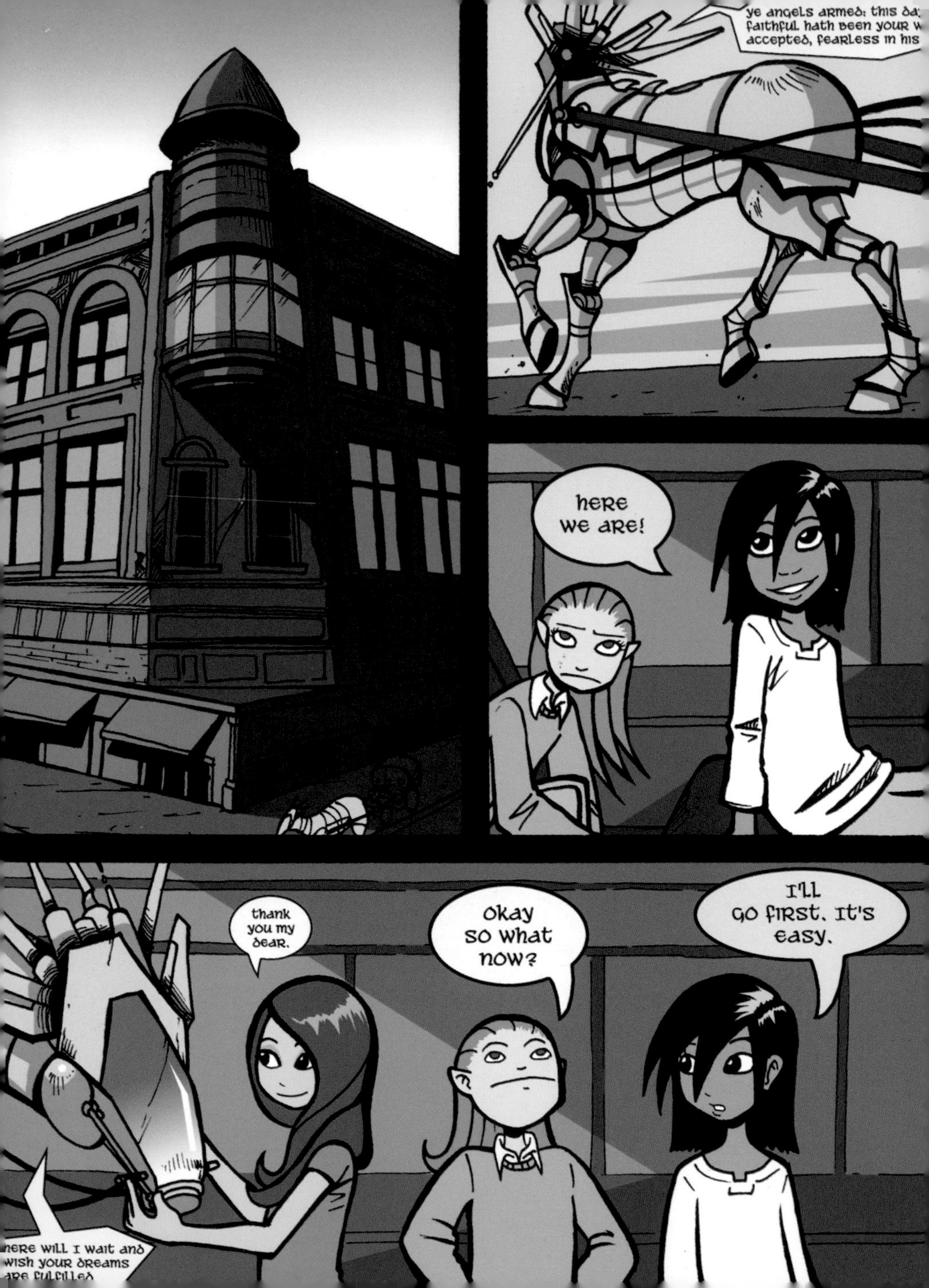
ye angels armed: this da
faithful hath been your w
accepted, fearless in his
here we are!
thank you my dear.
okay so what now?
I'll go first. It's easy.
here will I wait and wish your dreams are fulfilled

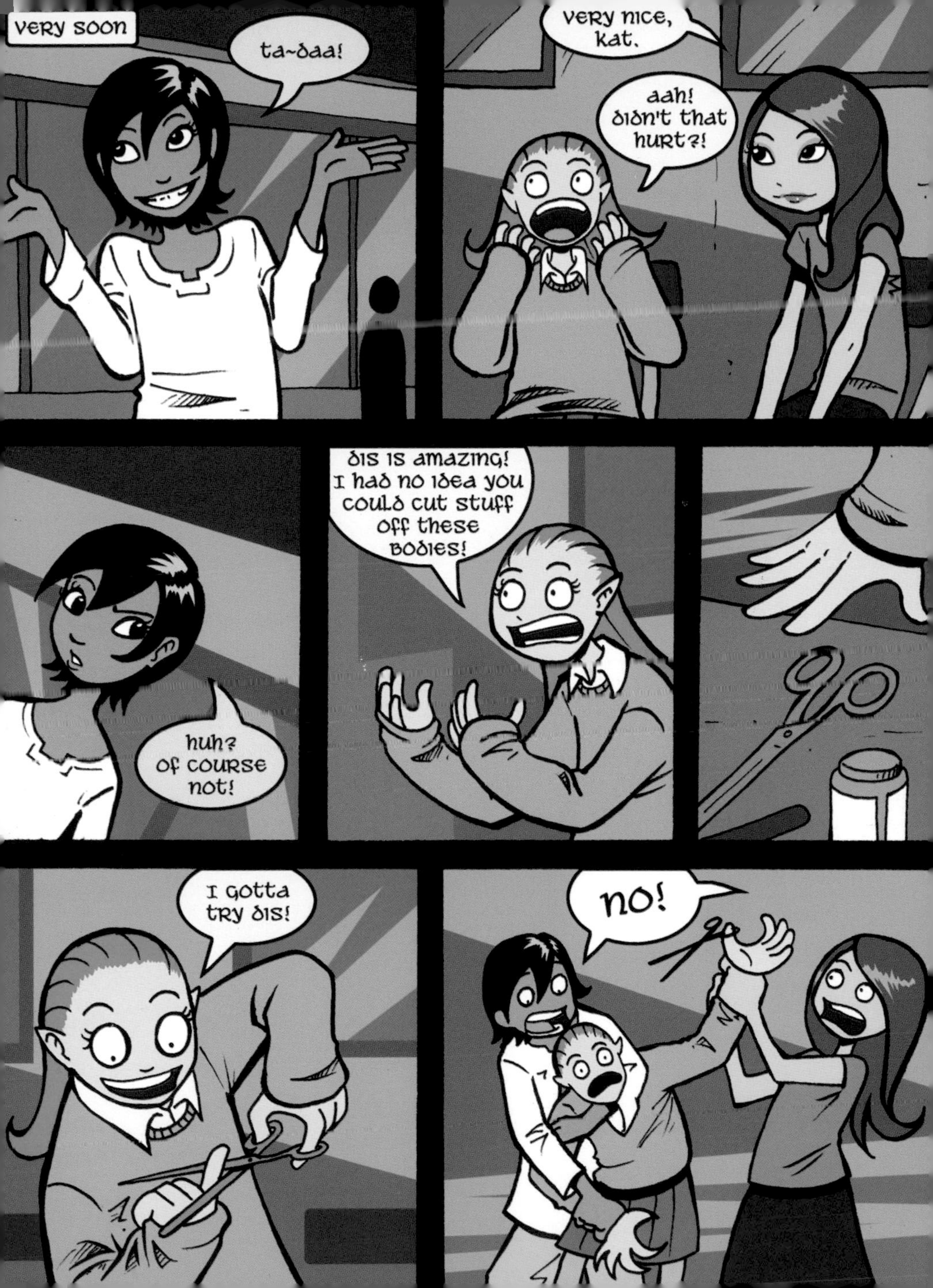
VERY SOON
ta~daa!
VERY NICE, KAT.
aah! didn't that hurt?!
dis is amazing! I had no idea you could cut stuff off these bodies!
huh? of course not!
I gotta try dis!
NO!

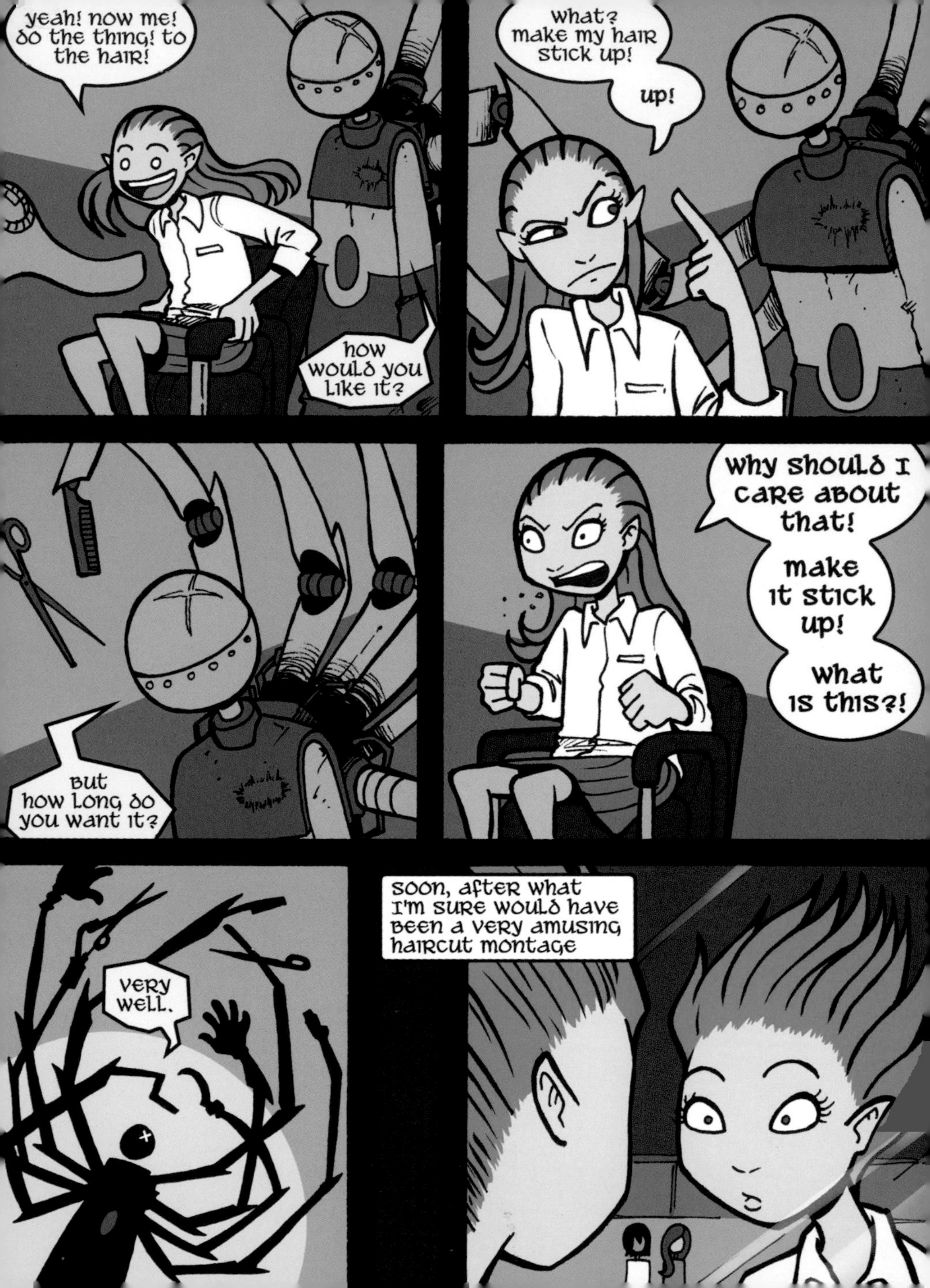
yeah! now me! do the thing! to the hair!
how would you like it?
what? make my hair stick up!
up!
but how long do you want it?
why should I care about that!
make it stick up!
what is this?!
very well.
soon, after what I'm sure would have been a very amusing haircut montage

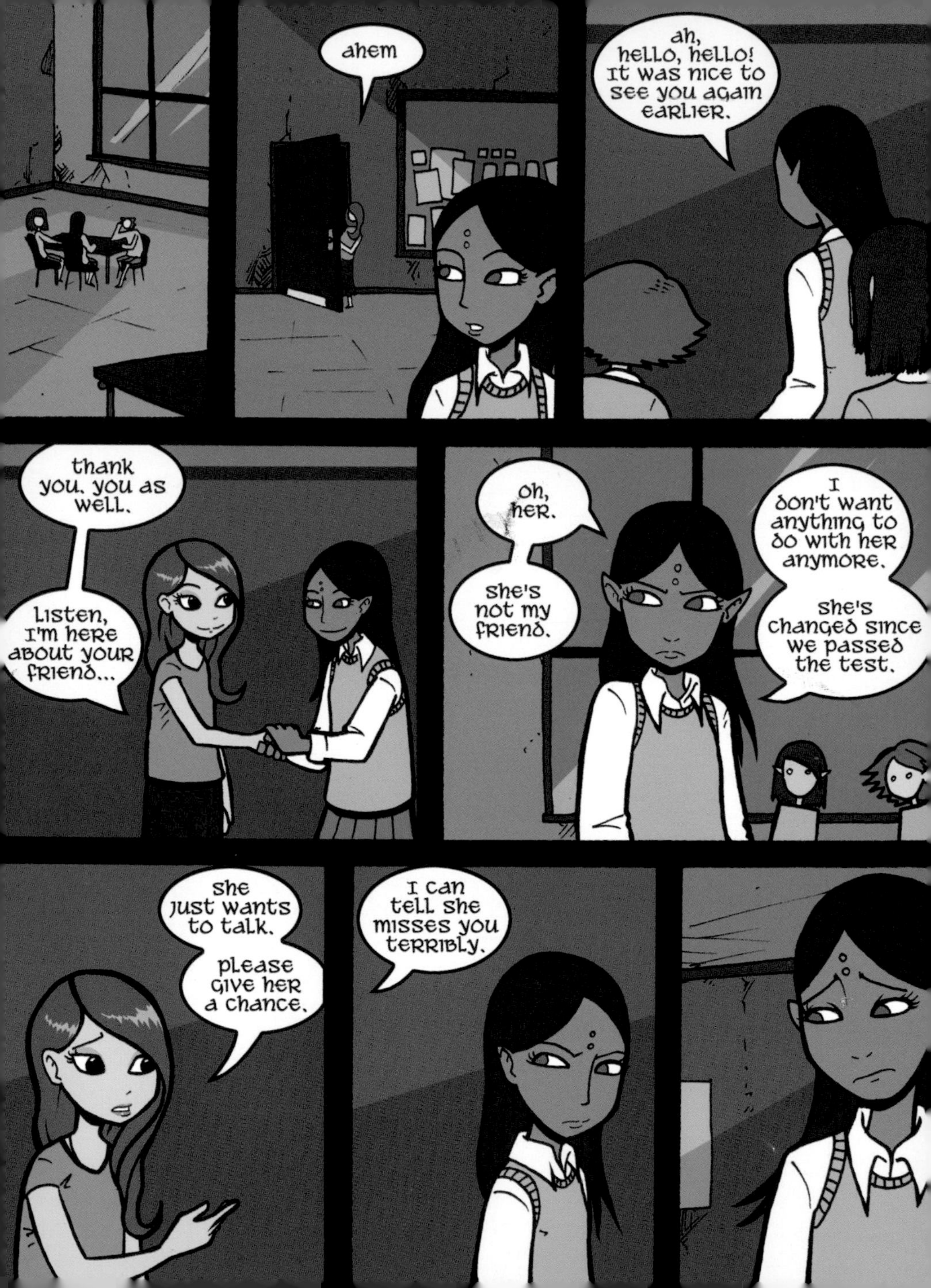
ahem
ah, hello, hello! It was nice to see you again earlier.
thank you. you as well.
Listen, I'm here about your friend...
oh, her.
she's not my friend.
I don't want anything to do with her anymore.
she's changed since we passed the test.
she just wants to talk.
please give her a chance.
I can tell she misses you terribly.

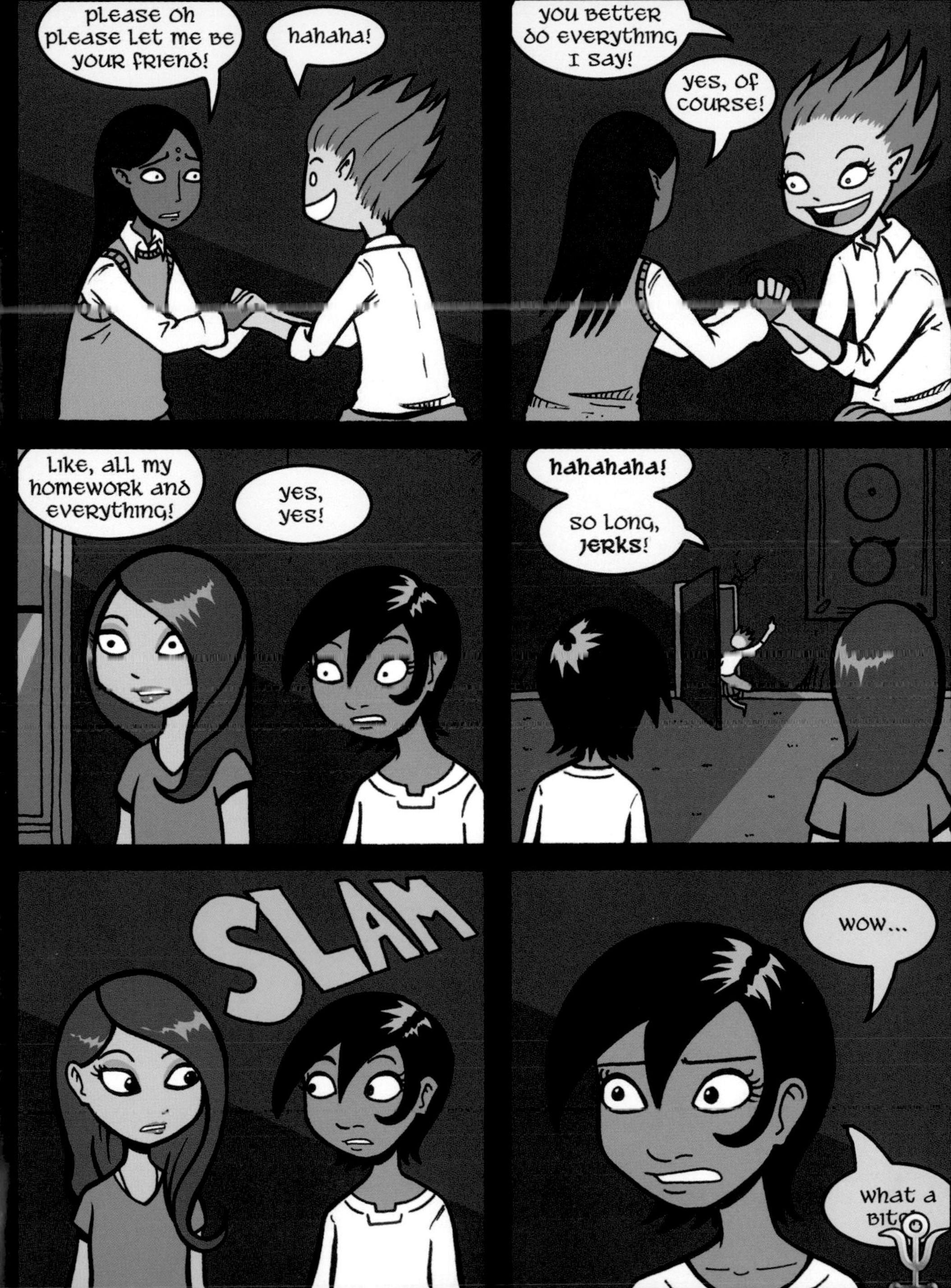
please oh please let me be your friend!
hahaha!
you better do everything I say!
yes, of course!
like, all my homework and everything!
yes, yes!
hahahaha!
so long, jerks!
SLAM
wow...
what a

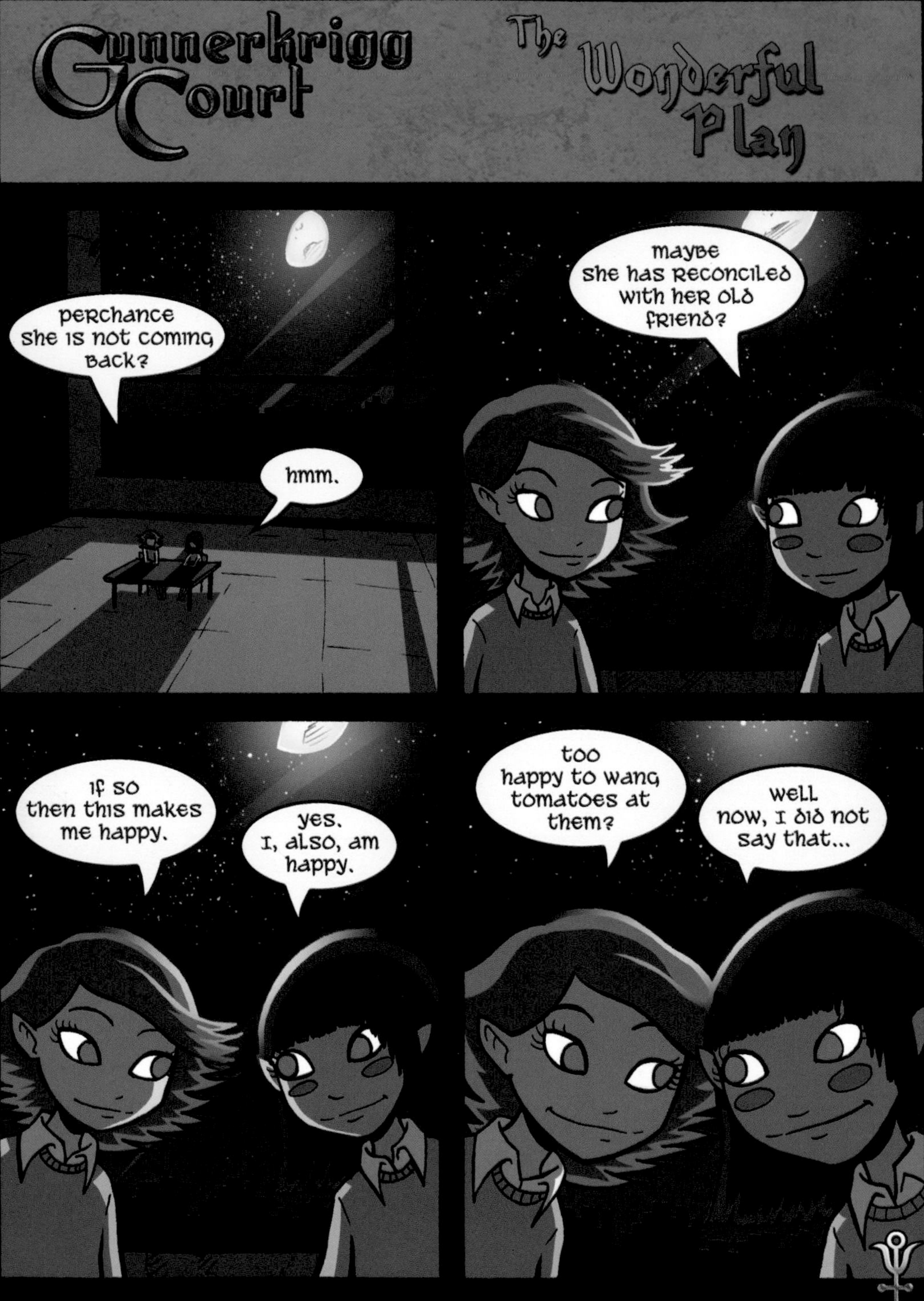
Gunnerkrigg Court
The Wonderful Plan
perchance she is not coming back?
hmm.
maybe she has reconciled with her old friend?
if so then this makes me happy.
yes. I, also, am happy.
too happy to wang tomatoes at them?
well now, I did not say that...

Gunnerkrigg Court

Chapter 16:

A Ghost Story

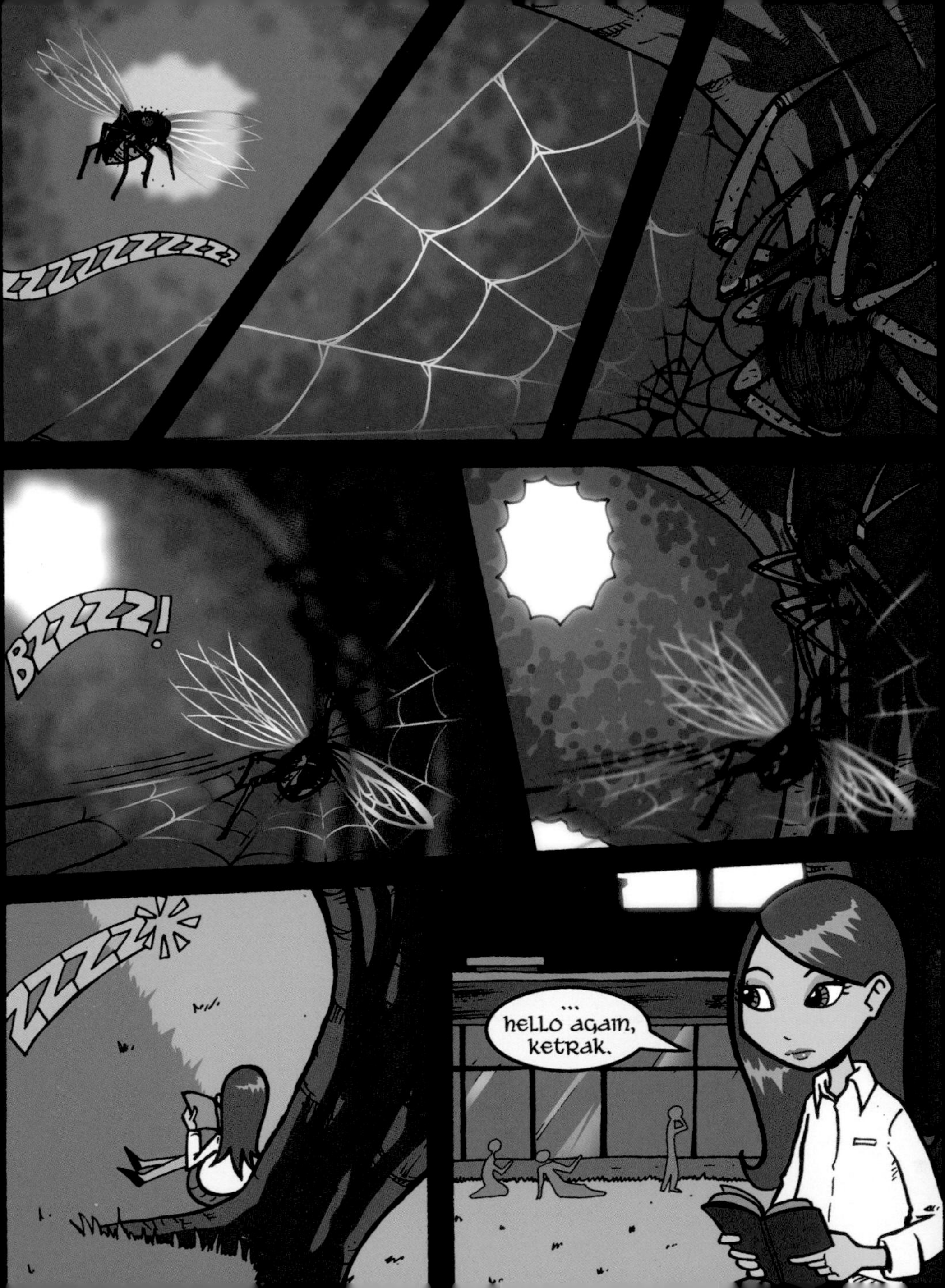
ZZZZZZZZZZZ
BZZZZZ!
ZZZZZZ
...
hello again,
ketrak.

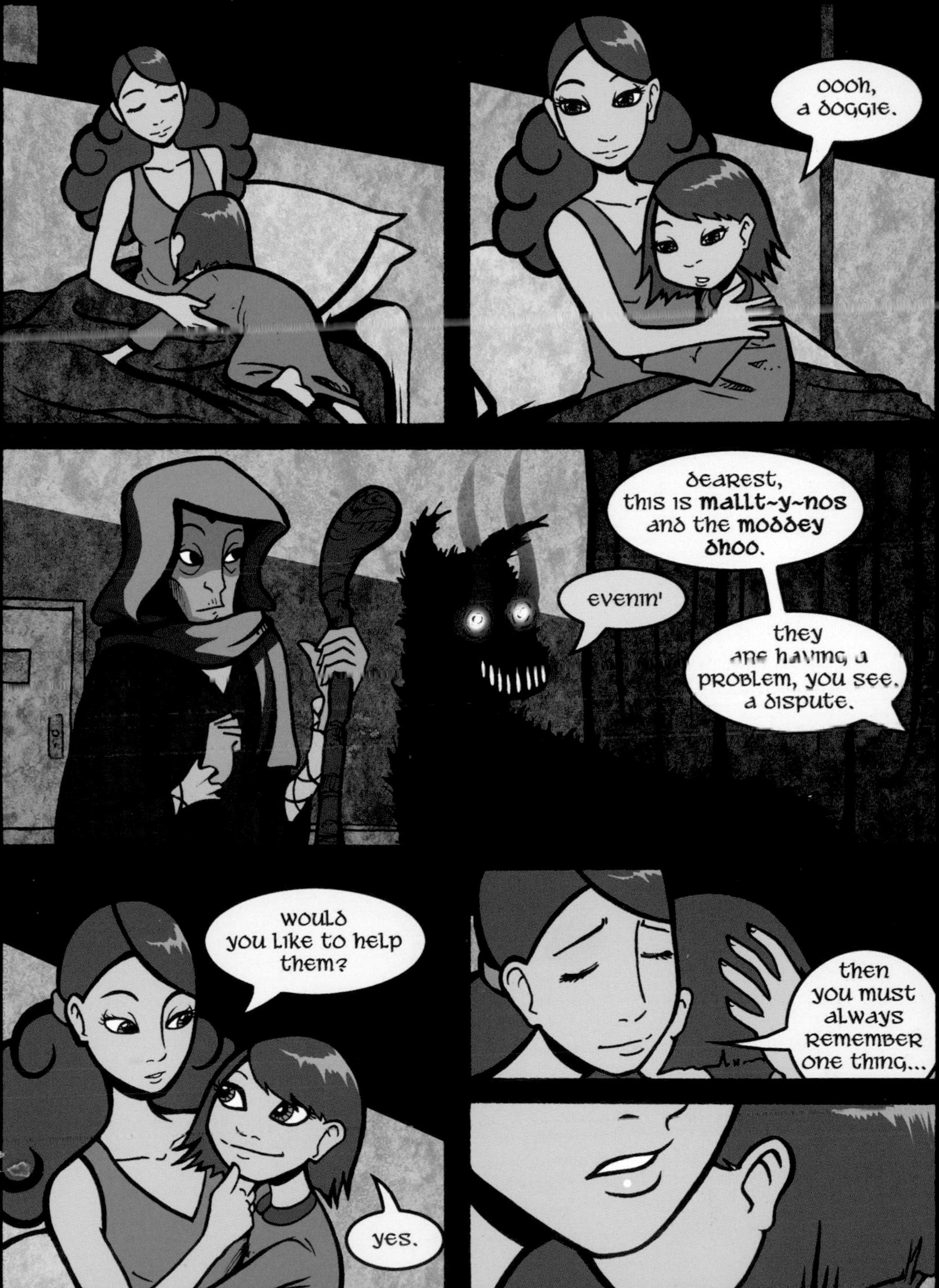
oooh, a doggie.
dearest, this is mallt-y-nos and the moddey dhoo.
evenin'
they are having a problem, you see. a dispute.
would you like to help them?
yes.
then you must always remember one thing...

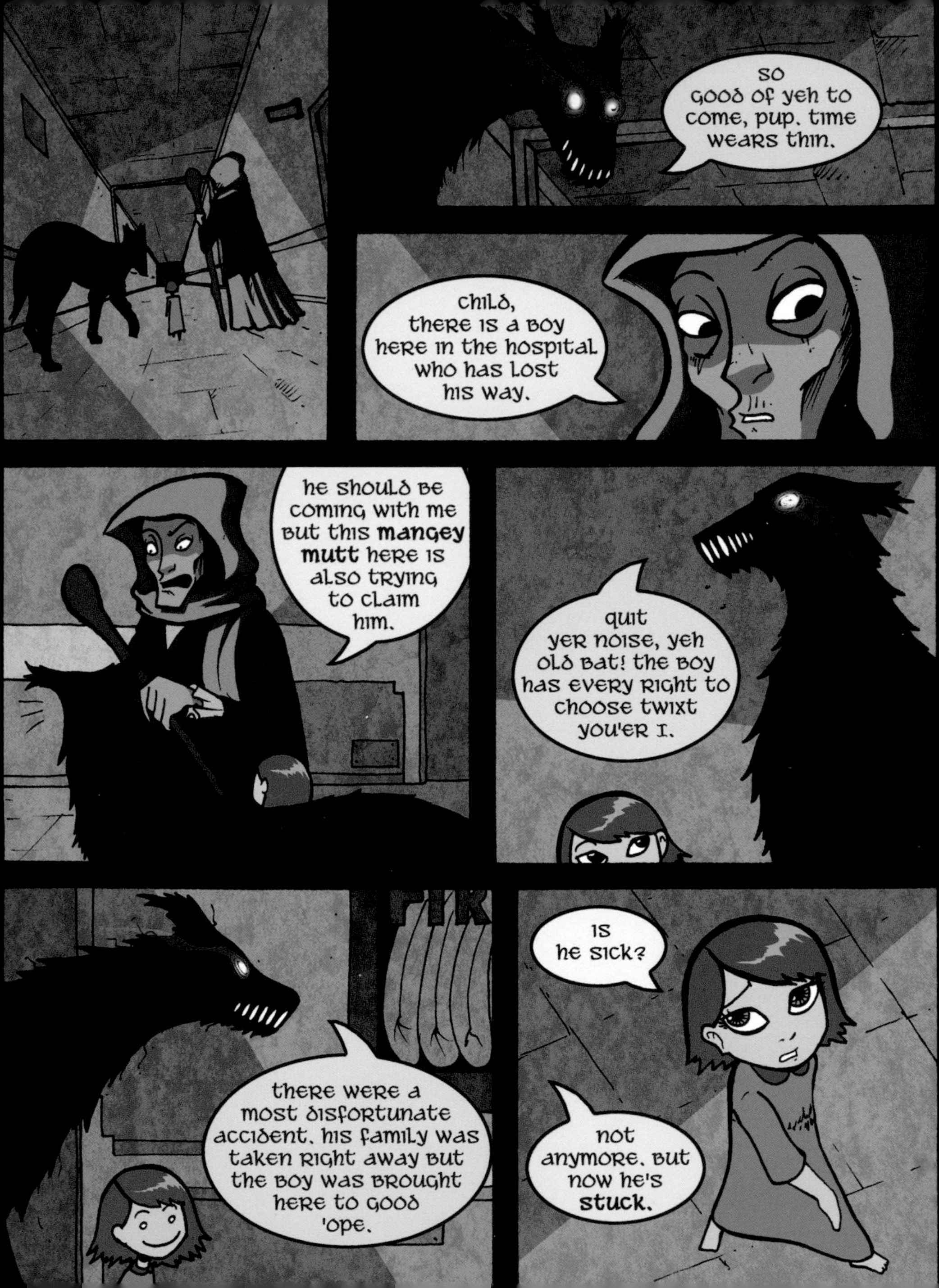
so good of yeh to come, pup. time wears thin.
child, there is a boy here in the hospital who has lost his way.
he should be coming with me but this **mangey mutt** here is also trying to claim him.
quit yer noise, yeh old bat! the boy has every right to choose twixt you'er I.
there were a most disfortunate accident. his family was taken right away but the boy was brought here to good 'ope.
is he sick?
not anymore. but now he's **stuck**.

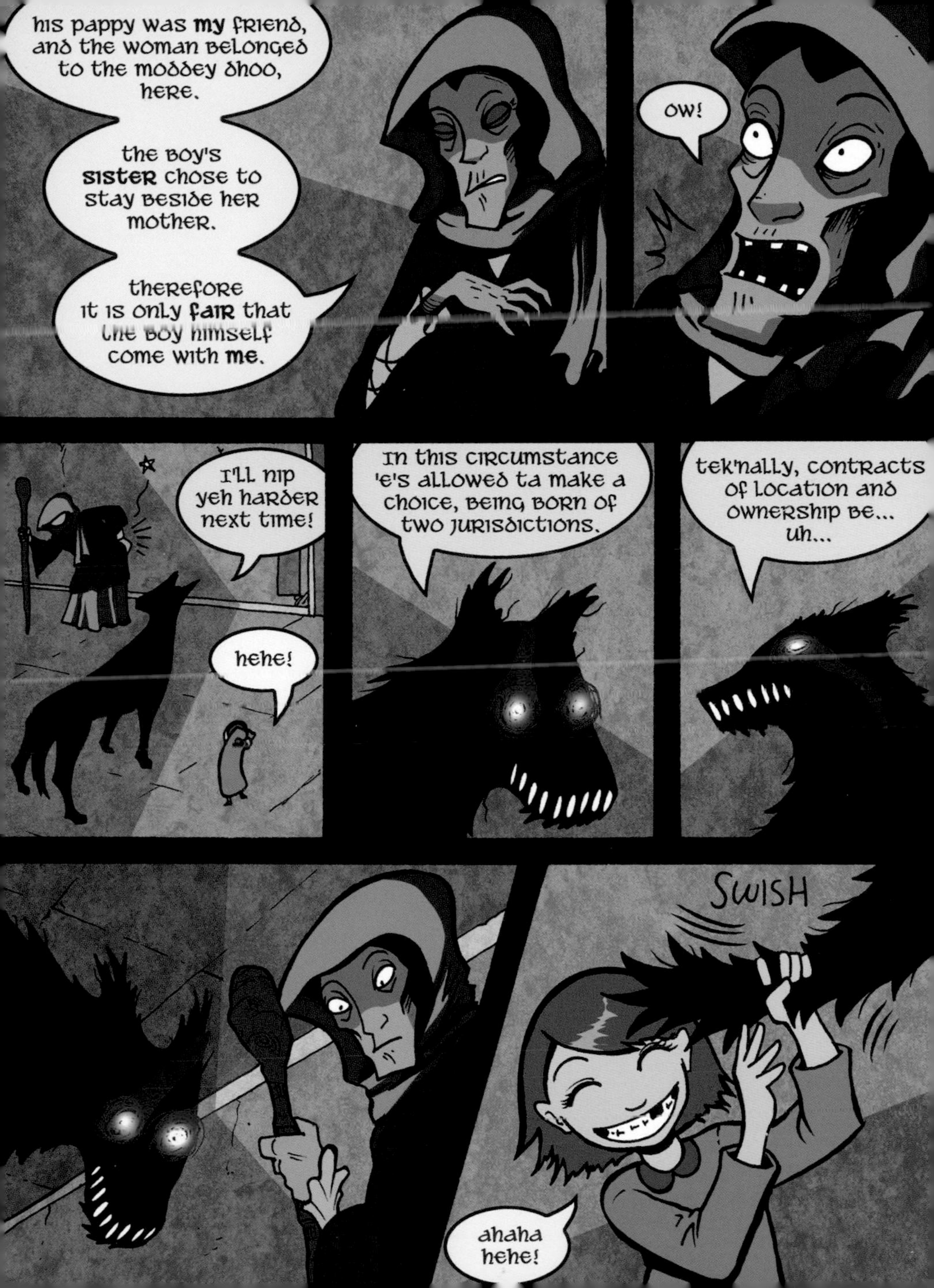

his pappy was my friend, and the woman belonged to the moddey dhoo, here.
the boy's sister chose to stay beside her mother.
therefore it is only fair that the boy himself come with me.
OW!
I'll nip yeh harder next time!
hehe!
In this circumstance 'e's allowed ta make a choice, being born of two jurisdictions.
tek'nally, contracts of location and ownership be... uh...
SWISH
ahaha hehe!

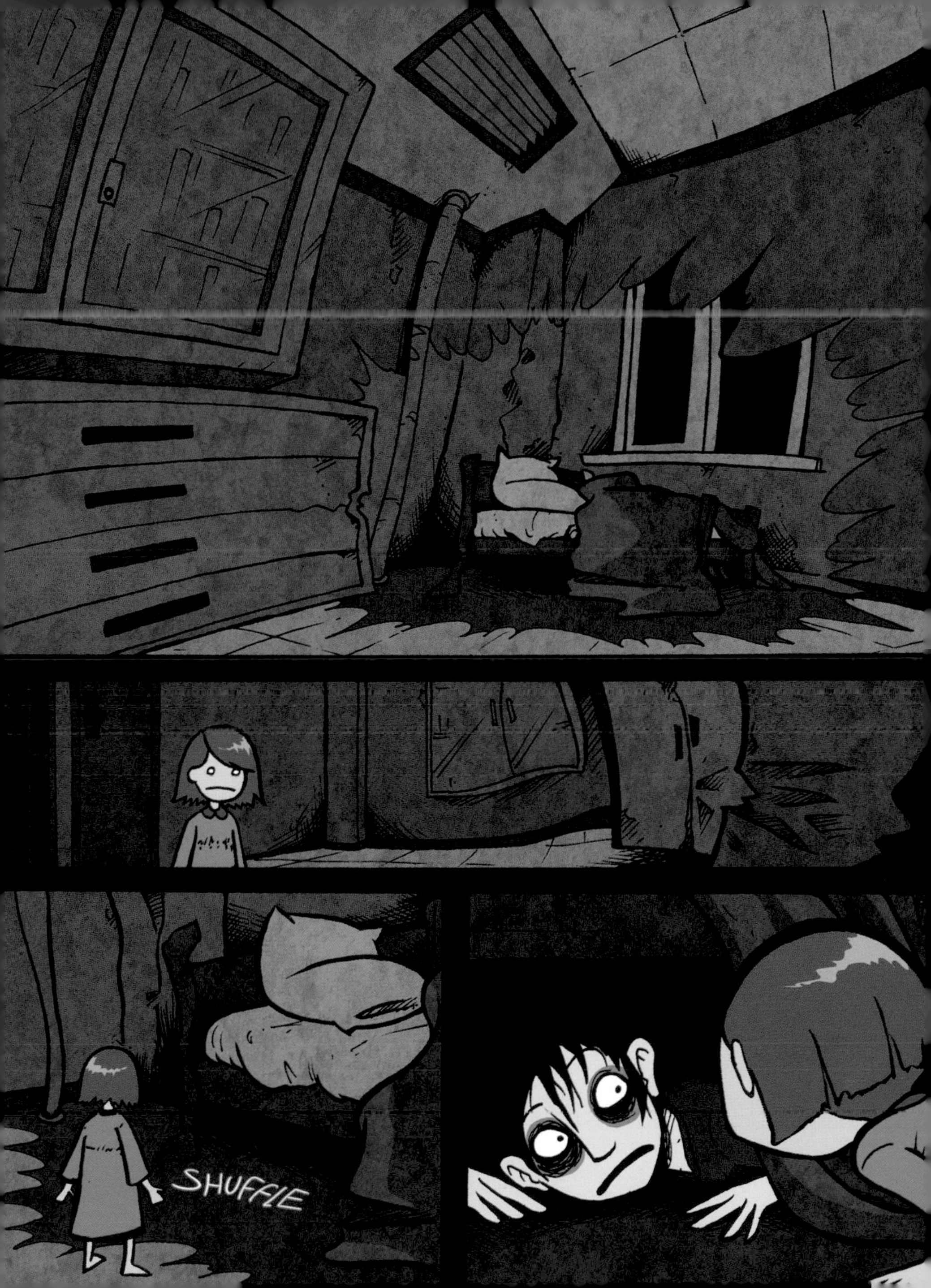
SHUFFLE

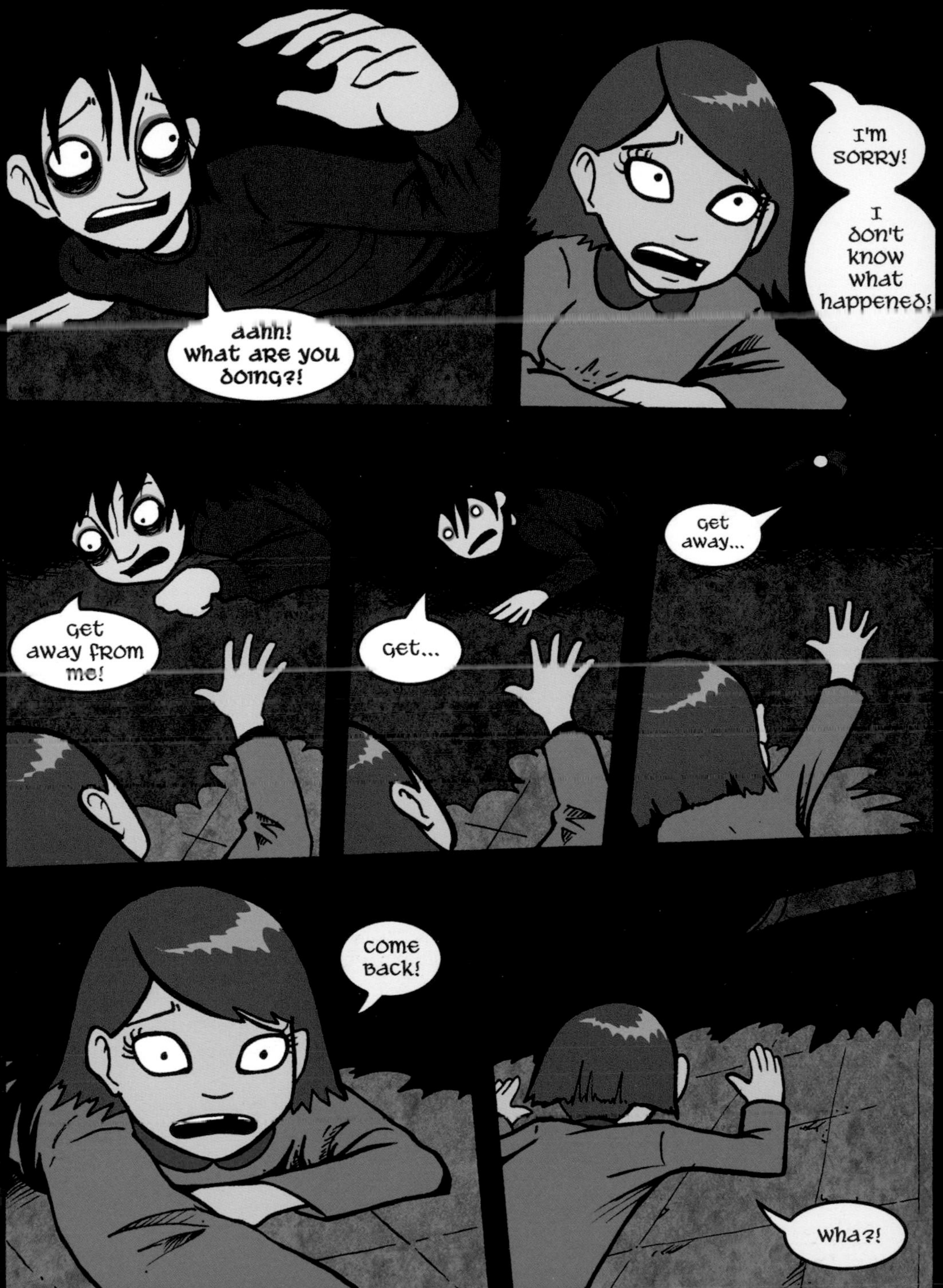
aahh! what are you doing?!
I'm SORRY!
I don't know what happened!
Get away from me!
Get...
Get away...
Come back!
Wha?!

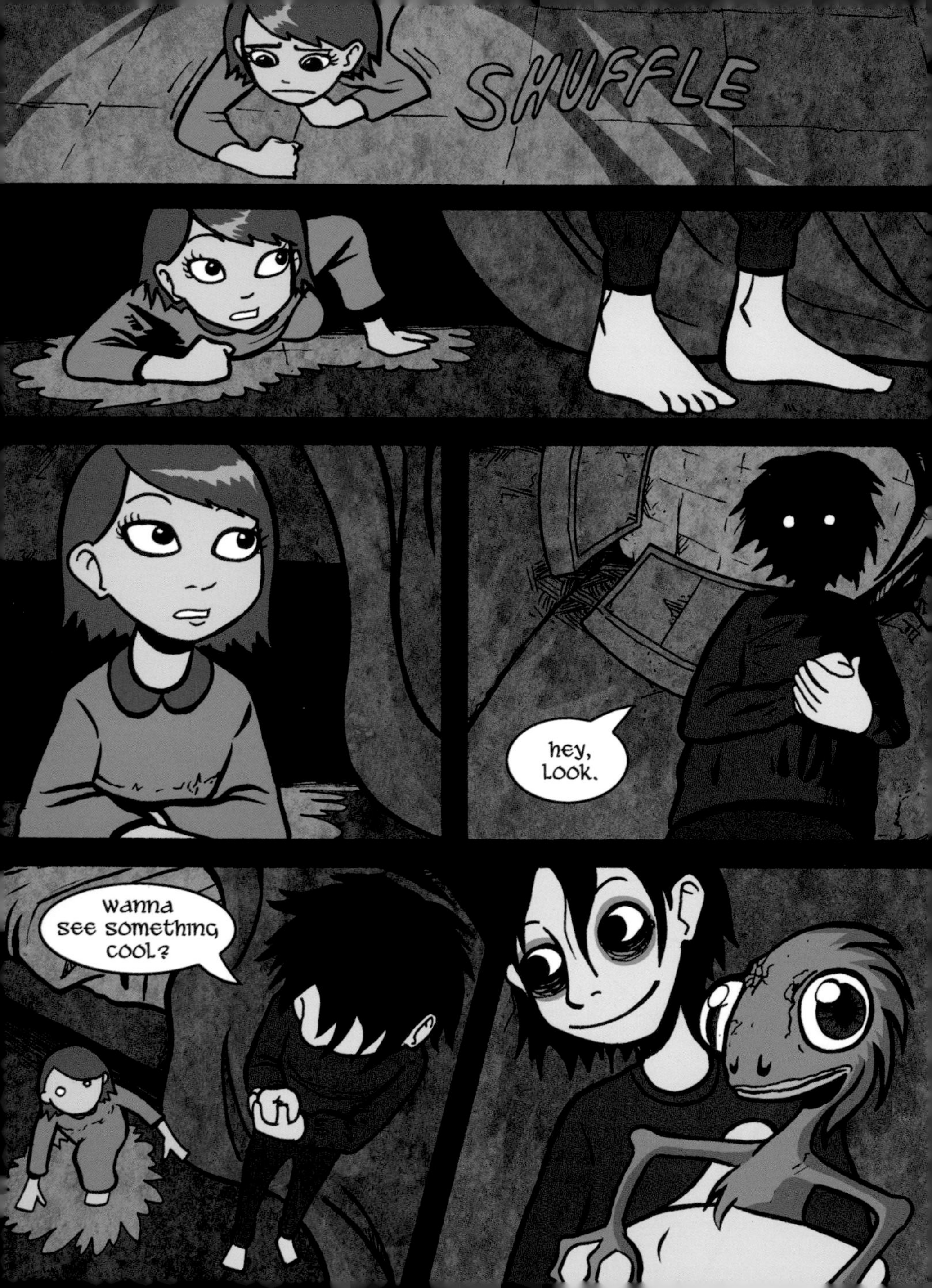
SHUFFLE
hey, look.
wanna see something cool?

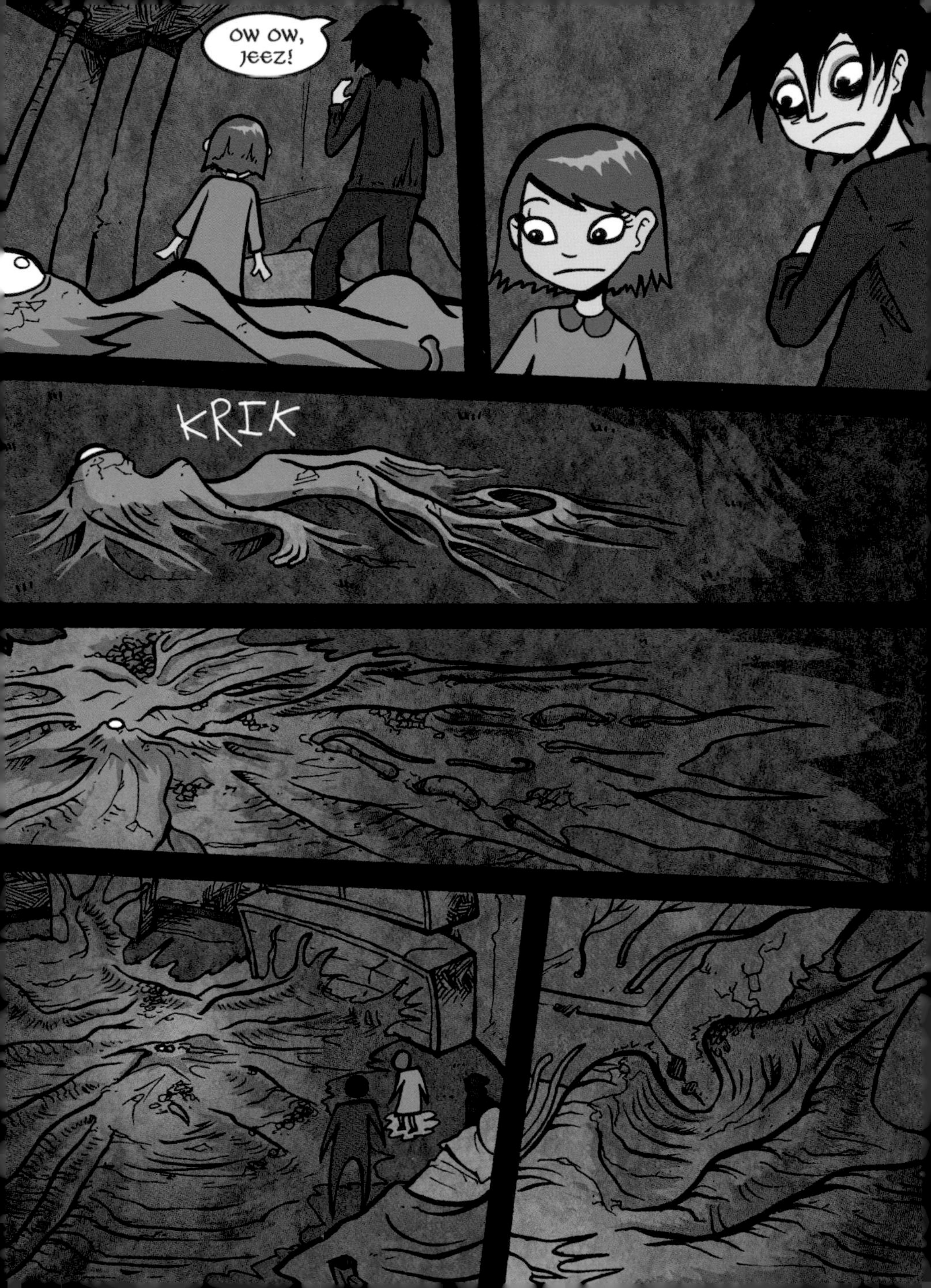
OW OW, JEEZ!
KRIK

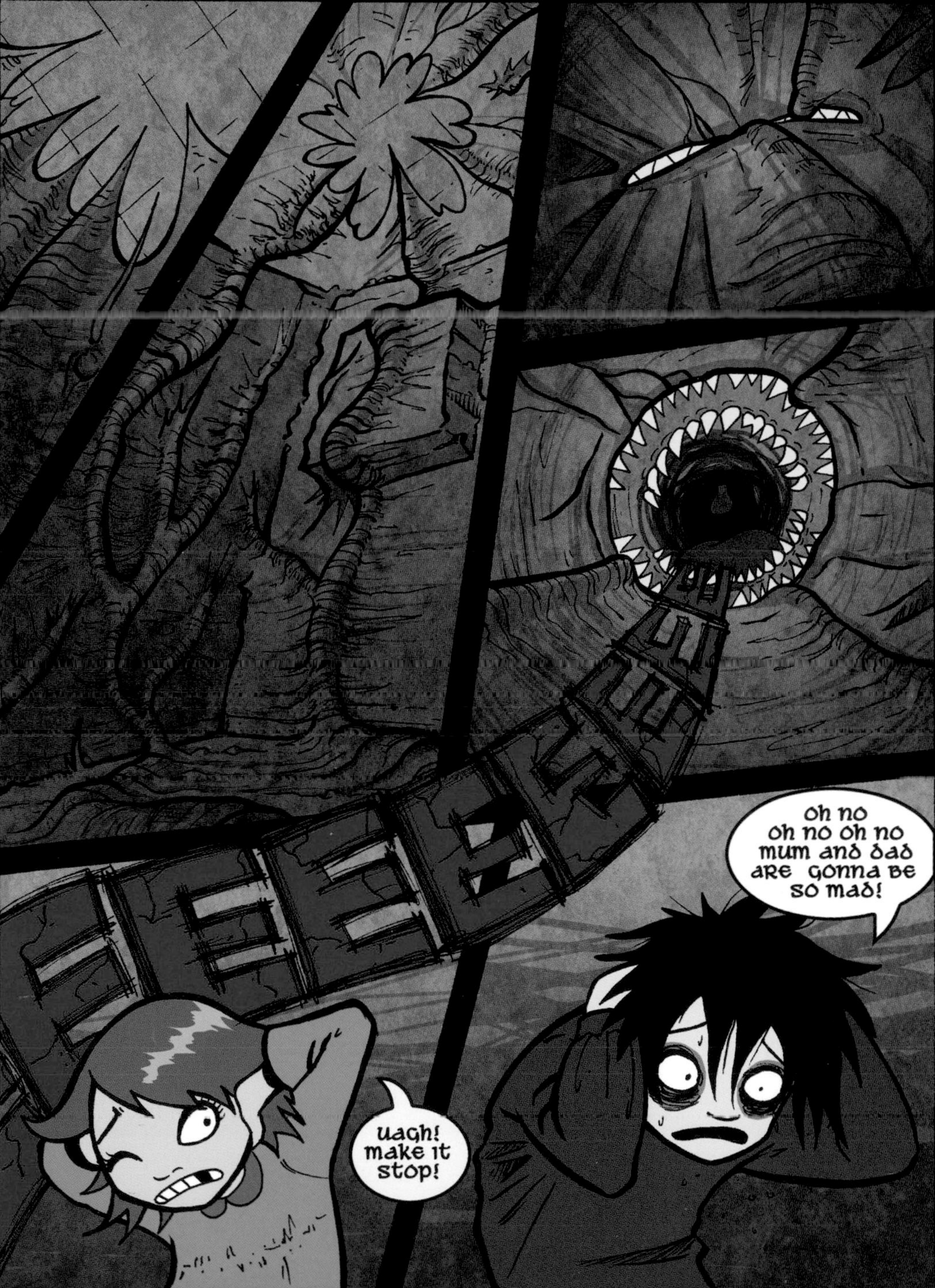
oh no
oh no oh no
mum and dad
are gonna be
so mad!
uagh!
make it
stop!

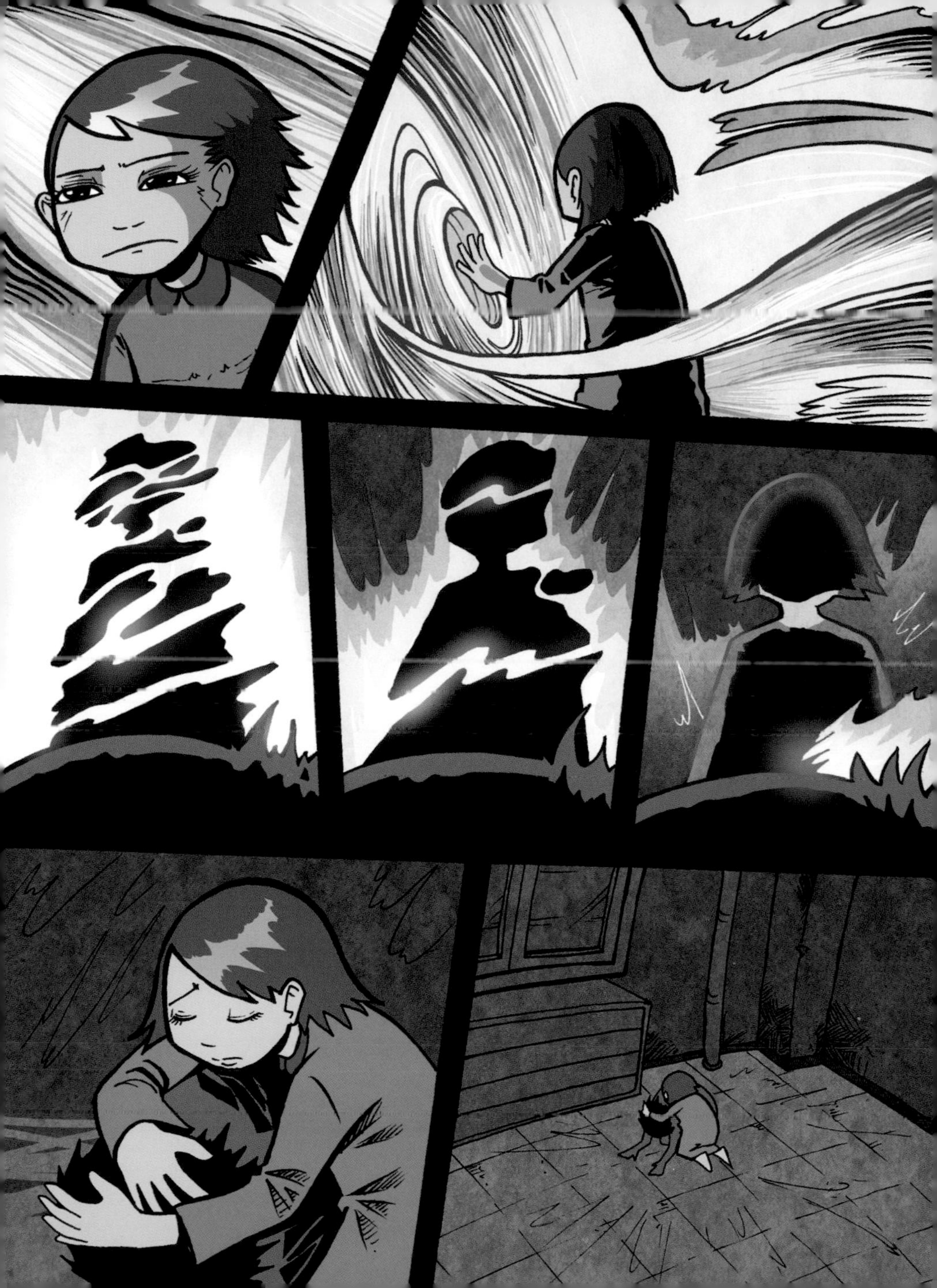

Black Dogs of the British Isles

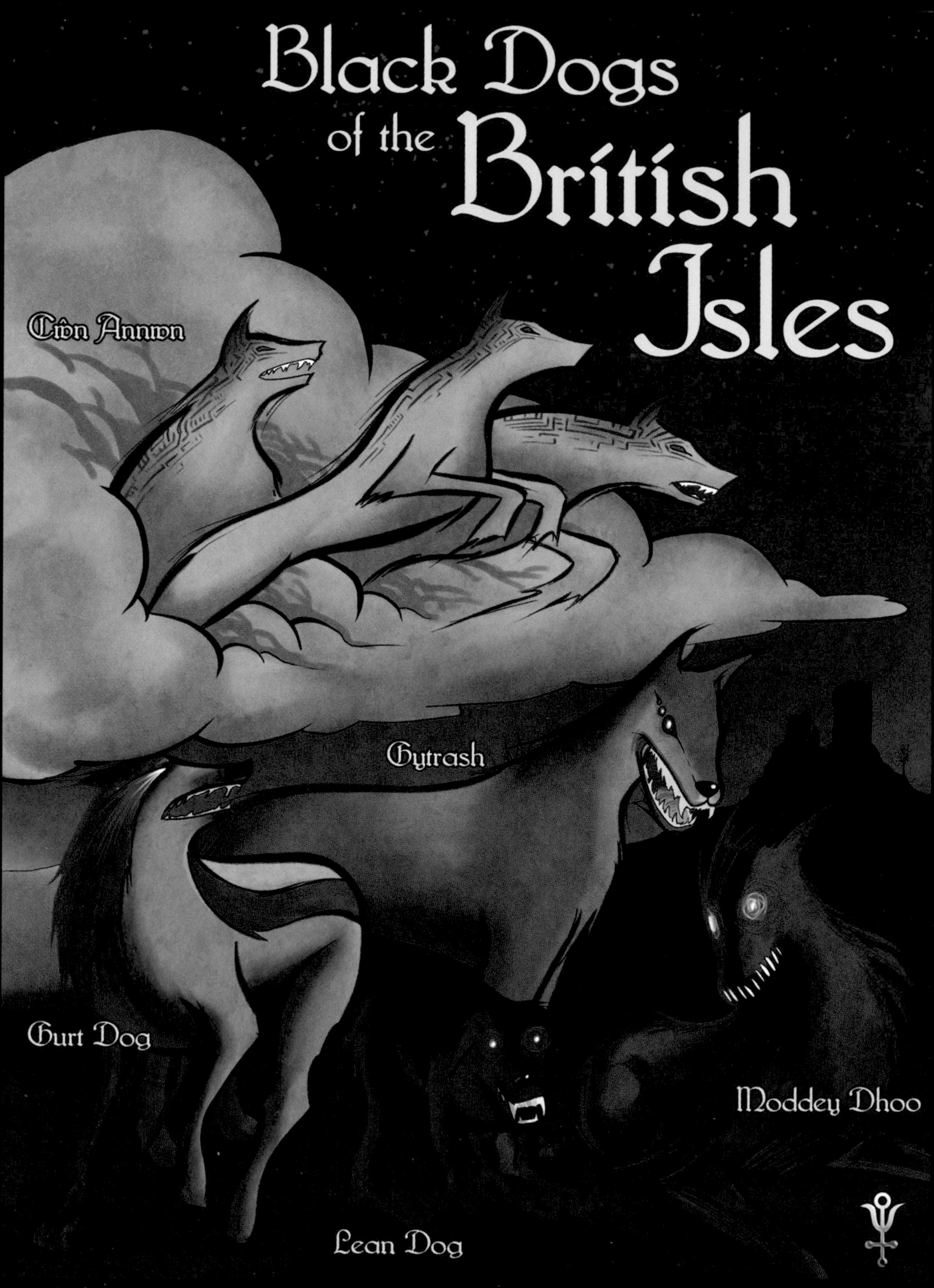
Cŵn Annwn
Gytrash
Gurt Dog
Moddey Dhoo
Lean Dog

Gunnerkrigg Court

Chapter 17:

The Medium Beginning

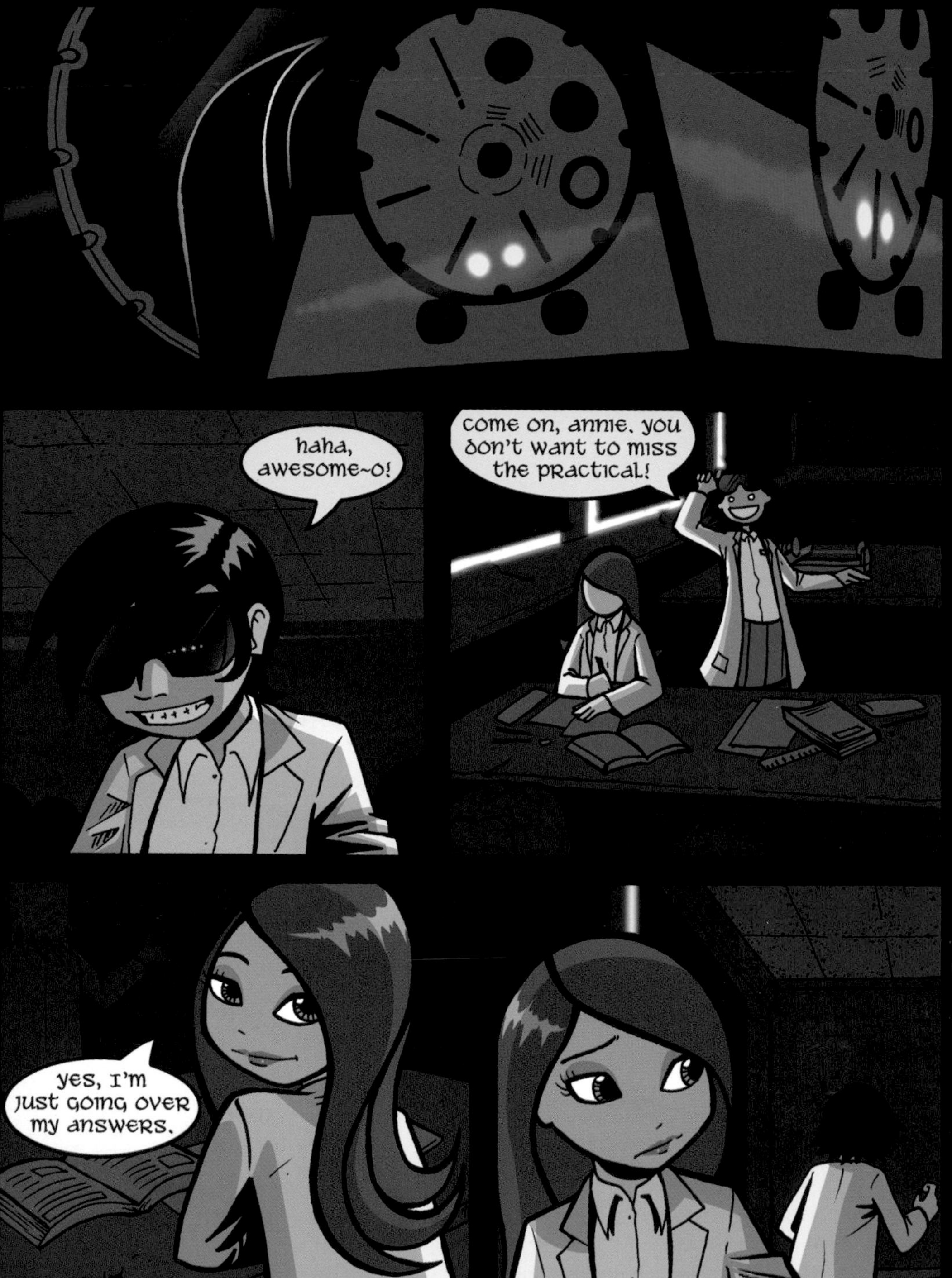
haha, awesome~o!
come on, annie. you don't want to miss the practical!
yes, I'm just going over my answers.

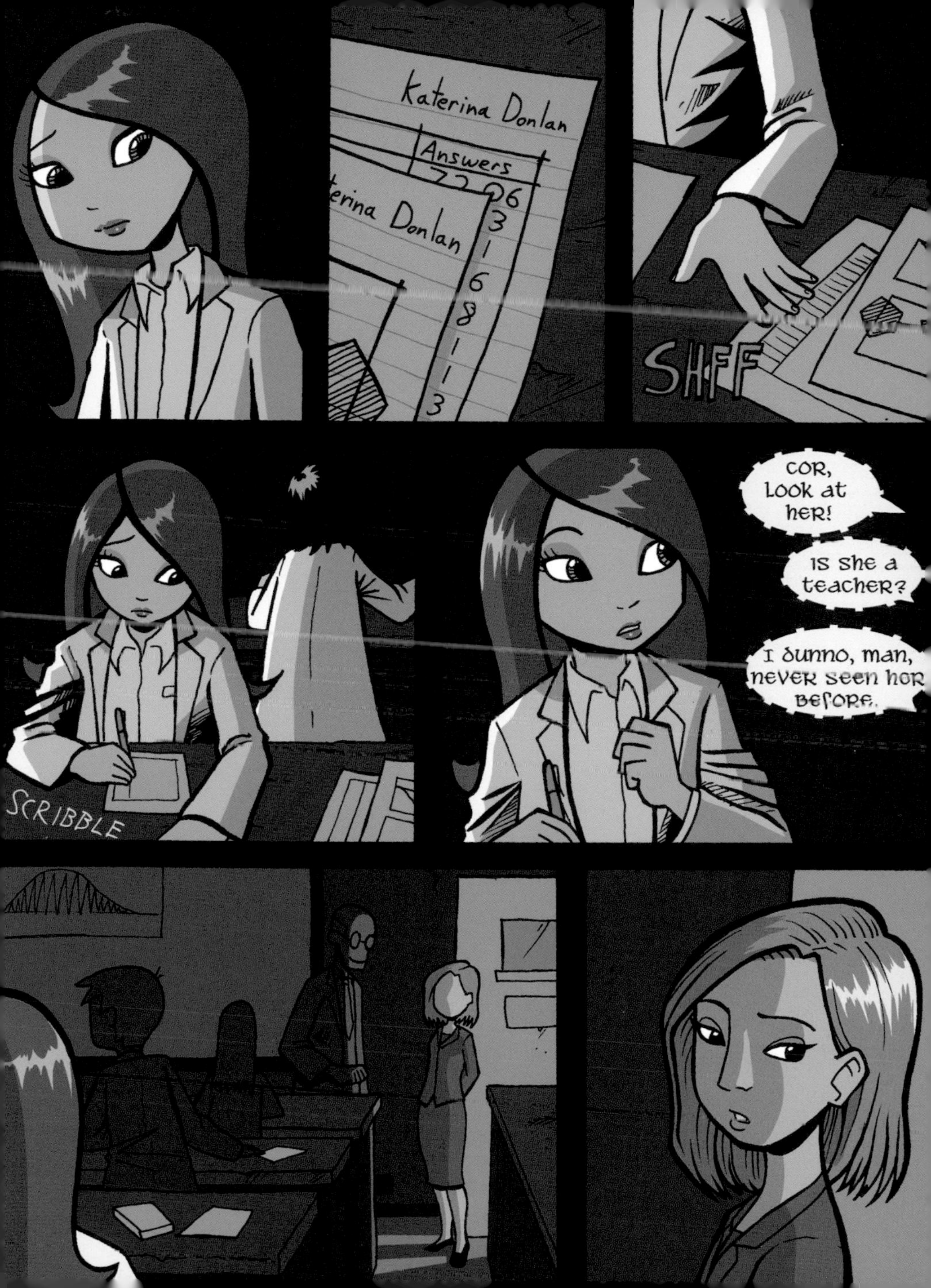
Katerina Donlan
Answers
Katerina Donlan
SHFF
SCRIBBLE
COR, LOOK AT HER!
IS SHE A TEACHER?
I DUNNO, MAN, NEVER SEEN HER BEFORE.

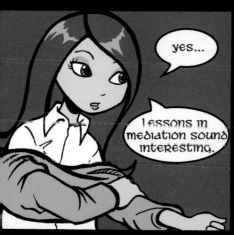

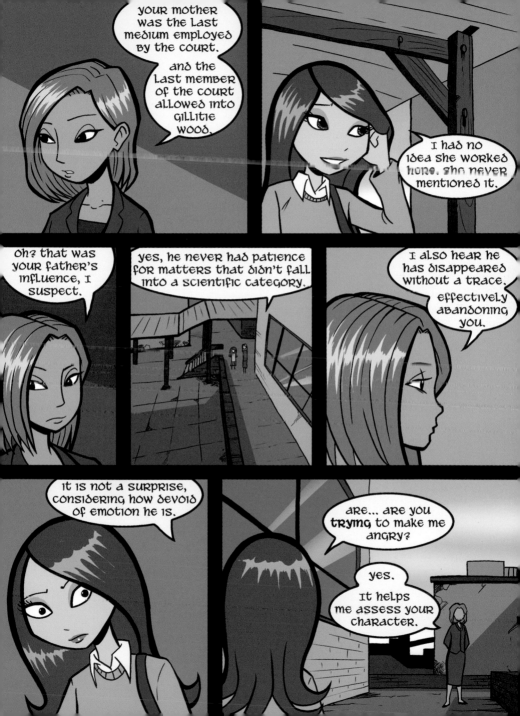

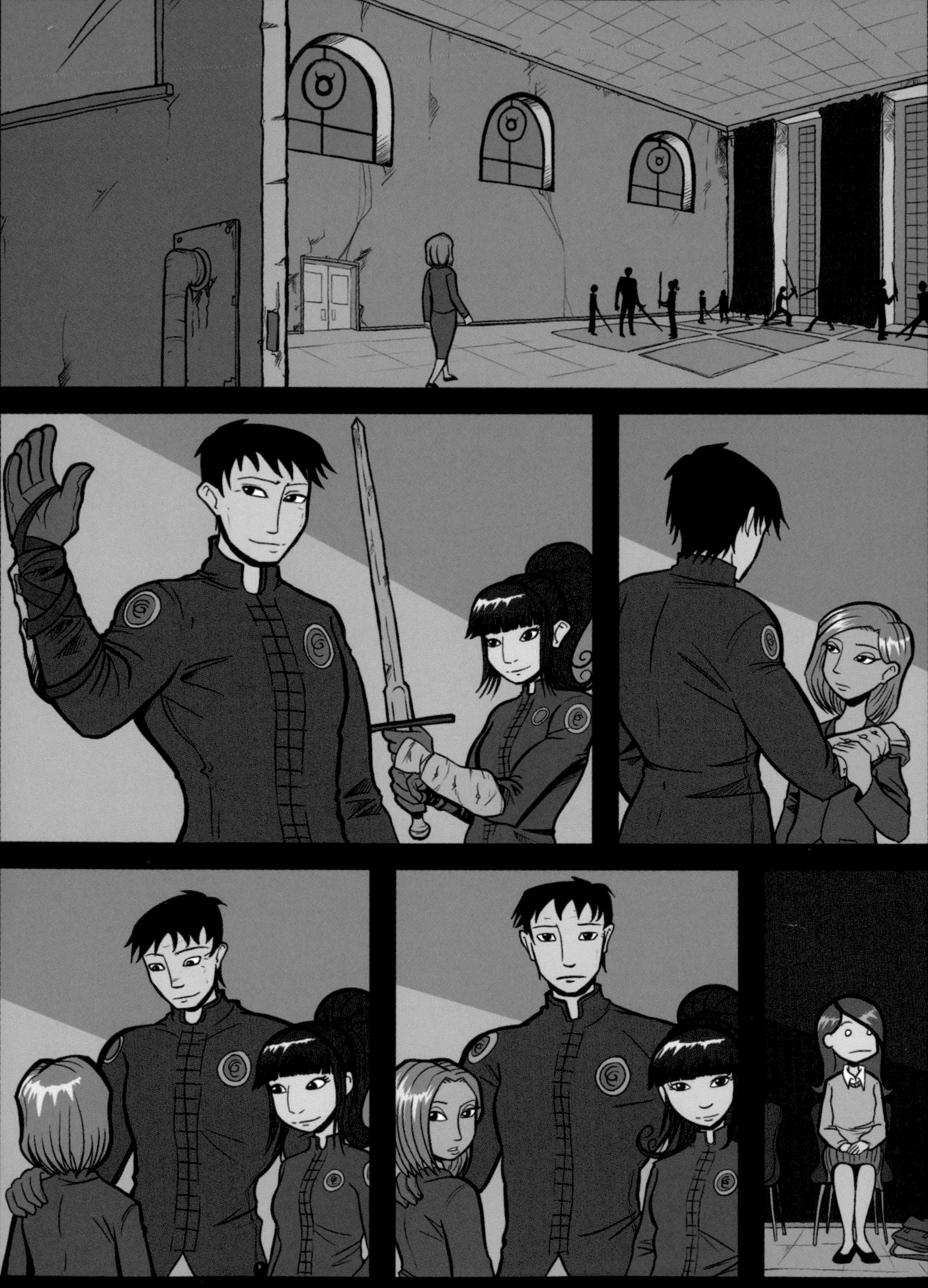

I'VE noticed an odd duality while I've been at the court.

In the subjects taught, the students, and... **things**... that happen.

FOR a school of science, there is much that science does not explain.

exactly.

In many places, my friend Kat says it's the alchemical symbol for bismuth.

In the glass there, have you ever seen that symbol before?

It serves as a reminder that the court was founded on a union between technological and **etheric** design.

etheric design?

processes unexplained by the science of man.

66

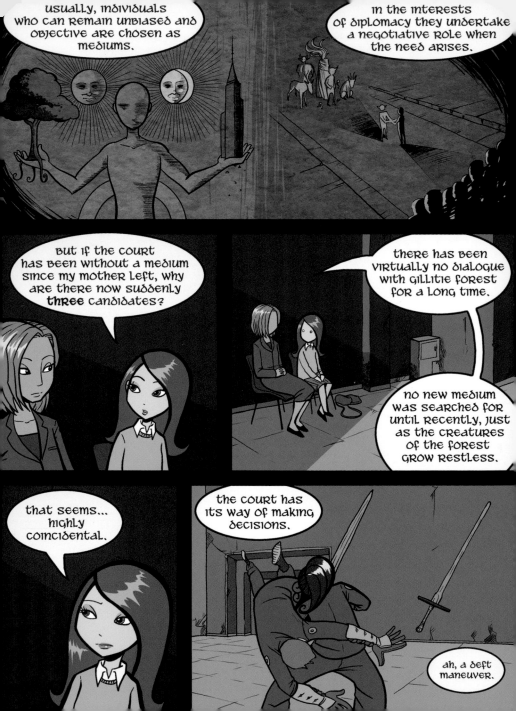

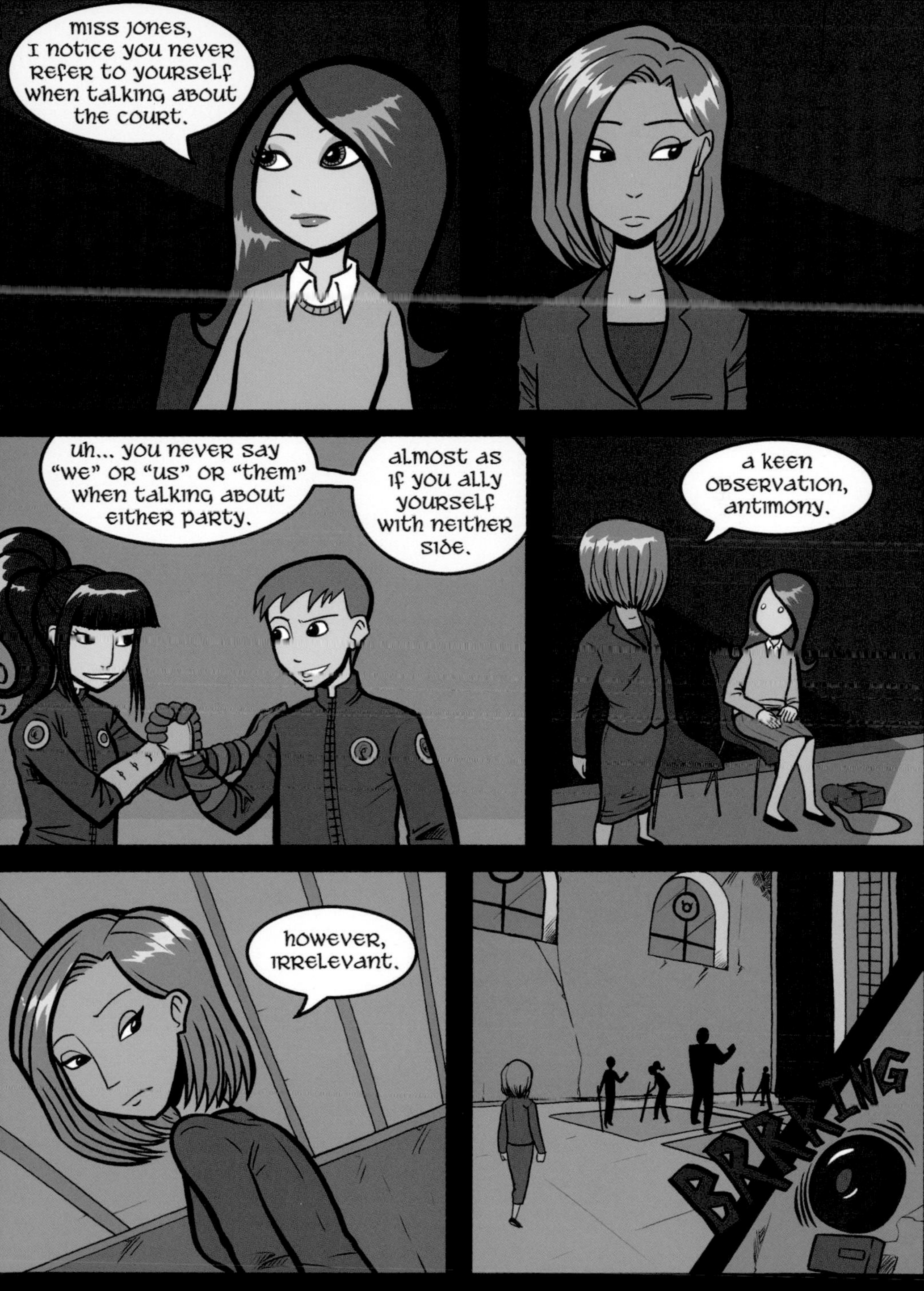
miss jones, I notice you never refer to yourself when talking about the court.
uh... you never say "we" or "us" or "them" when talking about either party.
almost as if you ally yourself with neither side.
a keen observation, antimony.
however, irrelevant.
BRRRING

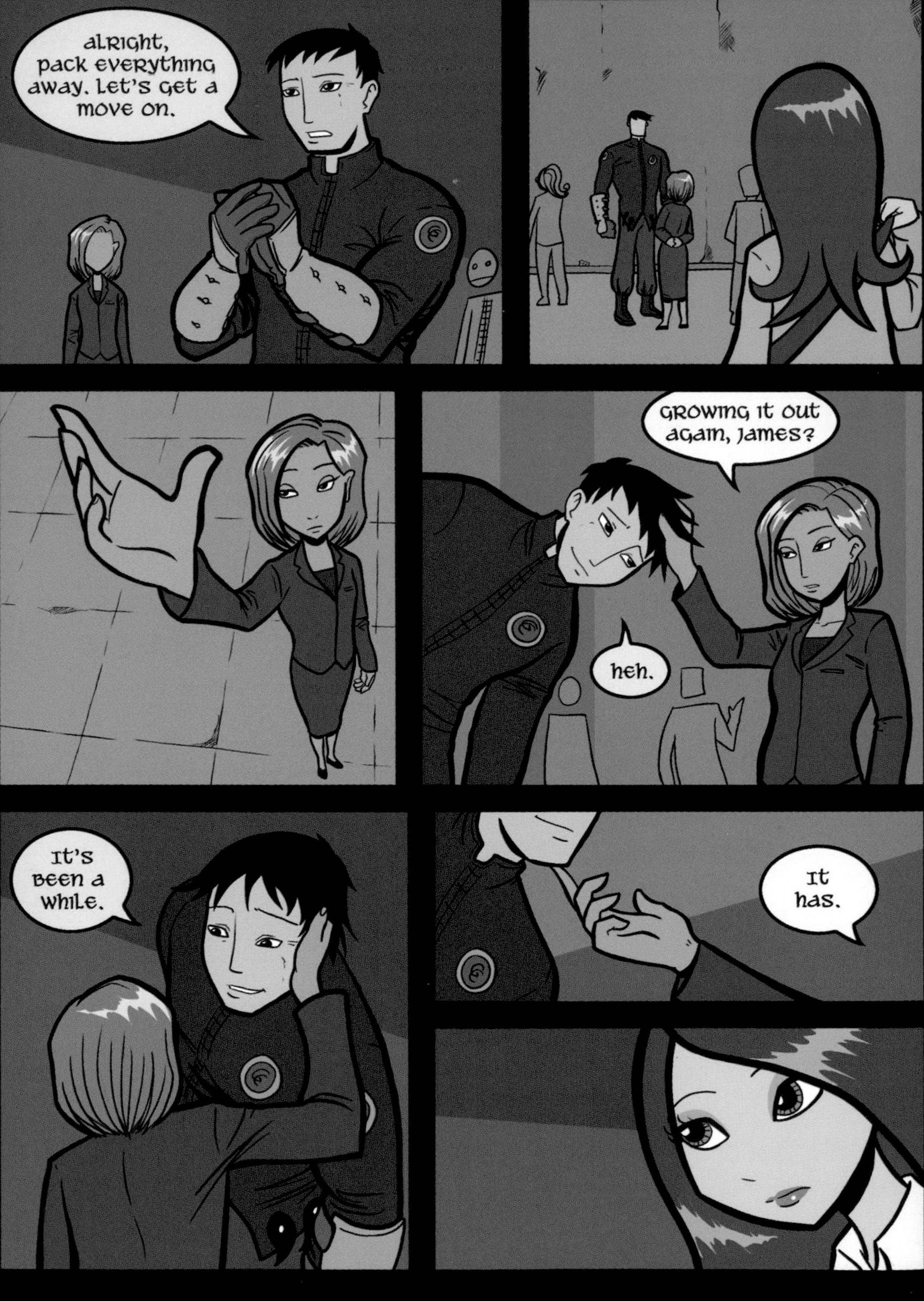
alRIGht, pack everythinG away. Let's Get a move on.
GROWING It out aGain, JAMES?
heh.
It's Been a whiLe.
It has.

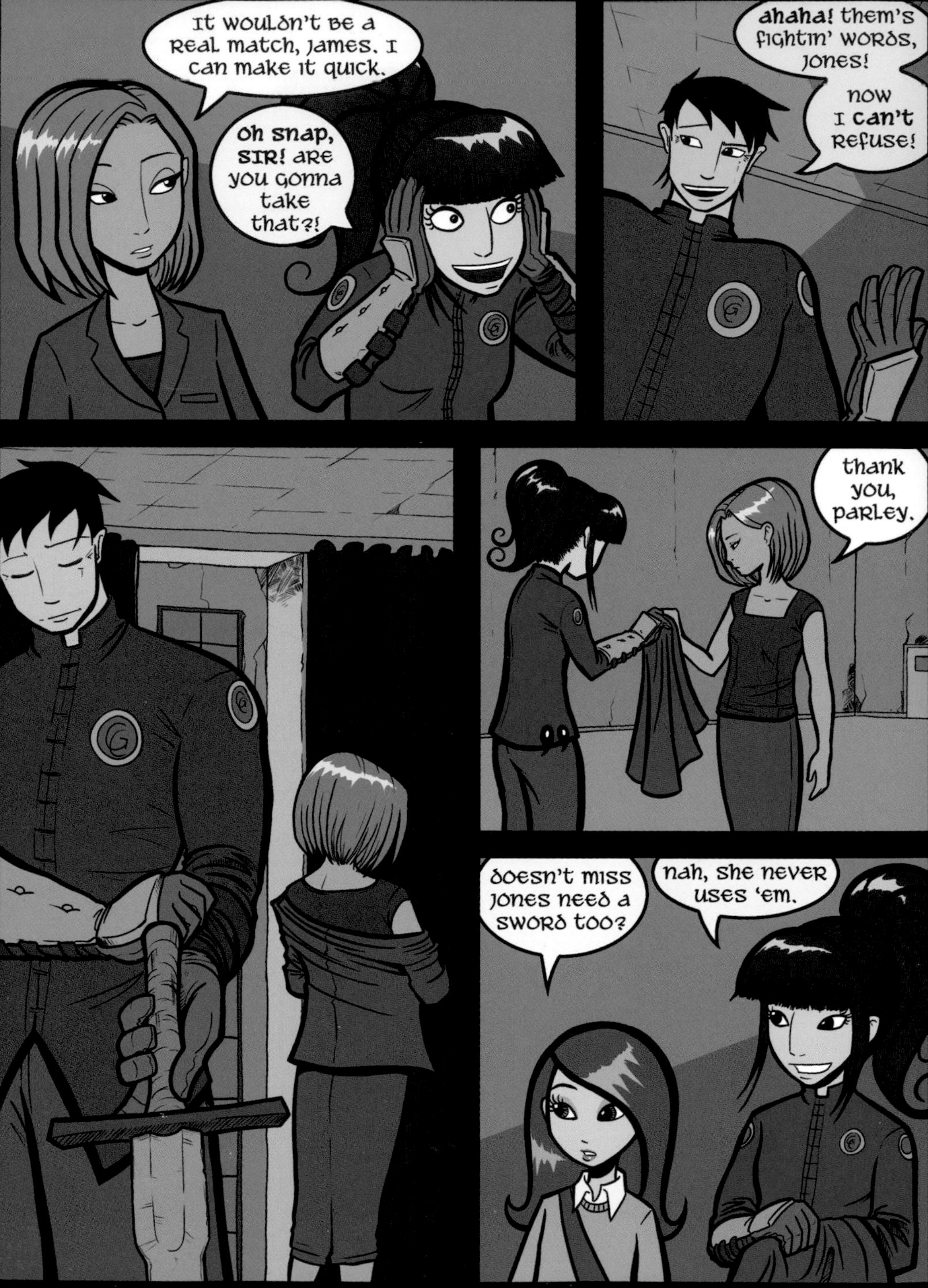
It wouldn't be a real match, James. I can make it quick.
Oh snap, SIR! are you gonna take that?!
ahaha! them's fightin' words, Jones!
now I can't refuse!
thank you, parley.
doesn't miss Jones need a sword too?
nah, she never uses 'em.

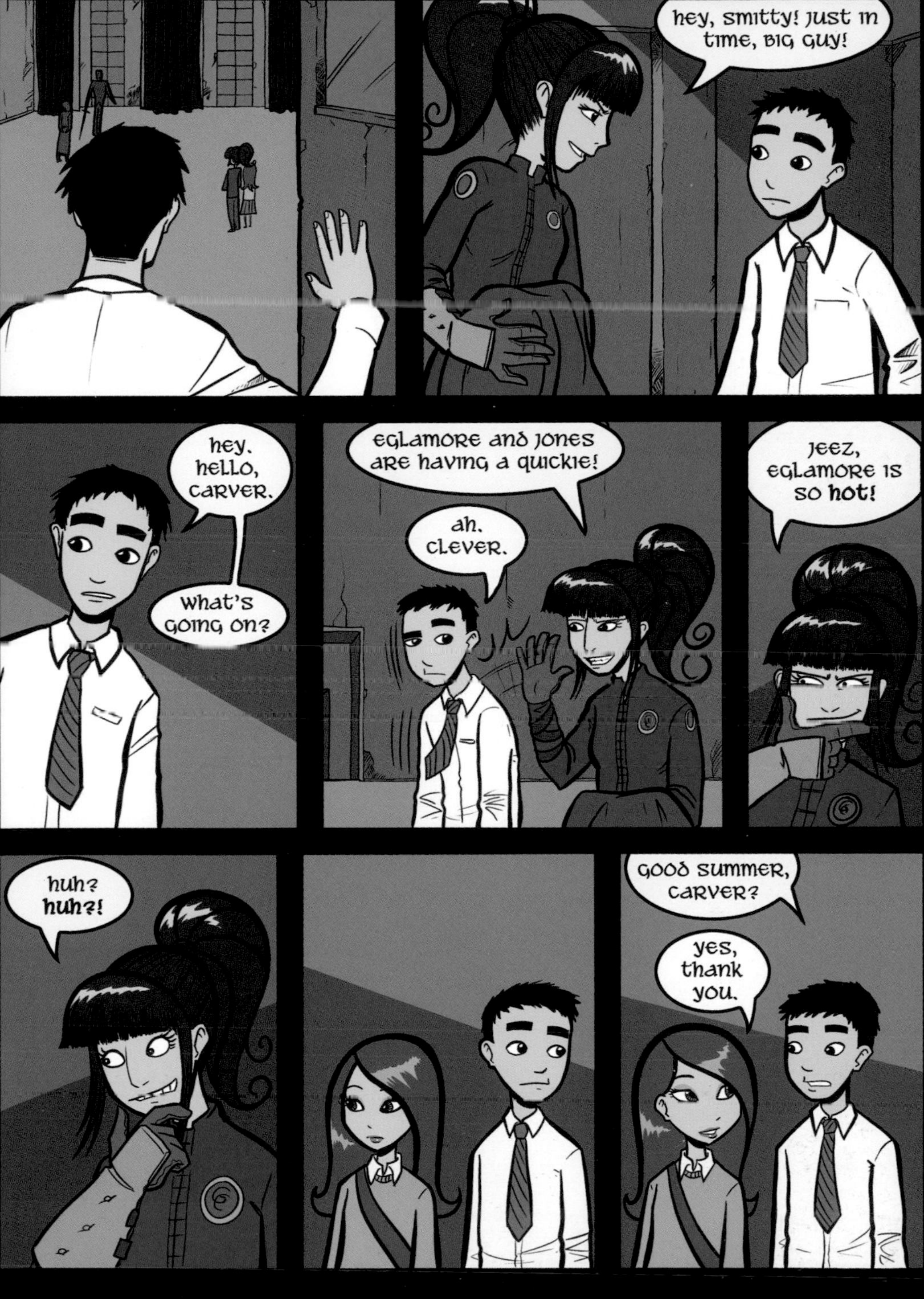
hey, smitty! just in time, big guy!
hey. hello, carver.
what's going on?
eglamore and jones are having a quickie!
ah. clever.
jeez, eglamore is so **hot!**
huh? **huh?!**
good summer, carver?
yes, thank you.

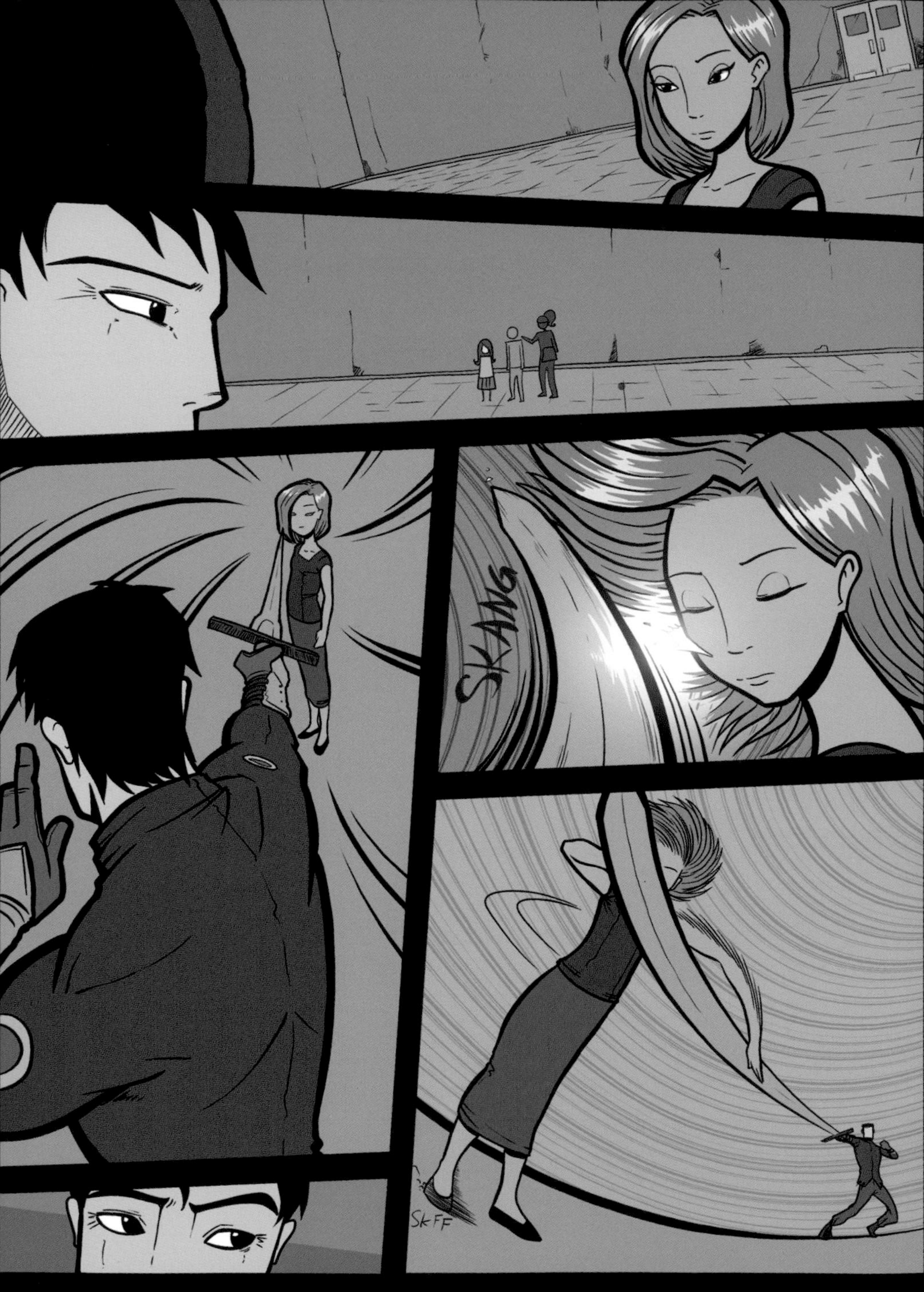
SKANG
SkFF

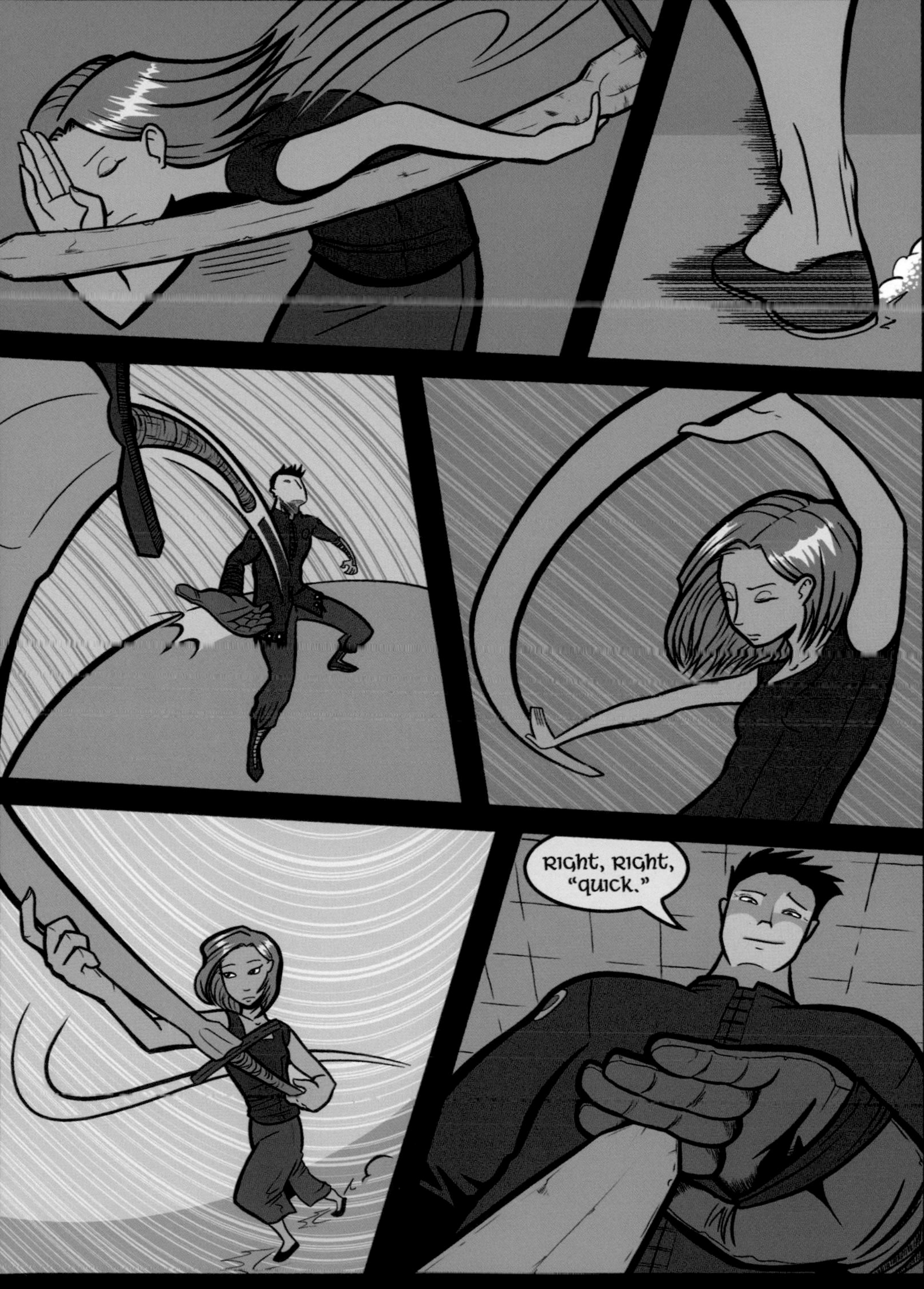
Right, right, "quick."

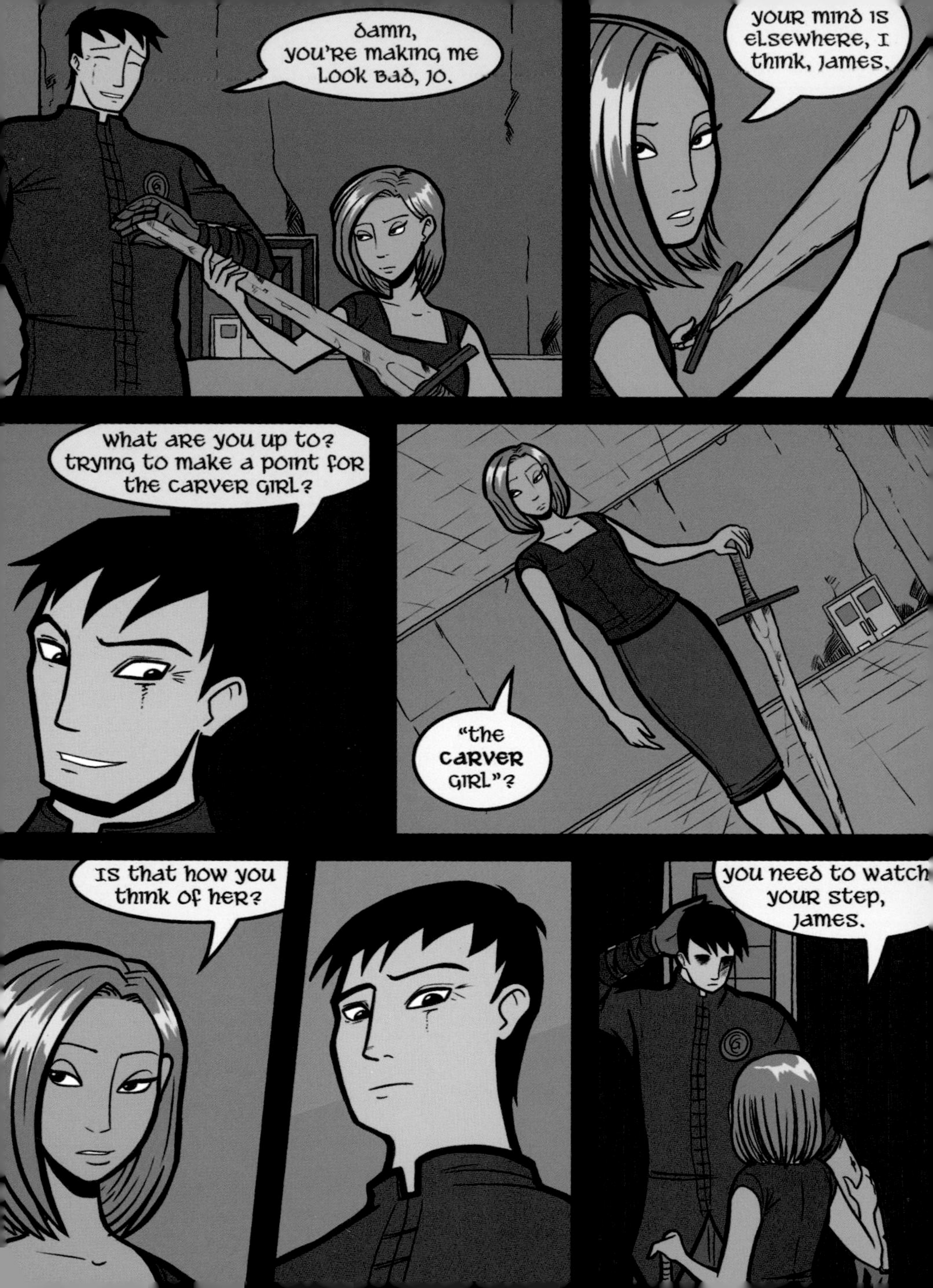
damn, you're making me look bad, jo.
your mind is elsewhere, I think, james.
what are you up to? trying to make a point for the carver girl?
"the carver girl"?
Is that how you think of her?
you need to watch your step, james.

GRABBING A SWORD BY THE BLADE ISN'T A VALID MOVE, IS IT?

IT IS FOR JONES!

NOT SOMETHING YOU WANT TO TRY YOURSELF!

AND I'M SURE THE BLADE GLANCED HER FACE...

YEAH, PROBABLY.

OH DAMN, HERE'S THE NEXT CLASS. I GOTTA GO GET CHANGED.

SMACK

TRY NOT TO GET TOO EXCITED THINKING ABOUT THAT, SMITS!

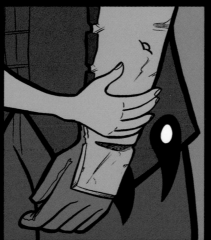

at least I can do something.

hey, shut up, man.

what is it you do, parley?

parley **senior** is the only person to have "officially" completed the **eugene gould psychic challenge.**

pfft, my dad is a **certified psychic.**

that's when they test your psychical ability in a lab.

he won like **five million quid** cos of it. put them suckers right outta business!

yeah, he's so good he predicted his **son, george** would also be psychic.

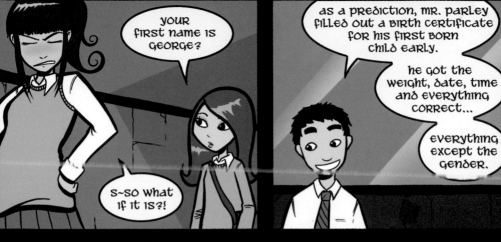

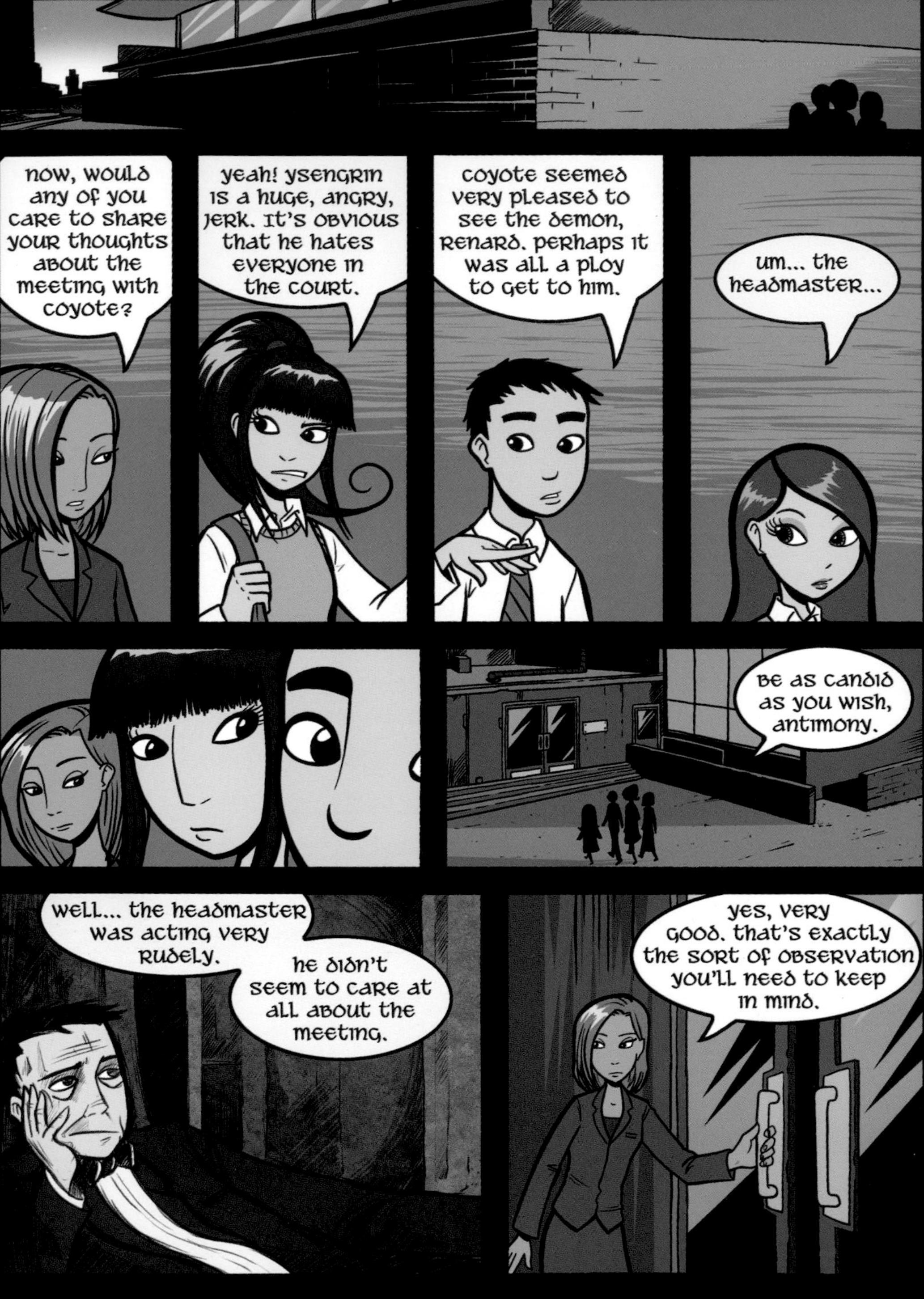
now, would any of you care to share your thoughts about the meeting with coyote?
yeah! ysengrin is a huge, angry, jerk. It's obvious that he hates everyone in the court.
coyote seemed very pleased to see the demon, renard. perhaps it was all a ploy to get to him.
um... the headmaster...
be as candid as you wish, antimony.
well... the headmaster was acting very rudely.
he didn't seem to care at all about the meeting.
yes, very good. that's exactly the sort of observation you'll need to keep in mind.

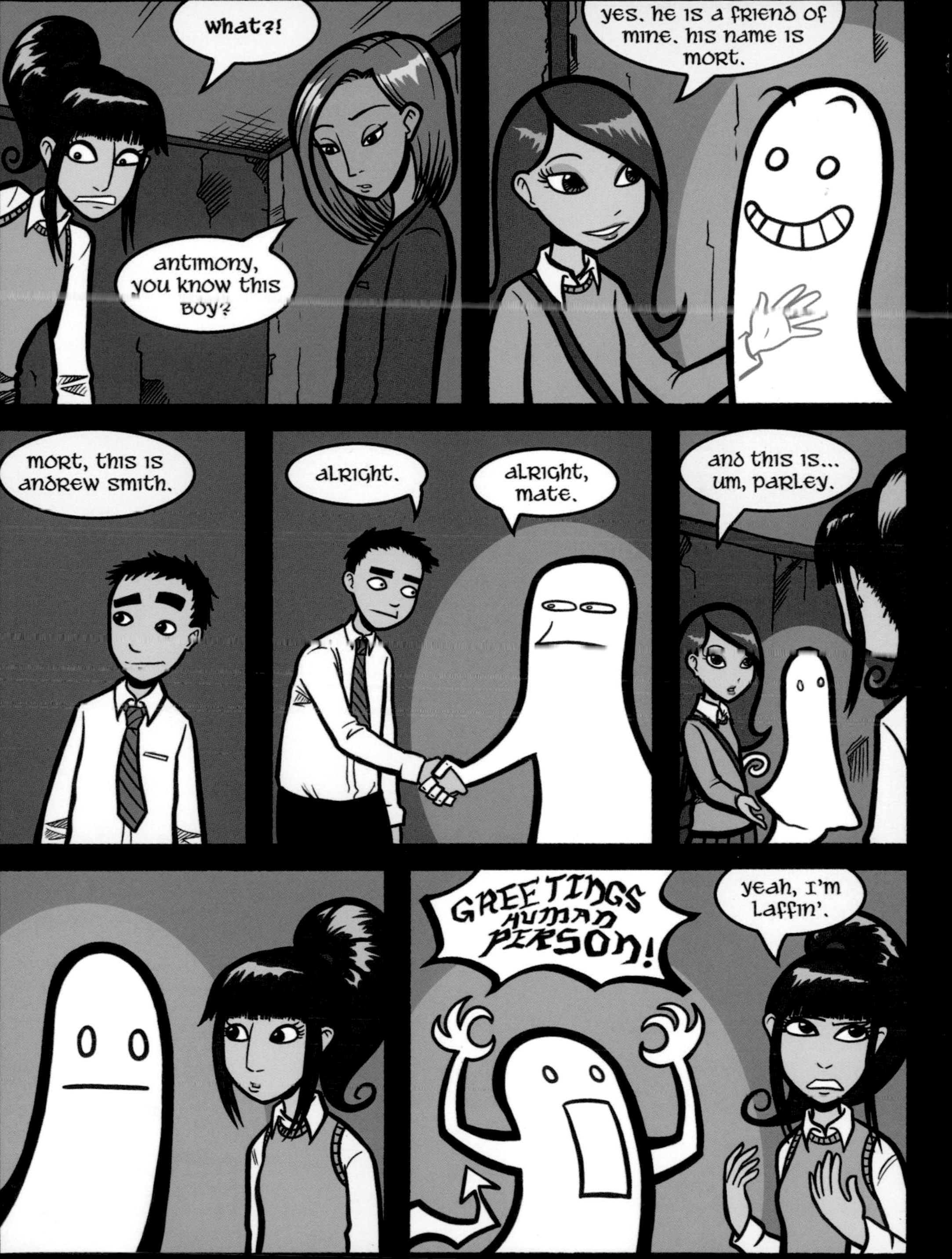
what?!
antimony, you know this boy?
yes. he is a friend of mine. his name is mort.
mort, this is andrew smith.
alright.
alright, mate.
and this is... um, parley.
GREETINGS HUMAN PERSON!
yeah, I'm laffin'.

SWORDS

Gunnerkrigg Court

there are many different types of sword

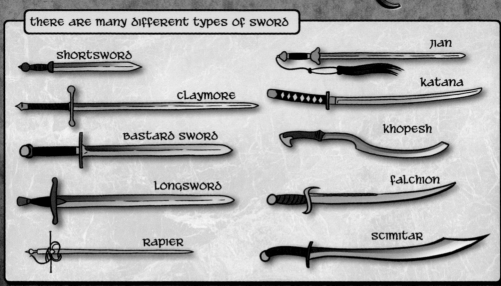

- shortsword
- claymore
- bastard sword
- longsword
- rapier
- jian
- katana
- khopesh
- falchion
- scimitar

anatomy of a sword:

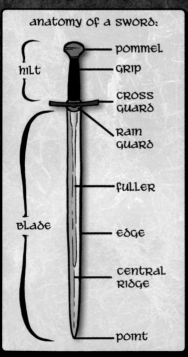

- pommel
- grip
- cross guard
- rain guard
- fuller
- edge
- central ridge
- point

hilt

blade

I think swords are neat do you think swords are neat!!

a sword is a tool designed to inflict pain or death on a fellow human!

often spiritualised and glorified, they also serve as a physical metaphor for humanity's eternal, savage thirst for destruction!

Gunnerkrigg Court

Chapter 18:

S1

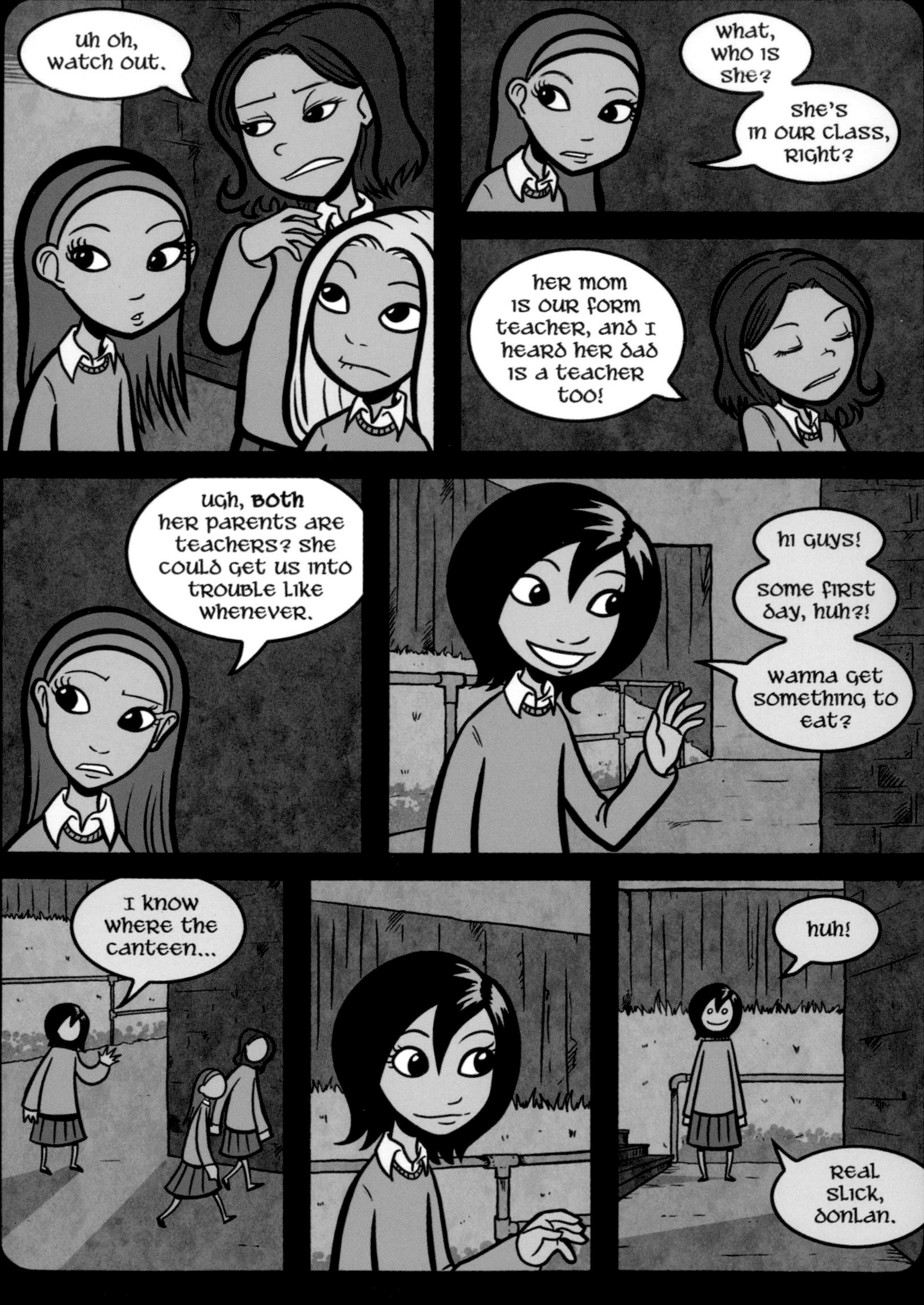
uh oh, watch out.
what, who is she?
she's in our class, right?
her mom is our form teacher, and I heard her dad is a teacher too!
ugh, **both** her parents are teachers? she could get us into trouble like whenever.
hi guys!
some first day, huh?!
wanna get something to eat?
I know where the canteen...
huh!
real slick, donlan.

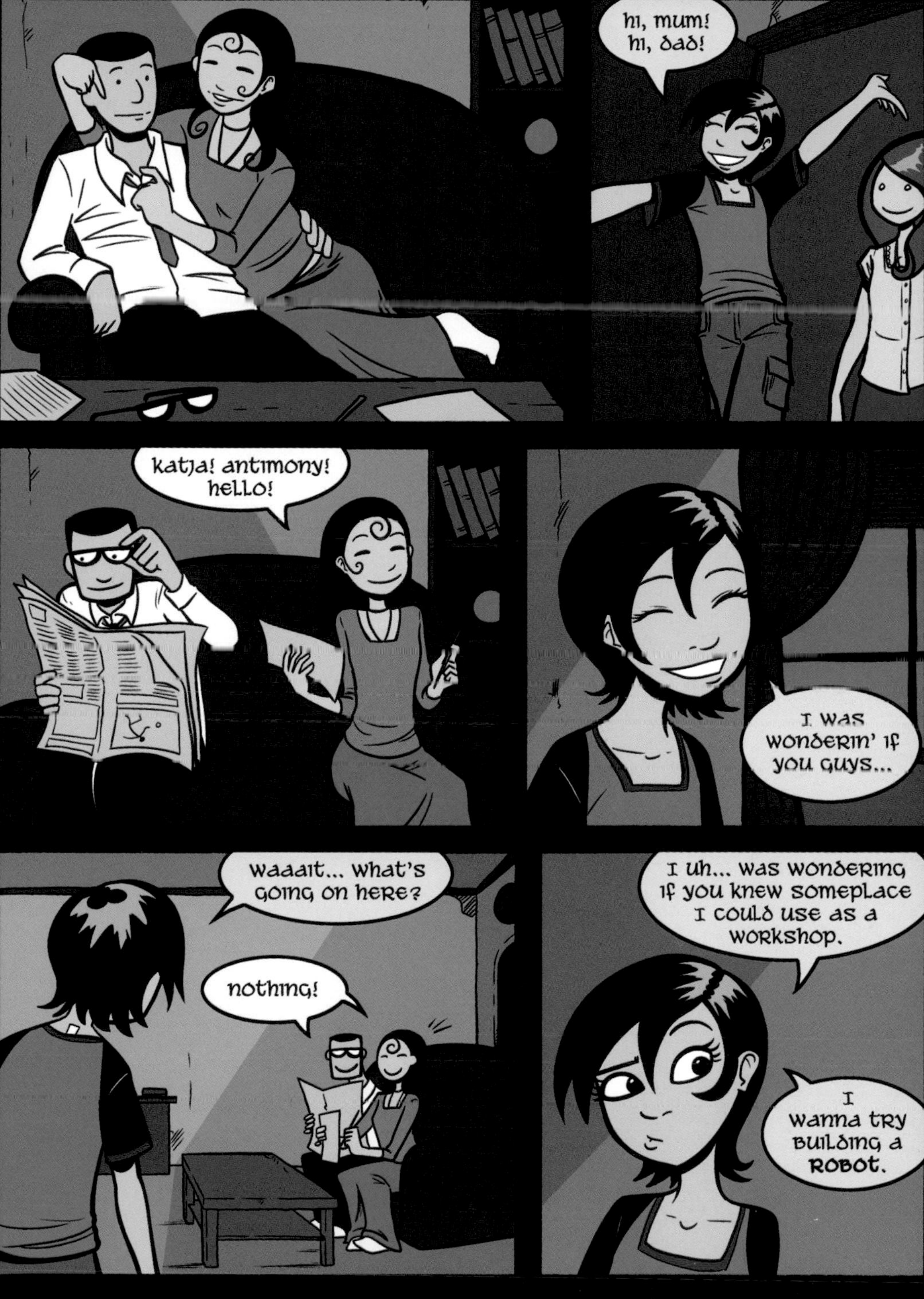

hi, mum! hi, dad!
katja! antimony! hello!
I was wonderin' if you guys...
Waaait... what's going on here?
nothing!
I uh... was wondering if you knew someplace I could use as a workshop.
I wanna try building a ROBOT.

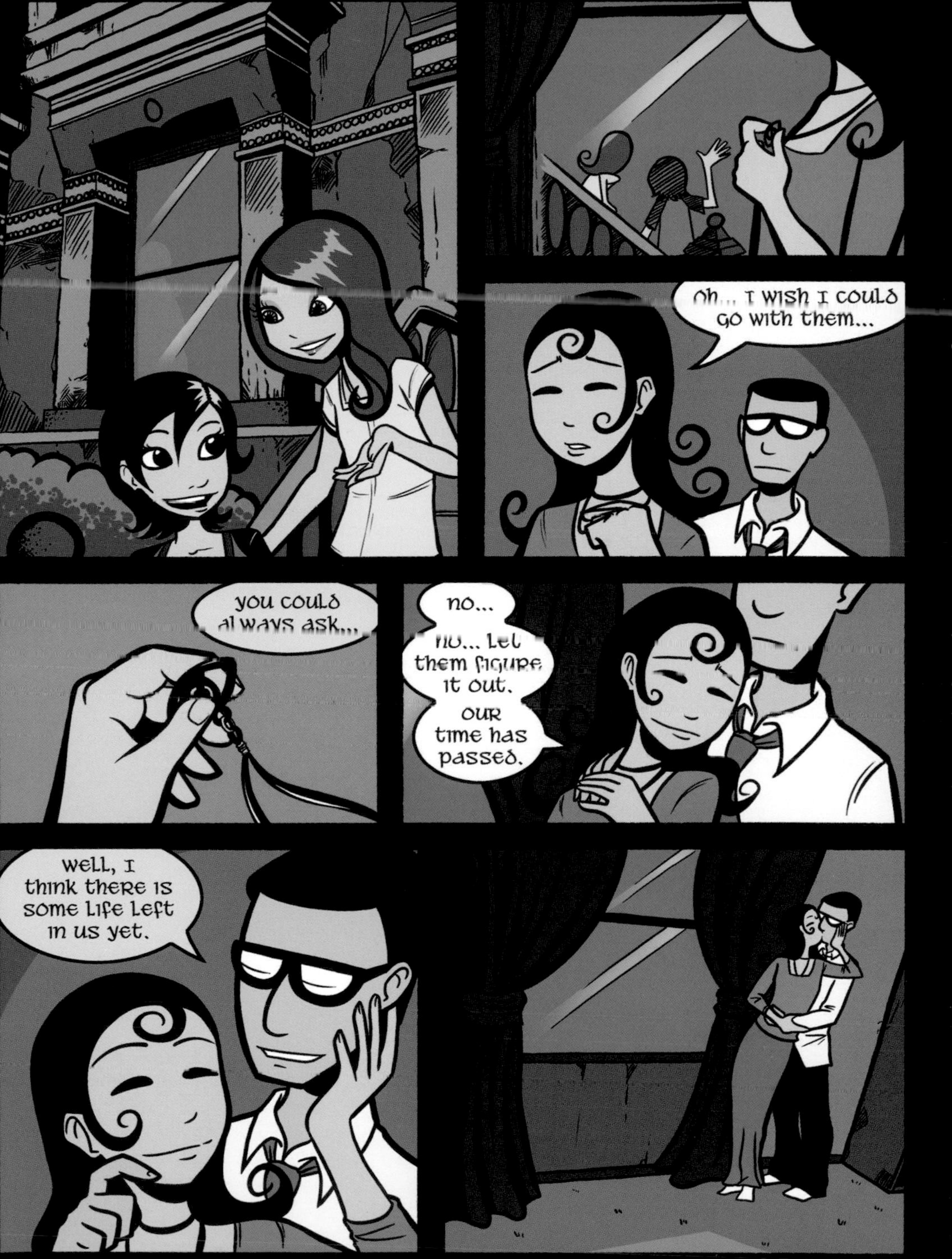
Oh... I wish I could go with them...
you could always ask...
no...
no... let them figure it out.
our time has passed.
well, I think there is some life left in us yet.

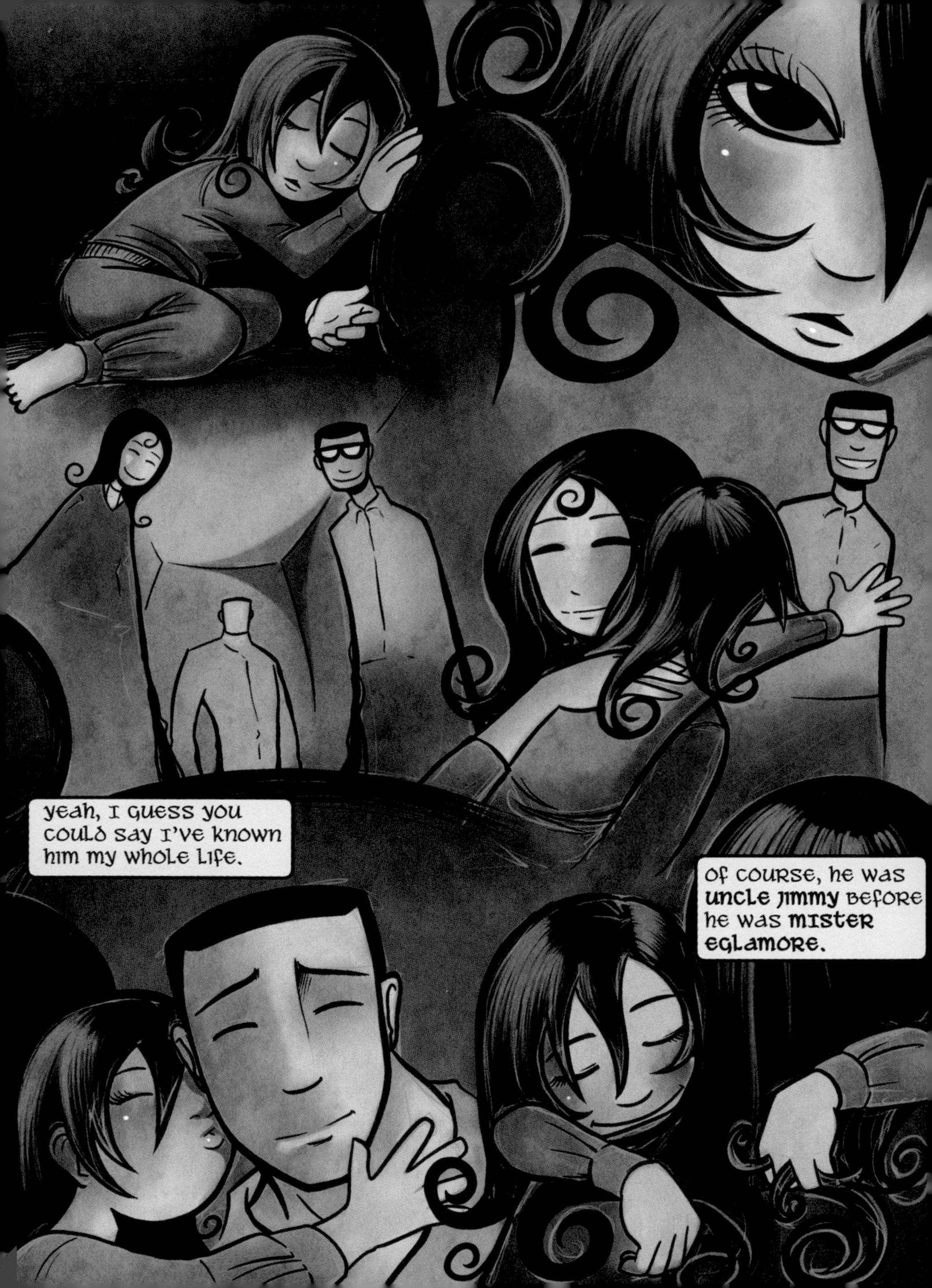
yeah, I guess you could say I've known him my whole life.
Of course, he was uncle jimmy before he was mister eglamore.

the human body is essentially a biological machine. it relies on contractile tissue for movement.

most of our robots have ultra high torque actuators in their joints. that's how they move.

so their point of locomotion is in their joints? that's not quite how muscles work.

haw! look at that!

hey! nice teddy!

are you off to nursery?

Born To Heckle

well, maybe hydraulics are closer to how... how a muscle...

hey you!

carrot top!

are you okay, kat?

those guys over there are being jerks.

hey! shut up!

ooooo!

haha!

Oh, we got to the bottom, finally.

This room must be very large. I can't see the walls or the ceiling.

I saw a plug on the end of this cable near the entrance. maybe it leads to...

Ah yes, a flood light.

I guess my mum set these up when she still worked here.

If you stay here with Reynardine and Robot, Shadow 2 and I will nip back and plug them in.

Won't be long!

heyyy ren~ar~deeen!
what is it?
that was pretty cute how you got all defensive about annie before.
you were all "insult you would they?!"
wh... no I wasn't! I said "us."
insult us, would they
no you didn't
yes I did!
hehe, okay then. whatever you say.
...
you are a good friend to her, katerina.
huh?
how is she doing in her studies?
does she have many other friends?
has anyone been giving her trouble?
has a boy caught her eye?

WOAH WOAH, WHERE DID ALL THIS COME FROM? ARE YOU LIKE HER DAD IN DISGUISE NOW?

UGH. PERISH THE THOUGHT. I WAS ONLY CURIOUS.

I ASSUMED YOU WOULD KNOW HER BEST, SINCE YOU SPEND SO MUCH TIME TOGETHER.

ALL SHE TALKS ABOUT IS YOU.

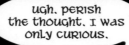

THIS IS A SET UP FOR ANOTHER LEWD JOKE, ISN'T IT? WHAT DO **YOU** CARE?

FORGET IT.

HUH! YOU'RE BEING SERIOUS AREN'T YOU?

I SAID FORGET IT.

YOU SHOULD STAY AS A WOLF MORE OFTEN, DUDE. YOU'RE MUCH NICER THIS WAY.

WELL, THE MIND IS NOTHING BUT A PLAYTHING OF THE BODY, CORRECT?

WHA?

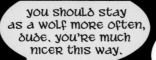

CHACK

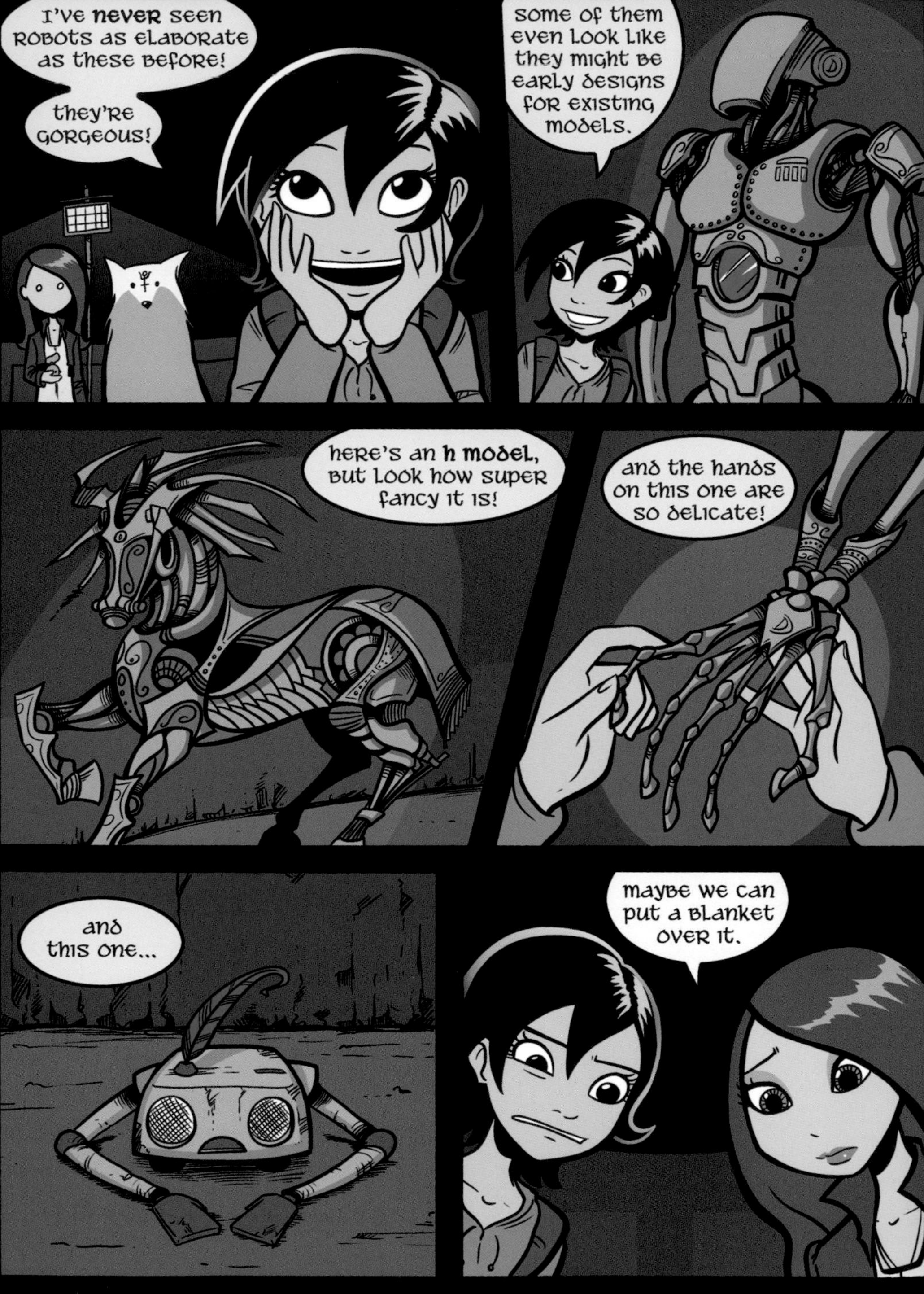
I'VE **NEVER** SEEN ROBOTS AS ELABORATE AS THESE BEFORE!
THEY'RE GORGEOUS!
SOME OF THEM EVEN LOOK LIKE THEY MIGHT BE EARLY DESIGNS FOR EXISTING MODELS.
HERE'S AN **H MODEL**, BUT LOOK HOW SUPER FANCY IT IS!
AND THE HANDS ON THIS ONE ARE SO DELICATE!
AND THIS ONE...
MAYBE WE CAN PUT A BLANKET OVER IT.

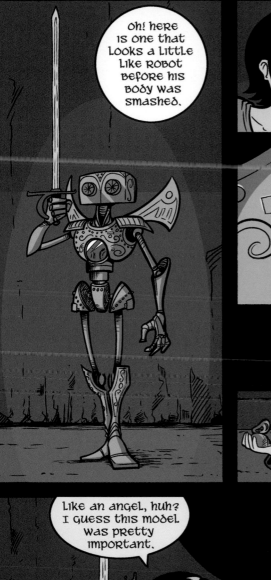

OH! HERE IS ONE THAT LOOKS A LITTLE LIKE ROBOT BEFORE HIS BODY WAS SMASHED.

VERY HANDSOME! I BET YOU GOT ALL THE GIRLBOTS BACK IN THE DAY, HUH!

AH! OH.. WELL..

YOU WERE S13, RIGHT, ROBOT?

LOOKS LIKE THIS WAS YOUR ORIGINAL DESIGN.

WHAT DOES THE S STAND FOR?

SERAPH, AS I RECALL.

LIKE AN ANGEL, HUH? I GUESS THIS MODEL WAS PRETTY IMPORTANT.

ANYWAY, LET'S SEE WHAT MAKES THESE GUYS TICK!

YOU MIGHT GET A NEW BODY SOONER THAN WE THOUGHT, ROBOT!

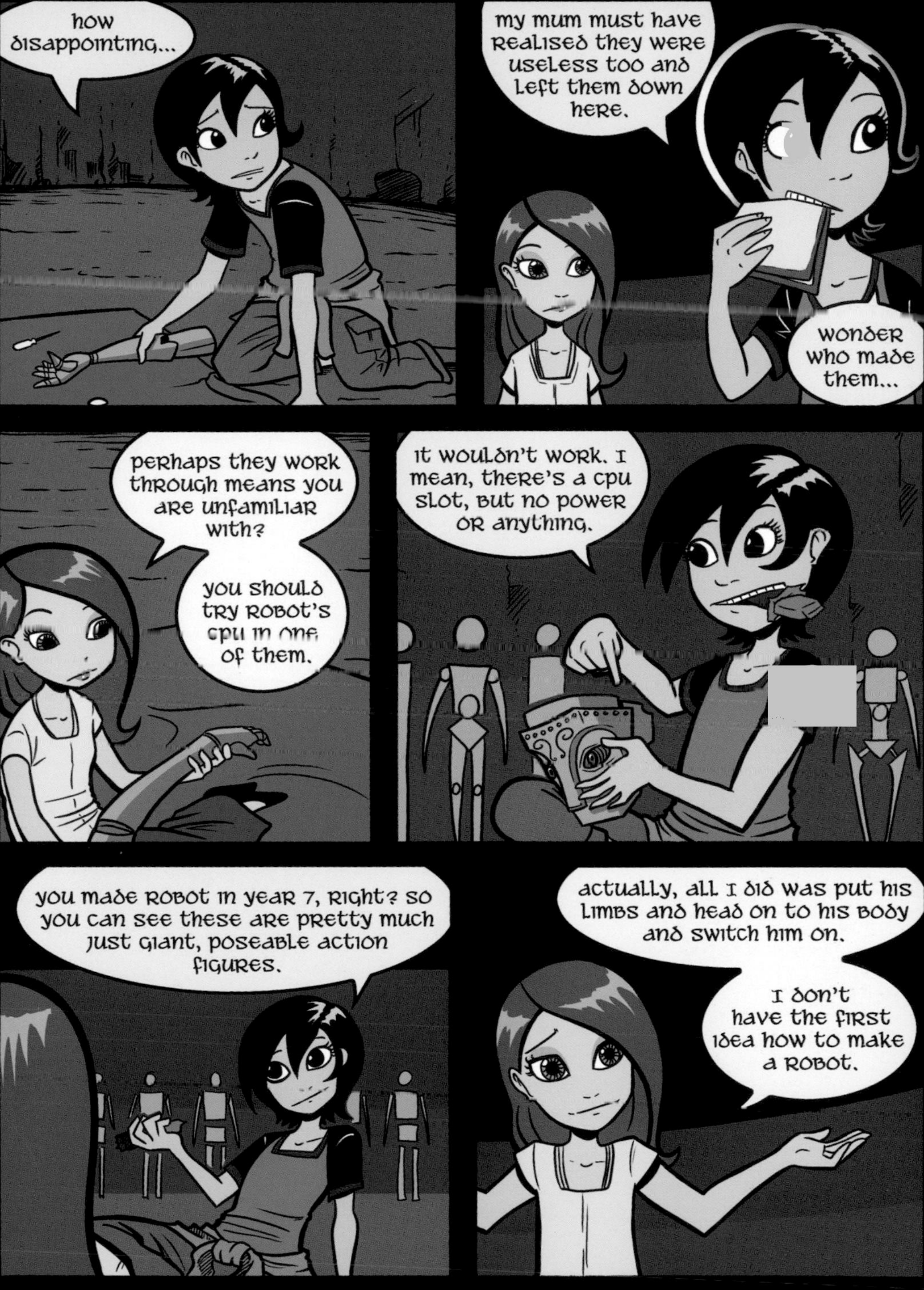
how disappointing...
my mum must have realised they were useless too and left them down here.
wonder who made them...
perhaps they work through means you are unfamiliar with?
you should try robot's cpu in one of them.
it wouldn't work. I mean, there's a cpu slot, but no power or anything.
you made robot in year 7, right? so you can see these are pretty much just giant, poseable action figures.
actually, all I did was put his limbs and head on to his body and switch him on.
I don't have the first idea how to make a robot.

SEE? NOTHING.

CLANG

WHAT IF YOU TRIED IT IN HIS ORIGINAL DESIGN?

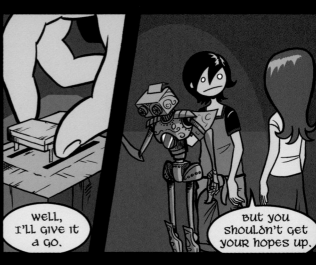

WELL, I'LL GIVE IT A GO.

BUT YOU SHOULDN'T GET YOUR HOPES UP.

SNAP

JEANNE!

JEANNE!

WHAAA?! THAT'S IMPOSSIBLE!

ROBOT!

KAT, I THINK SOMETHING'S WRONG WITH HIM!

I'LL SAY! HE'S RUNNIN' AROUND WHEN HE SHOULDN'T BE!

CLANK

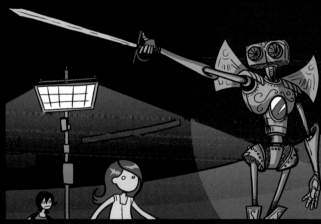

ROBOT?

ROBOT, WHO IS JEANNE?

HOOOOOH

SHE DIED AND WE DID NOTHING.

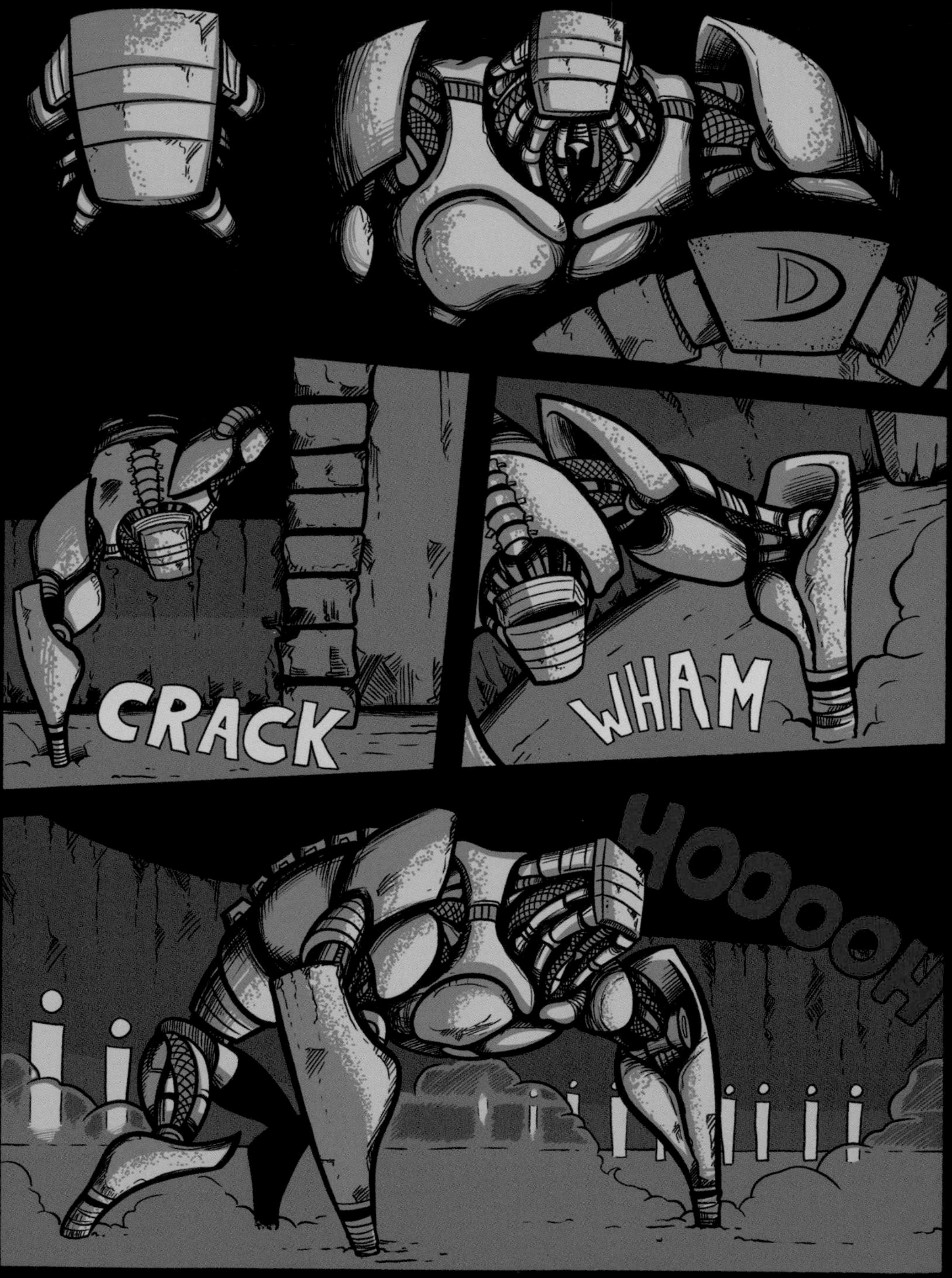
CRACK
WHAM
HOOOOOH

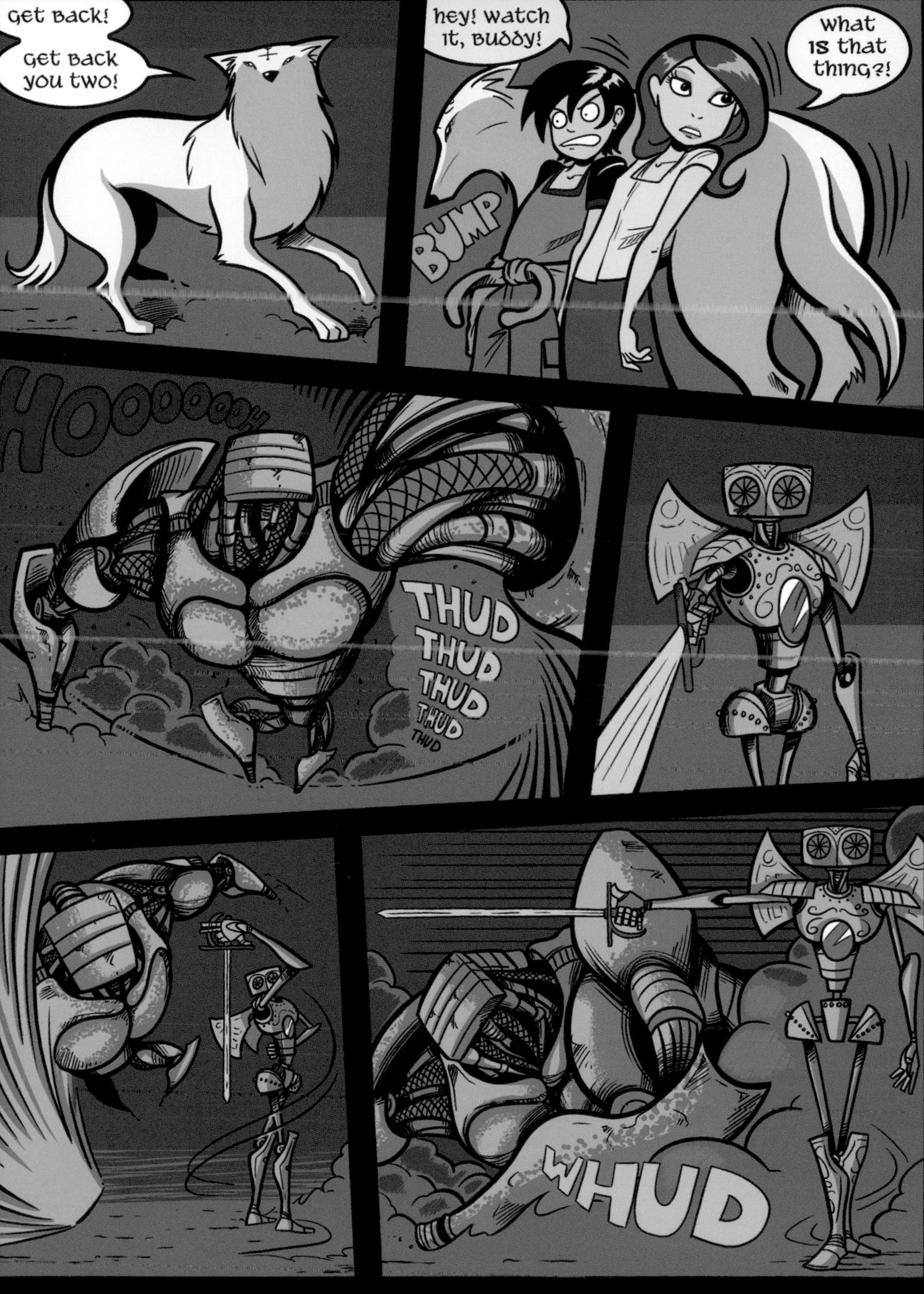
get back!
get back you two!
hey! watch it, buddy!
BUMP
What is that thing?!
HOOOOOOW
THUD THUD THUD THUD THUD
WHUD

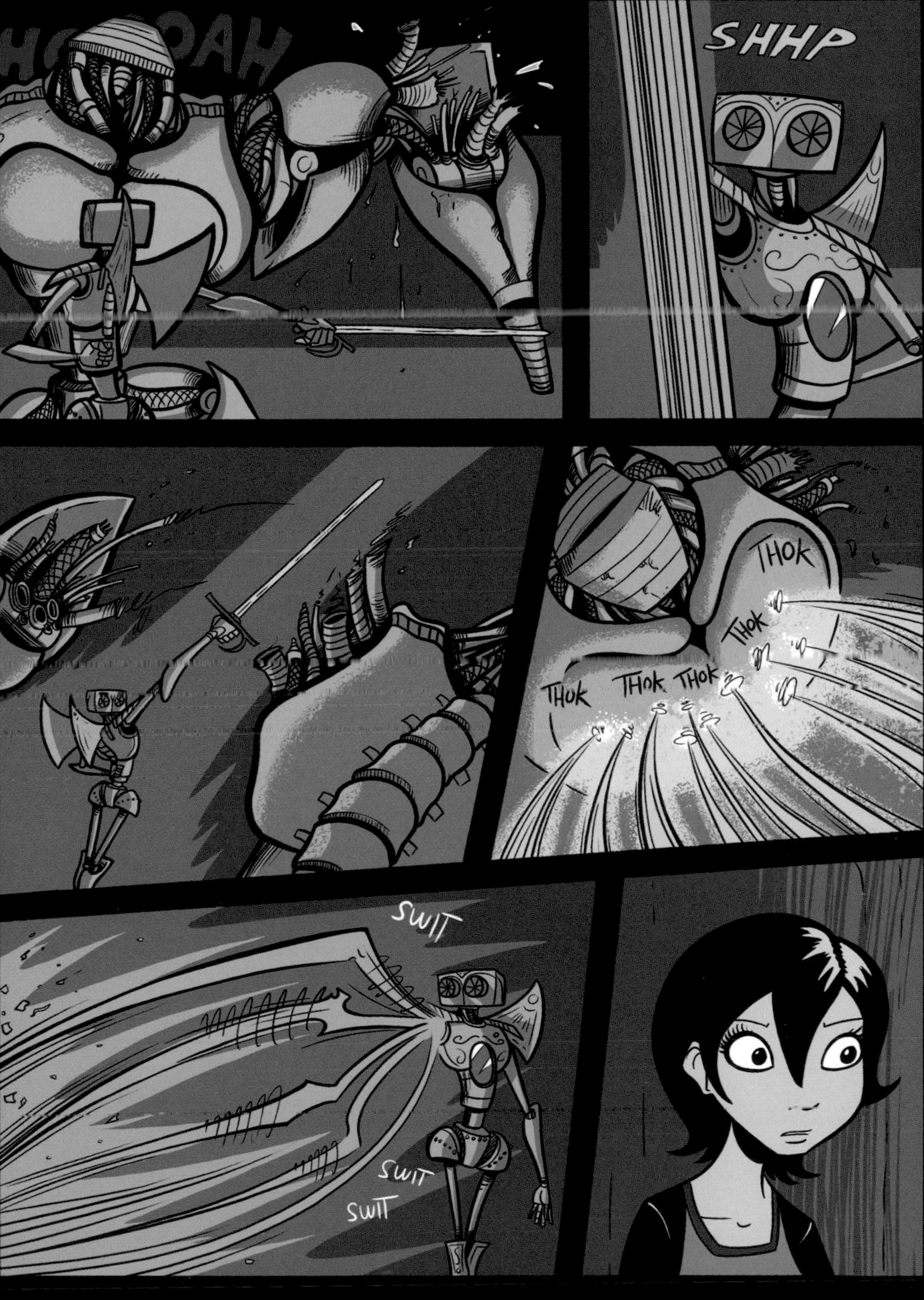
SHHP
THOK
THOK
THOK
THOK
THOK
SWIT
SWIT
SWIT

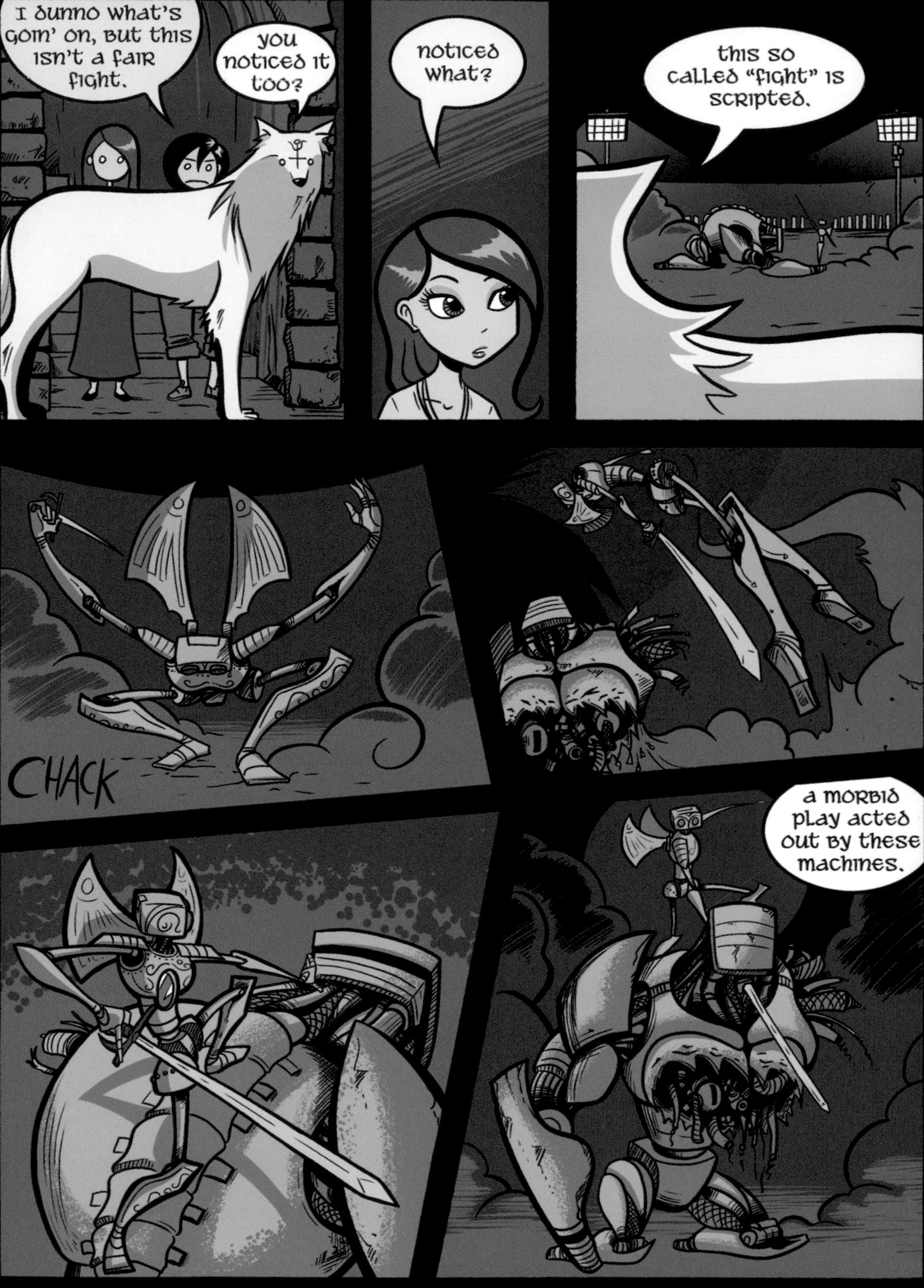
I dunno what's goin' on, but this isn't a fair fight.
you noticed it too?
noticed what?
this so called "fight" is scripted.
CHACK
a morbid play acted out by these machines.

ZASH

CLAP

CLAP

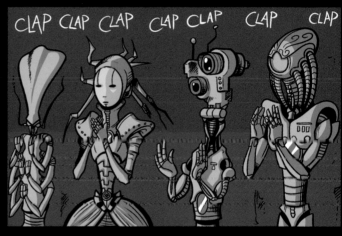

CLAP CLAP CLAP CLAP CLAP CLAP CLAP

now they're all moving!

CLAP
CLAP

CLAP

CLAP

CLAP

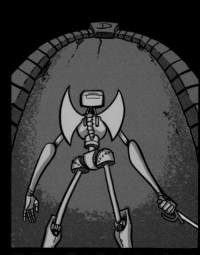

SLASH

WHAM

he's going into that hole!

Let's follow him.

hang on, let me get robot's mouse body.

there's a light up ahead...

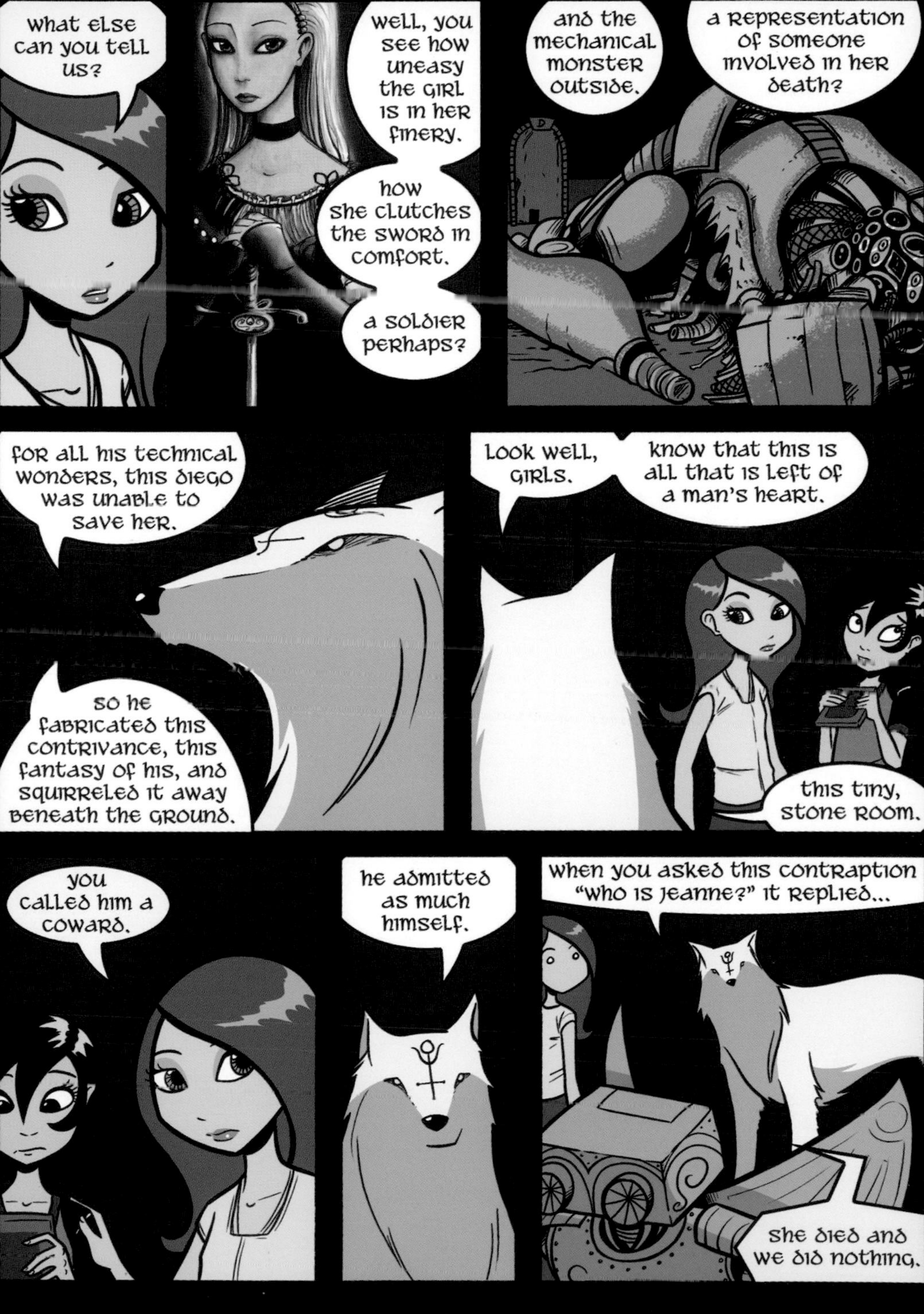
what else can you tell us?
well, you see how uneasy the girl is in her finery.
how she clutches the sword in comfort.
a soldier perhaps?
and the mechanical monster outside.
a representation of someone involved in her death?
for all his technical wonders, this diego was unable to save her.
so he fabricated this contrivance, this fantasy of his, and squirreled it away beneath the ground.
look well, girls.
know that this is all that is left of a man's heart.
this tiny, stone room.
you called him a coward.
he admitted as much himself.
when you asked this contraption "who is jeanne?" it replied...
she died and we did nothing.

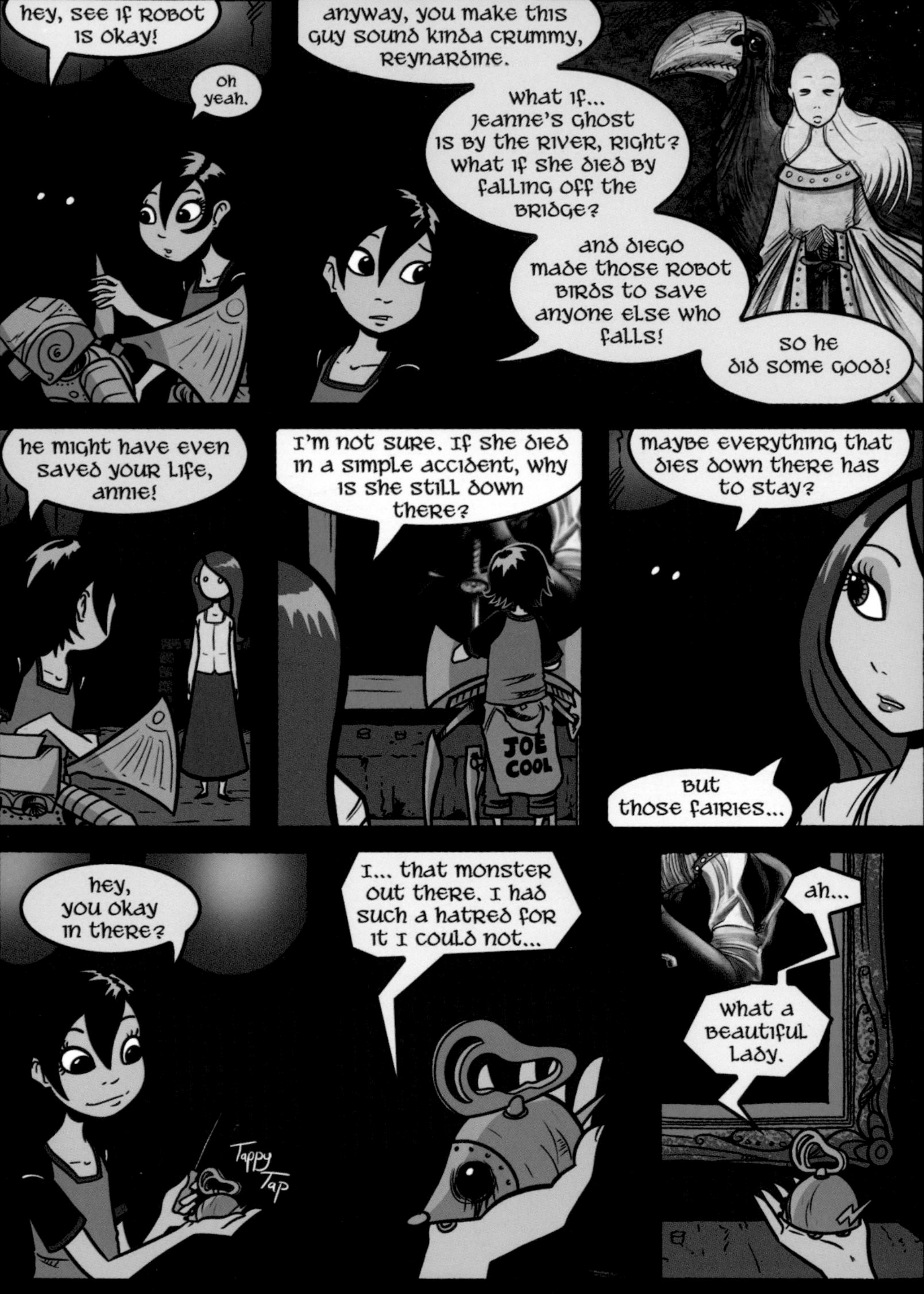
hey, see if robot is okay!
oh yeah.
anyway, you make this guy sound kinda crummy, Reynardine.
what if... Jeanne's ghost is by the river, right? what if she died by falling off the bridge?
and diego made those robot birds to save anyone else who falls!
so he did some good!
he might have even saved your life, annie!
I'm not sure. If she died in a simple accident, why is she still down there?
JOE COOL
maybe everything that dies down there has to stay?
but those fairies...
hey, you okay in there?
Tappy Tap
I... that monster out there. I had such a hatred for it I could not...
ah...
what a beautiful lady.

SAY, ROBOT, WHO LOOKS AFTER YOU GUYS? LIKE, WHO FIXES YOU WHEN YOU BREAK?

NOBODY.

THE COURT ROBOTS HAVE ALWAYS MAINTAINED THEMSELVES.

HUH! I GUESS WHEN DIEGO DIED YOU COULDN'T MAKE MORE OF YOURSELVES, SO YOU CHANGED TO SIMPLER DESIGNS.

ONE THING'S FOR SURE; THESE THINGS DON'T USE SERVOS OR HYDRAULICS OR ANYTHING LIKE THAT.

AND THESE OLD MODELS ARE SO COMPLEX I CAN'T FIGURE THEM OUT.

SOME KIND OF SUPERFAST REACTION MEMORY POLYMER?

THEY COULD BE POWERED BY ETHERIC MEANS.

YOU MEAN LIKE MAGIC?

COME ON, MAN, JUST BECAUSE SOMETHING ISN'T EXPLAINED YET DOESN'T MAKE IT MAGIC.

ah, I think I never get it!

just to get one of those robots to move. I wish I could see it!

CLICK

you'll figure it out, anny.

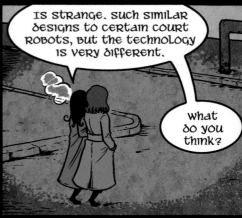

is strange, such similar designs to certain court robots, but the technology is very different.

what do you think?

yikes! don't ask me! I'm two short planks compared to you.

oh now! you and me are smart on different things! and when we work together, we are unstoppable!

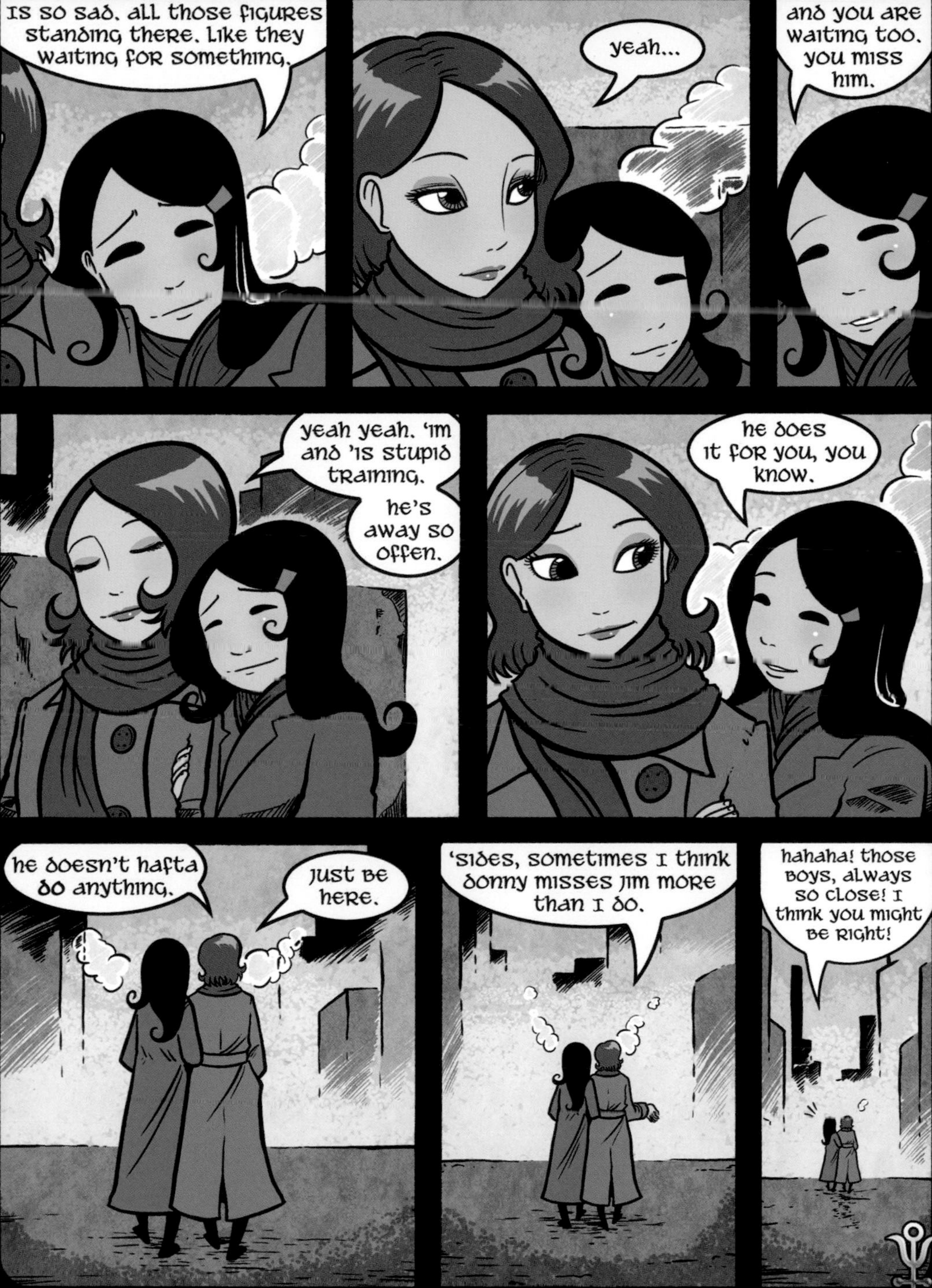
is so sad. all those figures standing there. like they waiting for something.
yeah...
and you are waiting too. you miss him.
yeah yeah. 'im and 'is stupid training.
he's away so offen.
he does it for you, you know.
he doesn't hafta do anything.
just be here.
'sides, sometimes I think donny misses jim more than I do.
hahaha! those boys, always so close! I think you might be right!

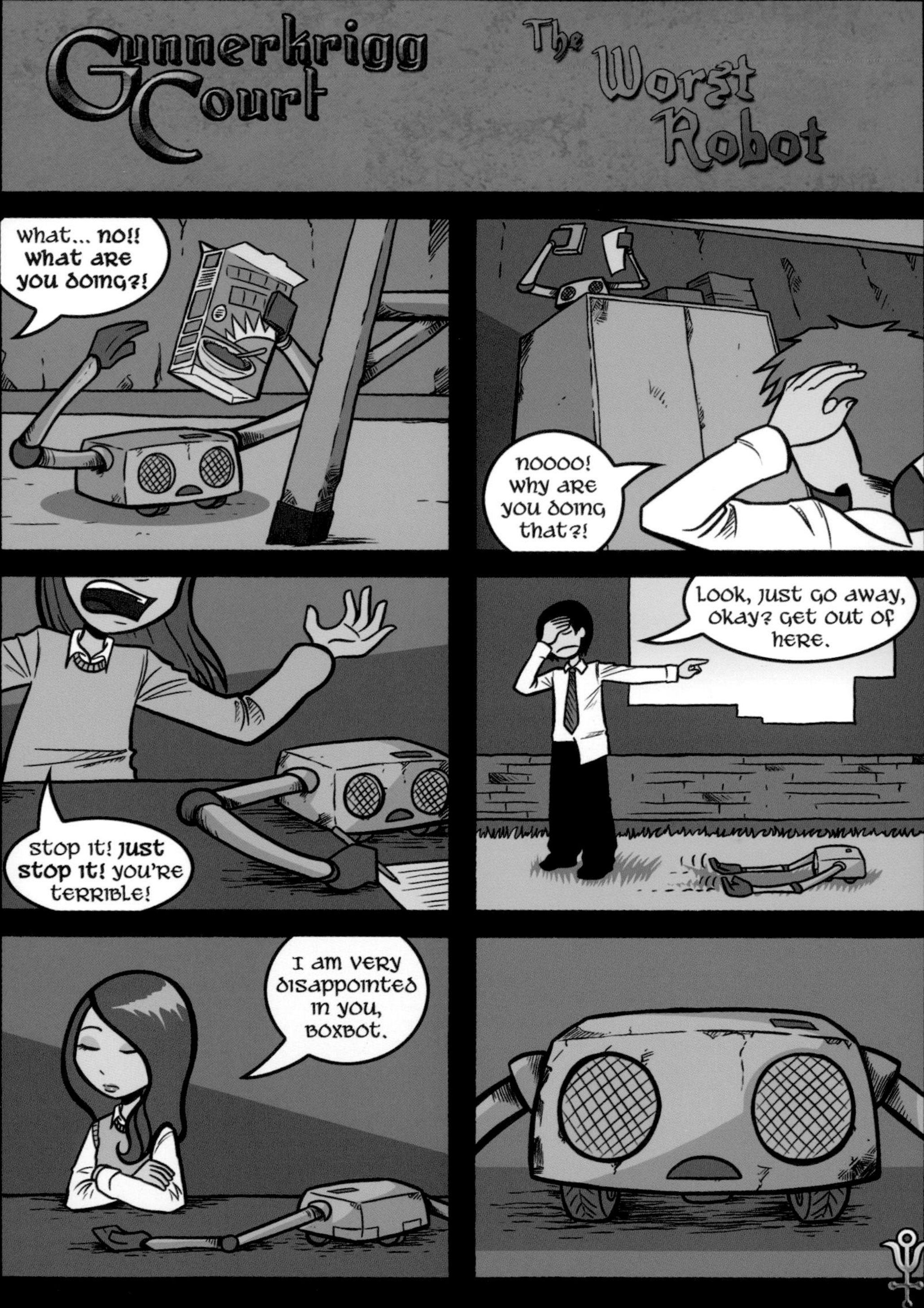
Gunnerkrigg Court
The Worst Robot
what... no!! what are you doing?!
noooo! why are you doing that?!
stop it! just stop it! you're terrible!
Look, just go away, okay? get out of here.
I am very disappointed in you, boxbot.

Gunnerkrigg Court

Chapter 19:

Power Station

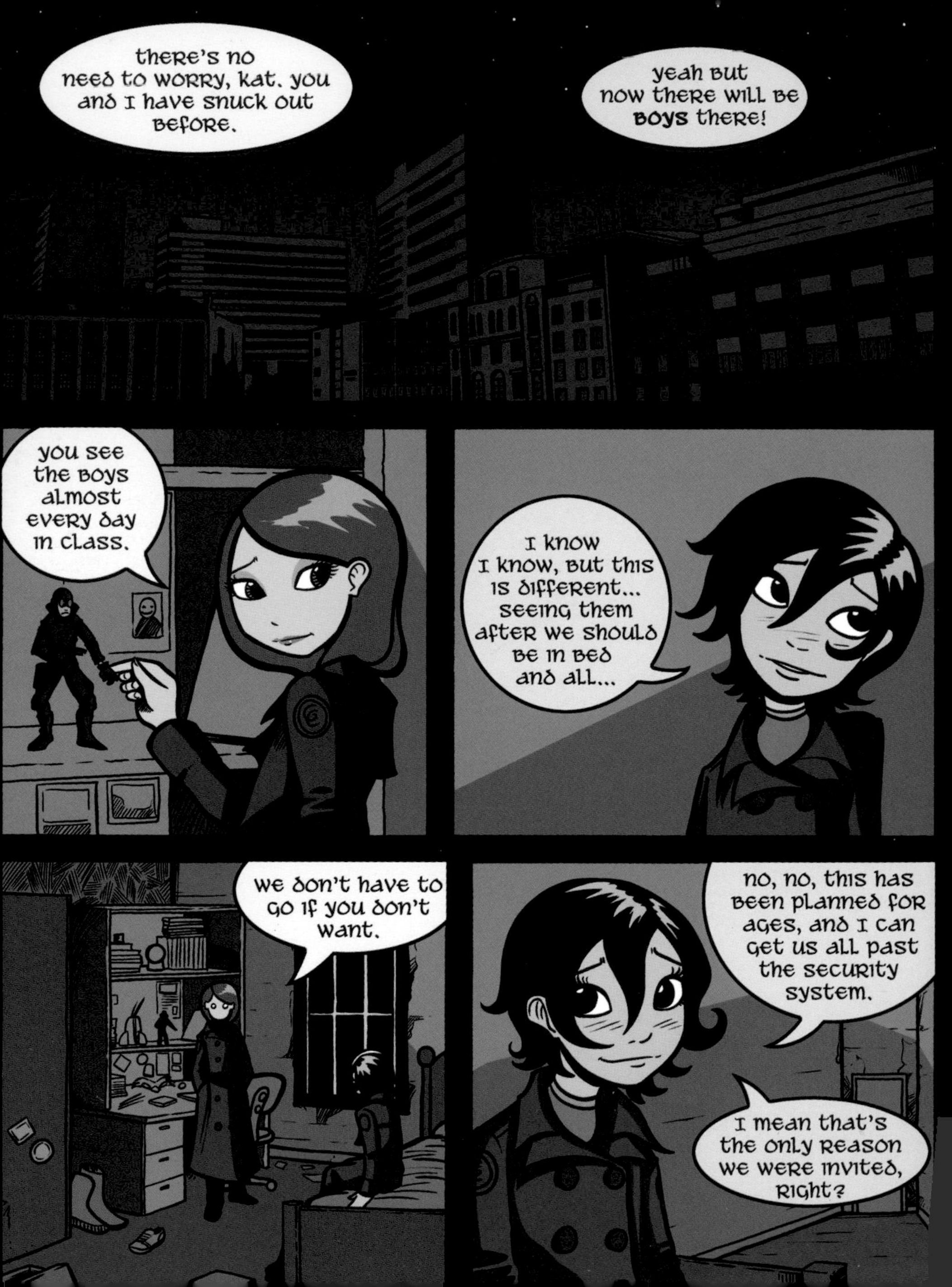
there's no need to worry, kat. you and I have snuck out before.
yeah but now there will be **boys** there!
you see the boys almost every day in class.
I know I know, but this is different... seeing them after we should be in bed and all...
we don't have to go if you don't want.
no, no, this has been planned for ages, and I can get us all past the security system.
I mean that's the only reason we were invited, right?

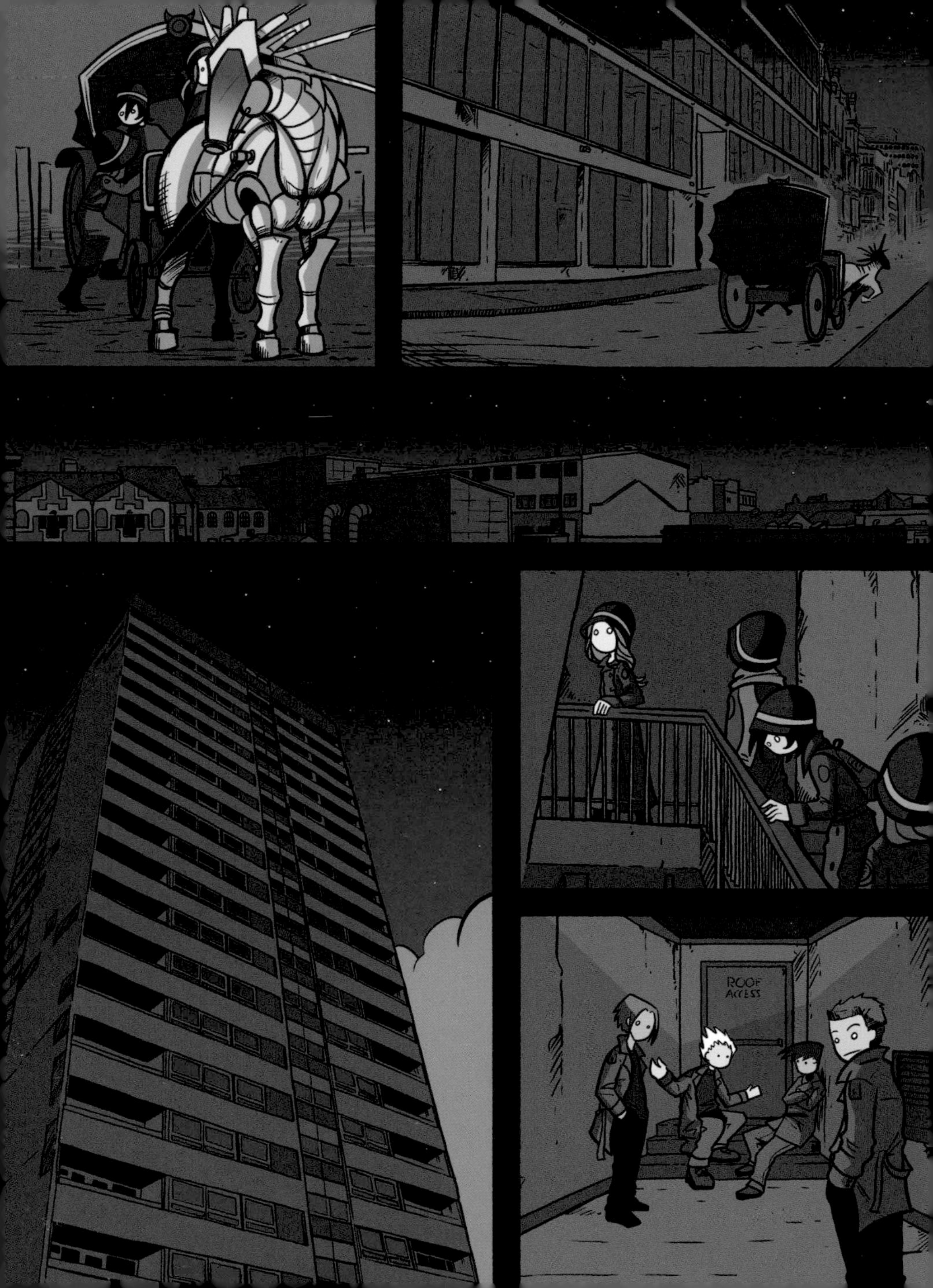
ROOF ACCESS

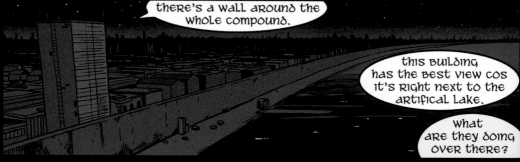

THERE'S A WALL AROUND THE WHOLE COMPOUND.

THIS BUILDING HAS THE BEST VIEW COS IT'S RIGHT NEXT TO THE ARTIFICAL LAKE.

WHAT ARE THEY DOING OVER THERE?

THEY'RE GEARIN' UP FOR AN EXPERIMENT.

WHAT KIND OF EXPERIMENT?

YOU'LL KNOW AS MUCH AS I DO WHEN YOU SEE IT.

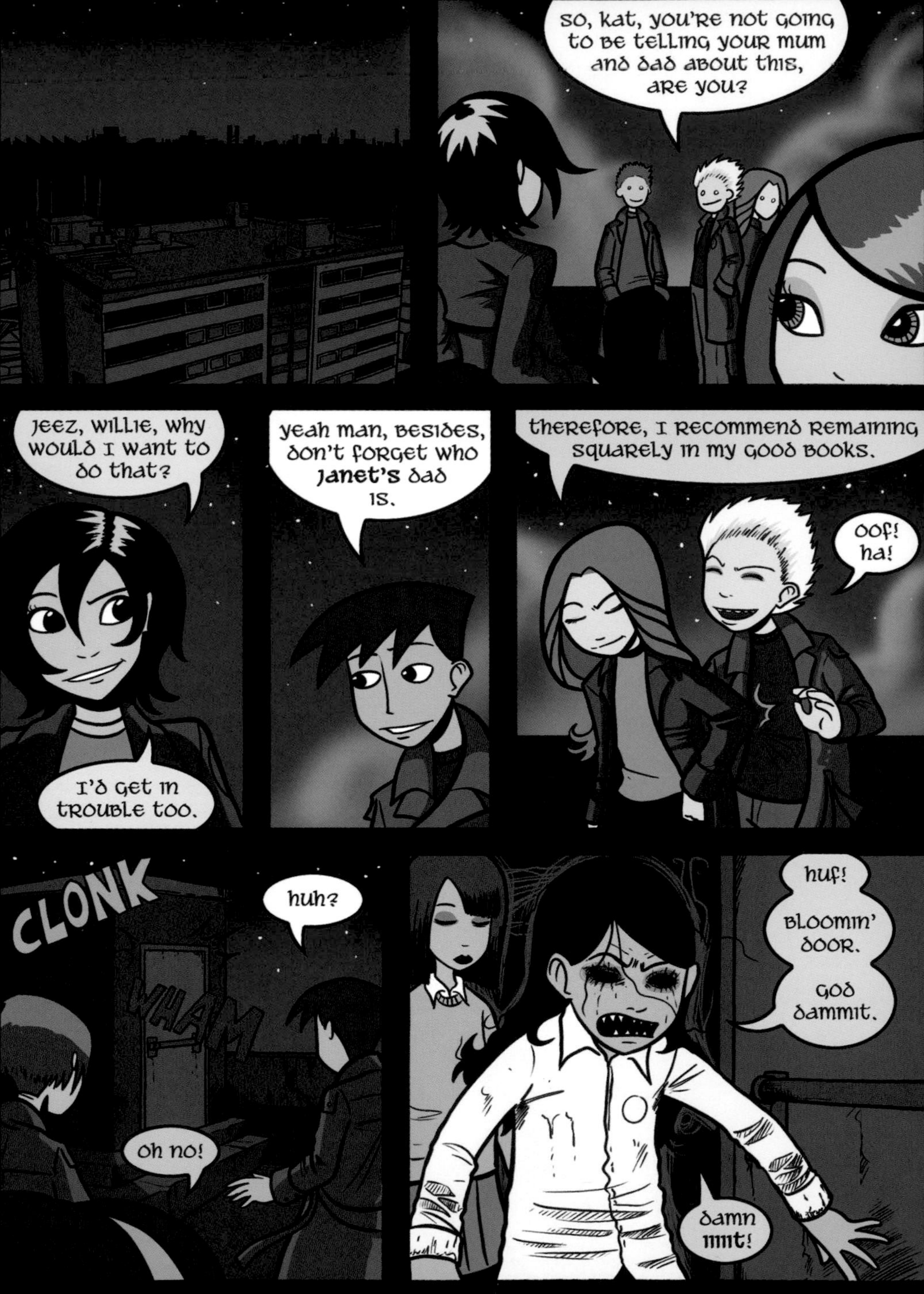
so, kat, you're not going to be telling your mum and dad about this, are you?
jeez, willie, why would I want to do that?
I'd get in trouble too.
yeah man, besides, don't forget who janet's dad is.
therefore, I recommend remaining squarely in my good books.
oof! ha!
CLONK
WHAM
huh?
oh no!
huf!
bloomin' door.
god dammit.
damn mmit!

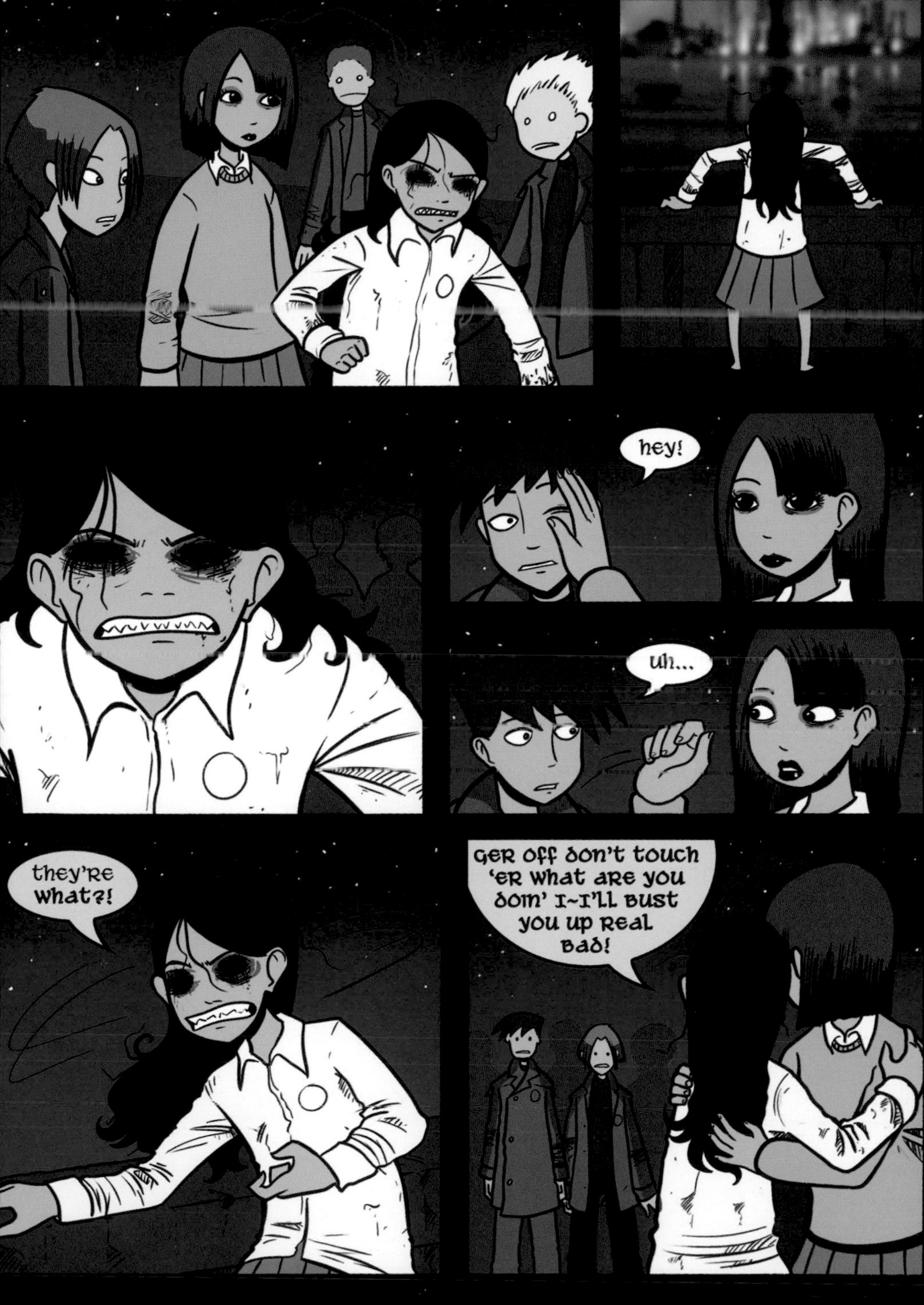
hey!
uh...
they're what?!
GER OFF DON'T TOUCH 'ER WHAT ARE YOU DOIN' I~I'LL BUST YOU UP REAL BAD!

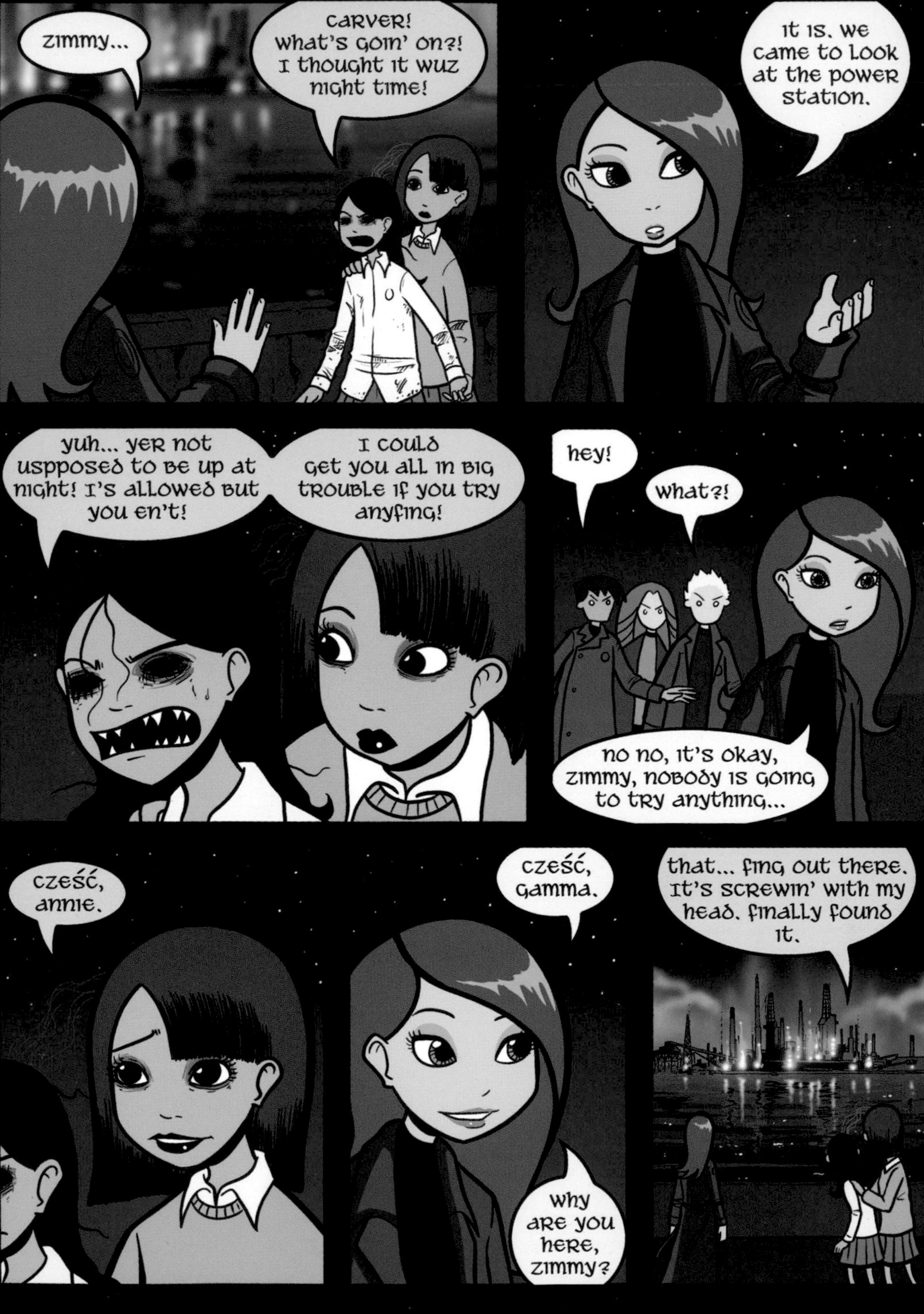
zimmy...
carver! what's goin' on?! I thought it wuz night time!
it is. we came to look at the power station.
yuh... yer not uspposed to be up at night! I's allowed but you en't!
I could get you all in big trouble if you try anyfing!
hey!
what?!
no no, it's okay, zimmy, nobody is going to try anything...
cześć, annie.
cześć, gamma.
why are you here, zimmy?
that... fing out there. It's screwin' with my head. finally found it.

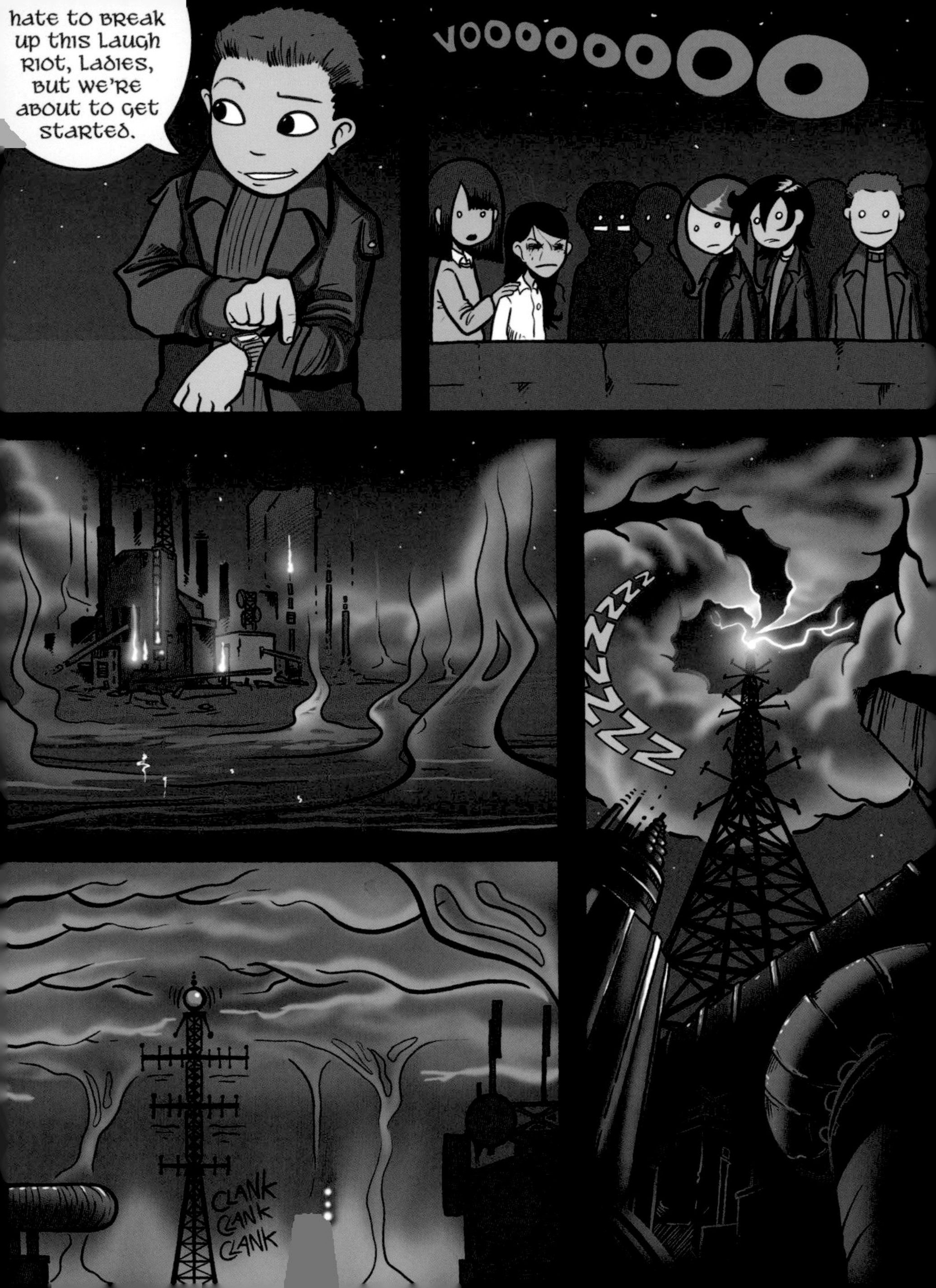
hate to break up this laugh riot, ladies, but we're about to get started.
VOOOOOOOOO
ZZZZZZZZZ
CLANK CLANK CLANK

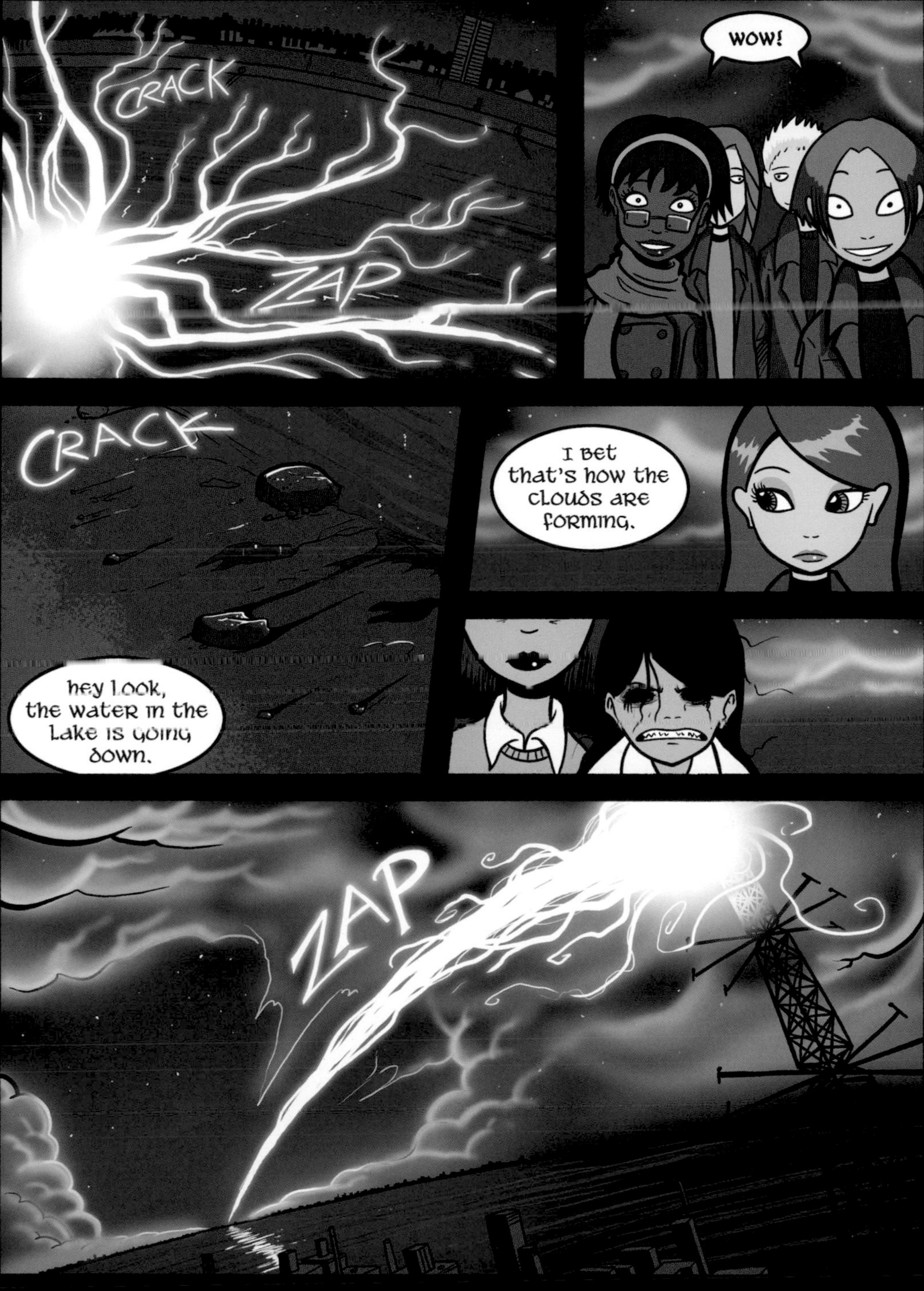
CRACK
ZAP
WOW!
CRACK
I bet that's how the clouds are forming.
hey look, the water in the lake is going down.
ZAP

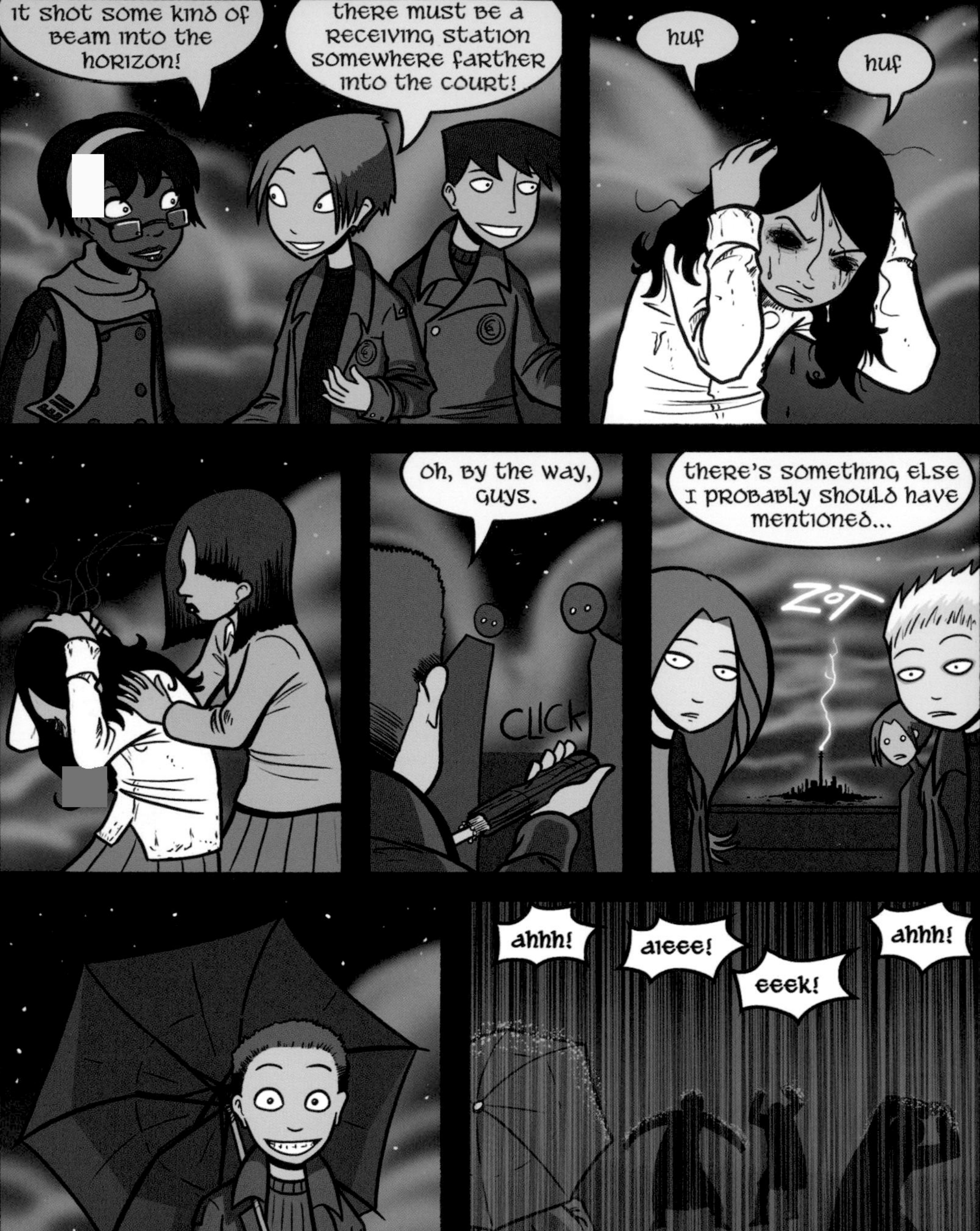

it shot some kind of beam into the horizon!
there must be a receiving station somewhere farther into the court!
huf
huf
oh, by the way, guys.
CLICK
there's something else I probably should have mentioned...
ZOT
ahhh!
aieee!
eeek!
ahhh!
BOOSH

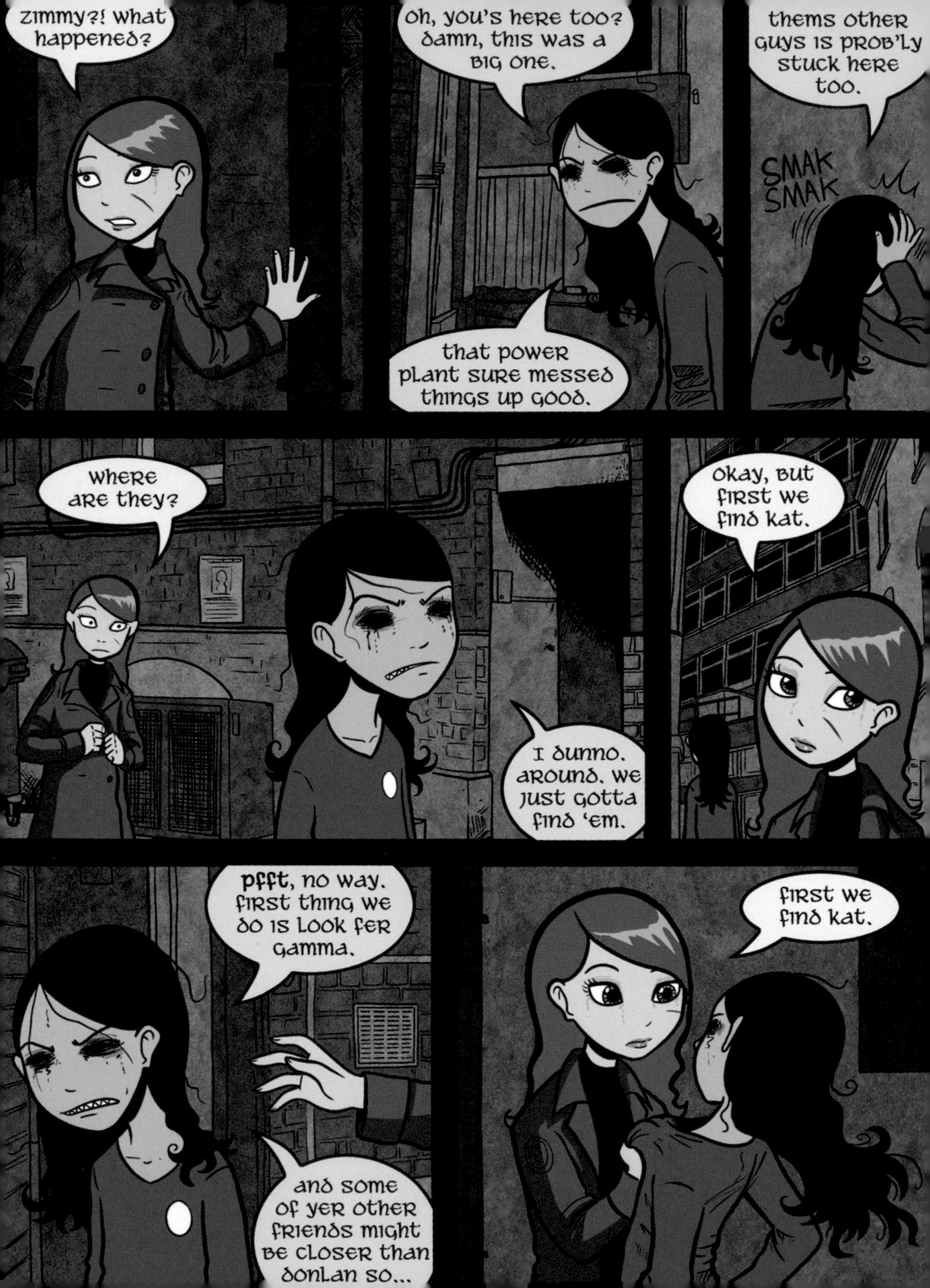
zimmy?! what happened?
oh, you's here too? damn, this was a big one.
that power plant sure messed things up good.
thems other guys is prob'ly stuck here too.
SMAK SMAK
where are they?
I dunno. around. we just gotta find 'em.
okay, but first we find kat.
pfft, no way. first thing we do is look fer gamma.
and some of yer other friends might be closer than donlan so...
first we find kat.

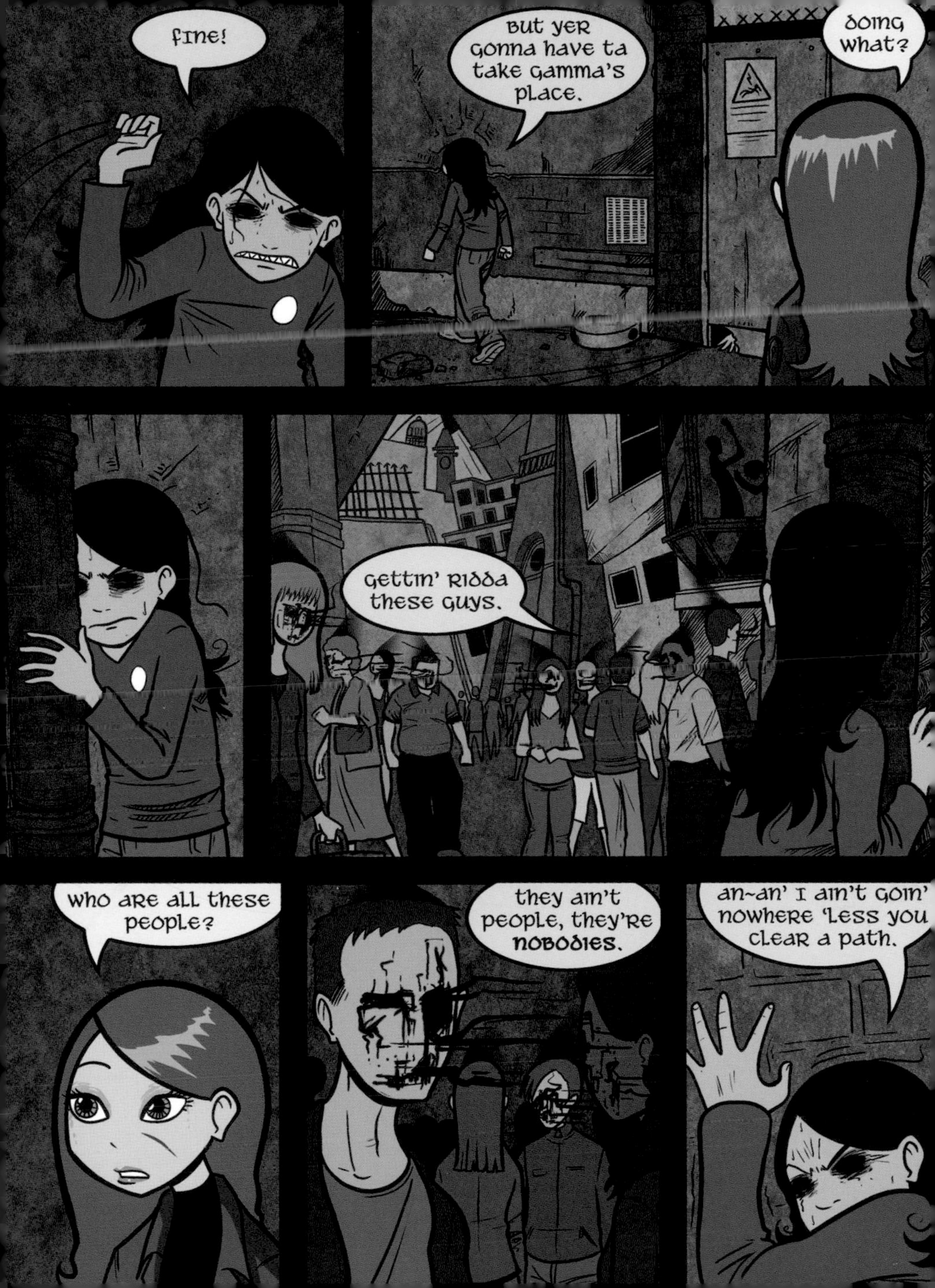
fine!
But yer gonna have ta take Gamma's place.
doing what?
Gettin' Ridda these guys.
who are all these people?
they ain't people, they're NOBODIES.
an~an' I ain't goin' nowhere 'less you clear a path.

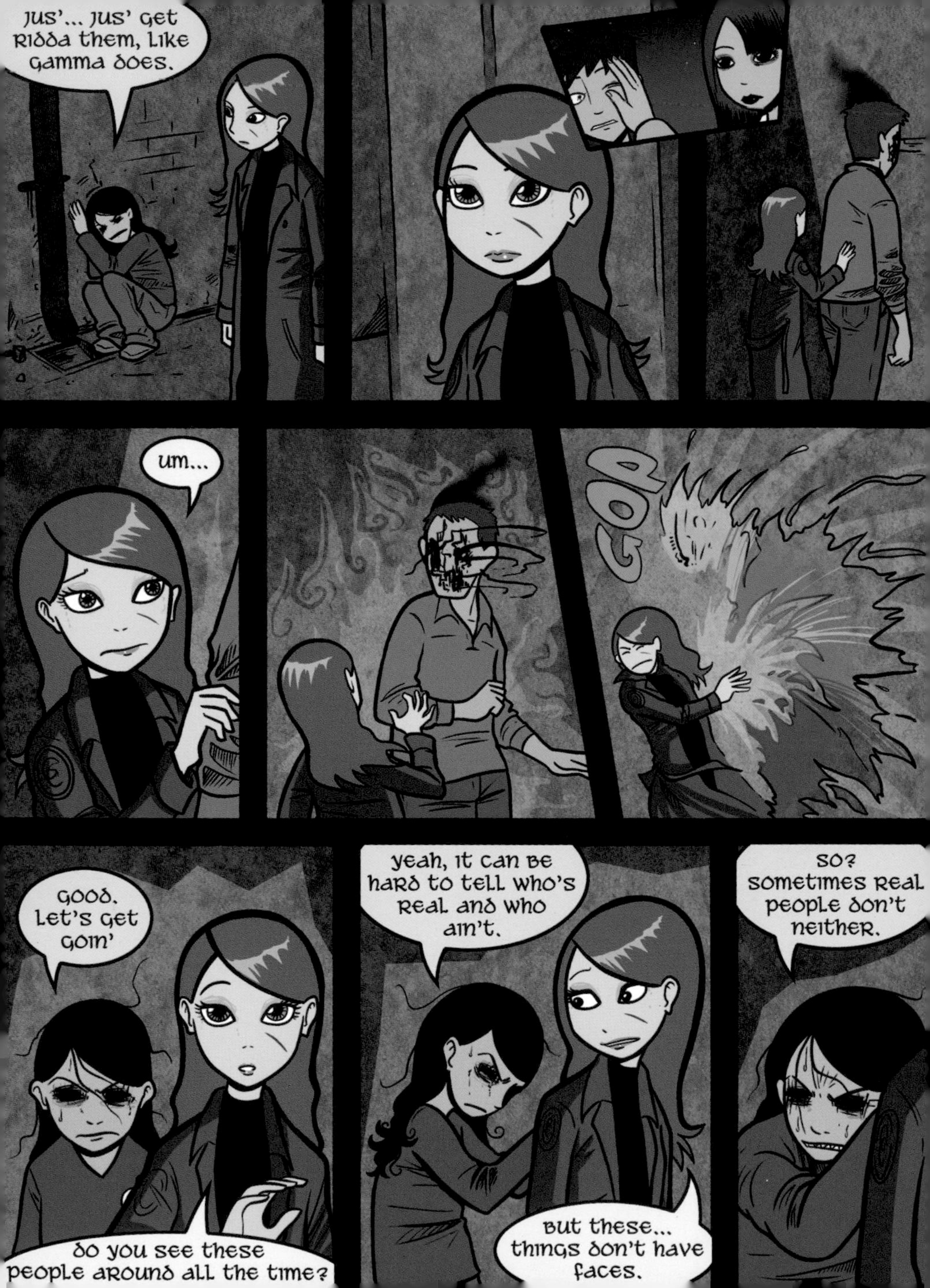
JUS'... JUS' GET RIDDA THEM, LIKE GAMMA DOES.
UM...
GOP
GOOD. LET'S GET GOIN'
DO YOU SEE THESE PEOPLE AROUND ALL THE TIME?
YEAH, IT CAN BE HARD TO TELL WHO'S REAL AND WHO AIN'T.
BUT THESE... THINGS DON'T HAVE FACES.
SO? SOMETIMES REAL PEOPLE DON'T NEITHER.

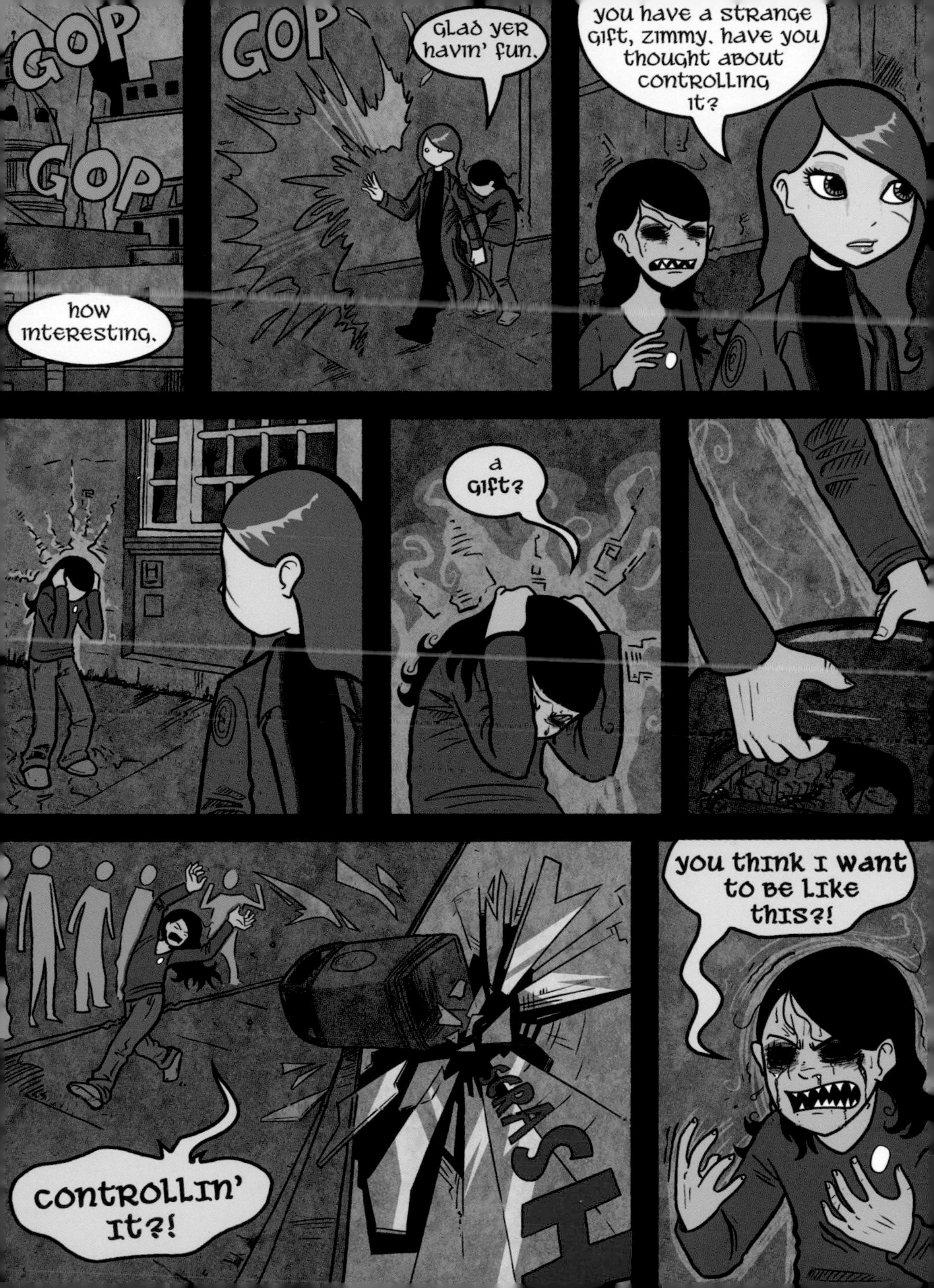
GOP
GOP
how interesting.
GOP
Glad yer havin' fun.
you have a strange gift, zimmy. have you thought about controlling it?
a gift?
controllin' it?!
SCRASH
you think I want to be like this?!

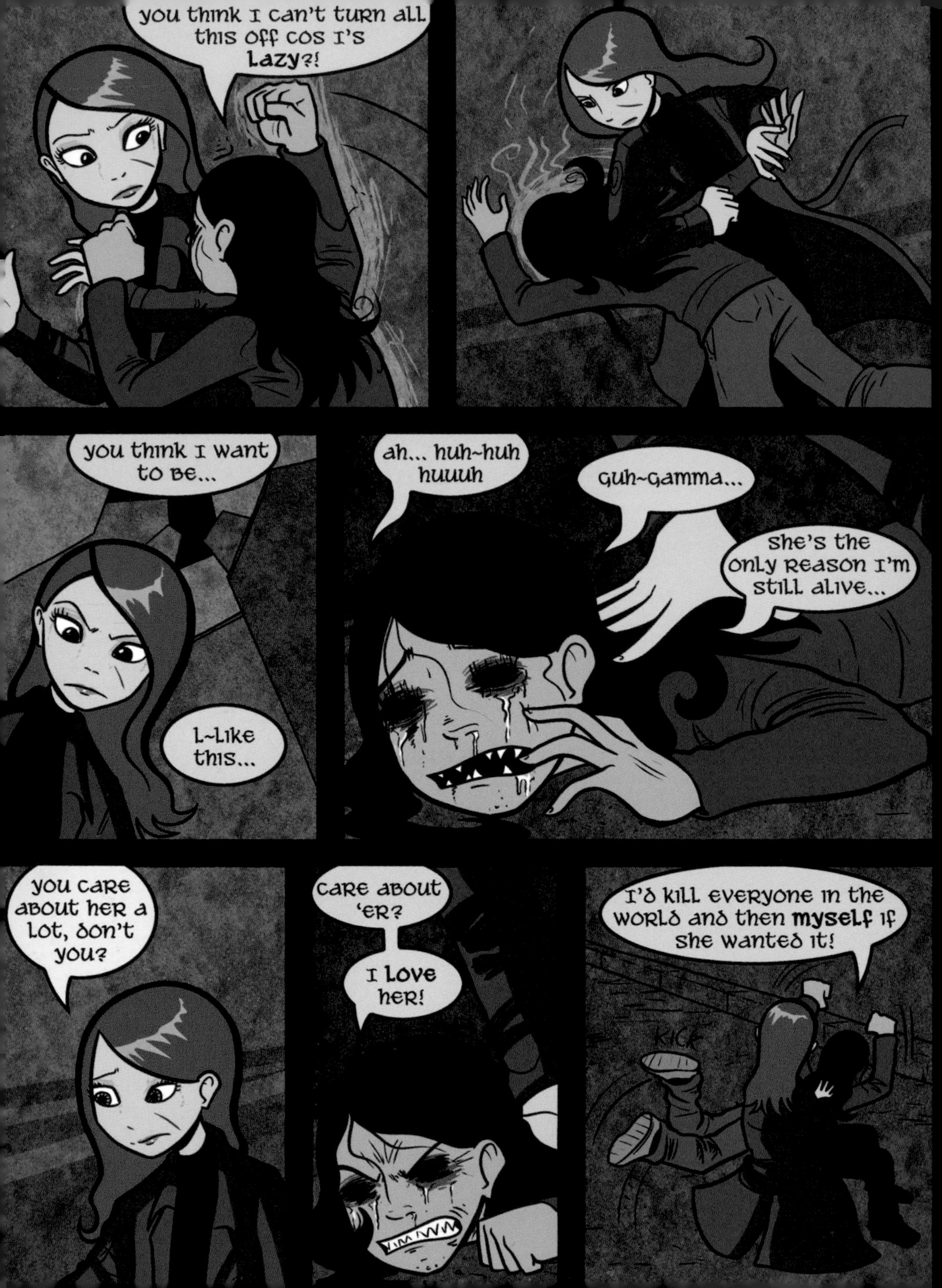
you think I can't turn all this off cos I's **lazy**?!
you think I want to be...
l-like this...
ah... huh-huh huuuh
guh-gamma...
she's the only reason I'm still alive...
you care about her a lot, don't you?
care about 'er?
I **love** her!
KICK
I'd kill everyone in the world and then **myself** if she wanted it!

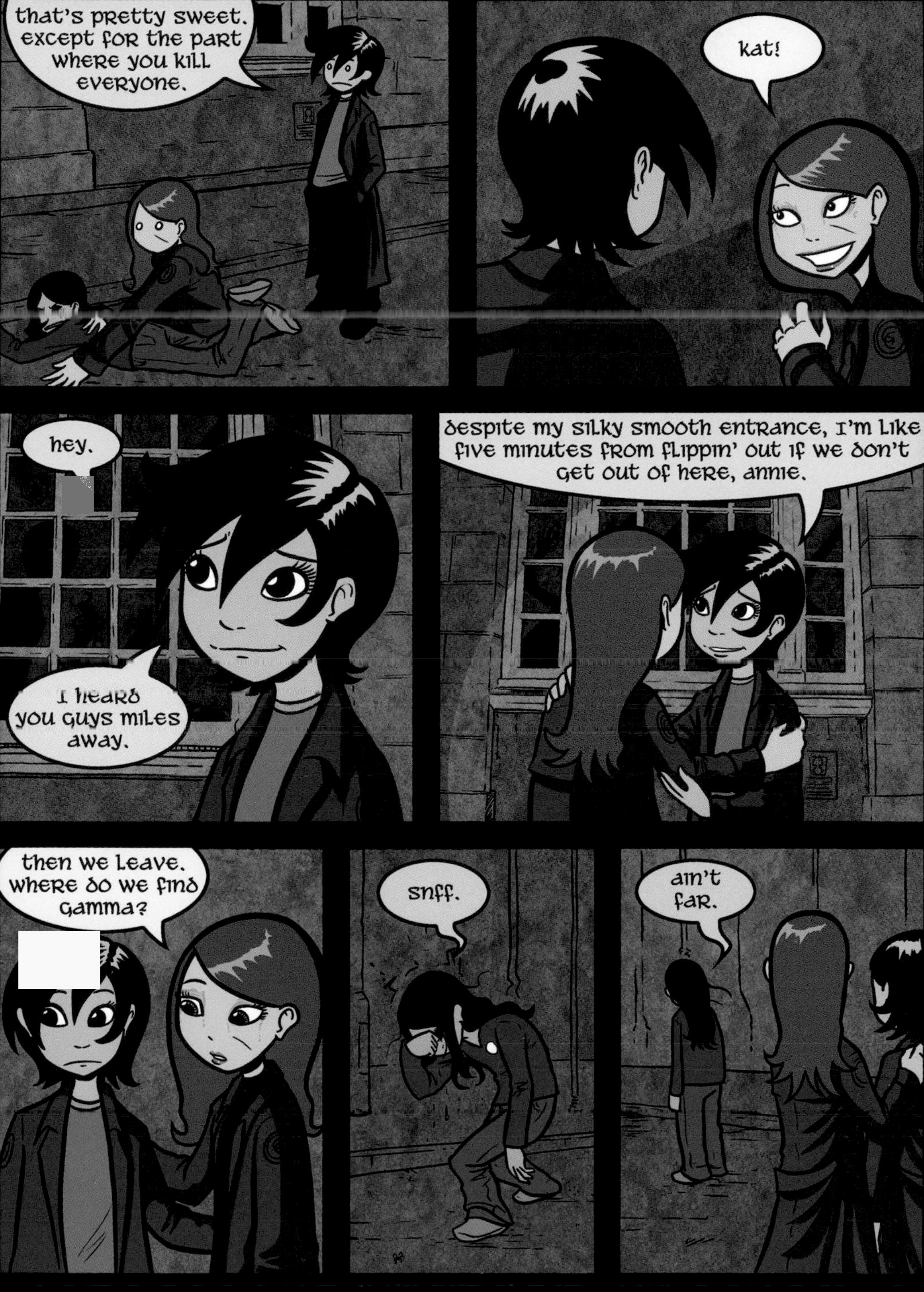
that's pretty sweet. except for the part where you kill everyone.
kat!
hey.
I heard you guys miles away.
despite my silky smooth entrance, I'm like five minutes from flippin' out if we don't get out of here, annie.
then we leave. where do we find gamma?
snff.
ain't far.

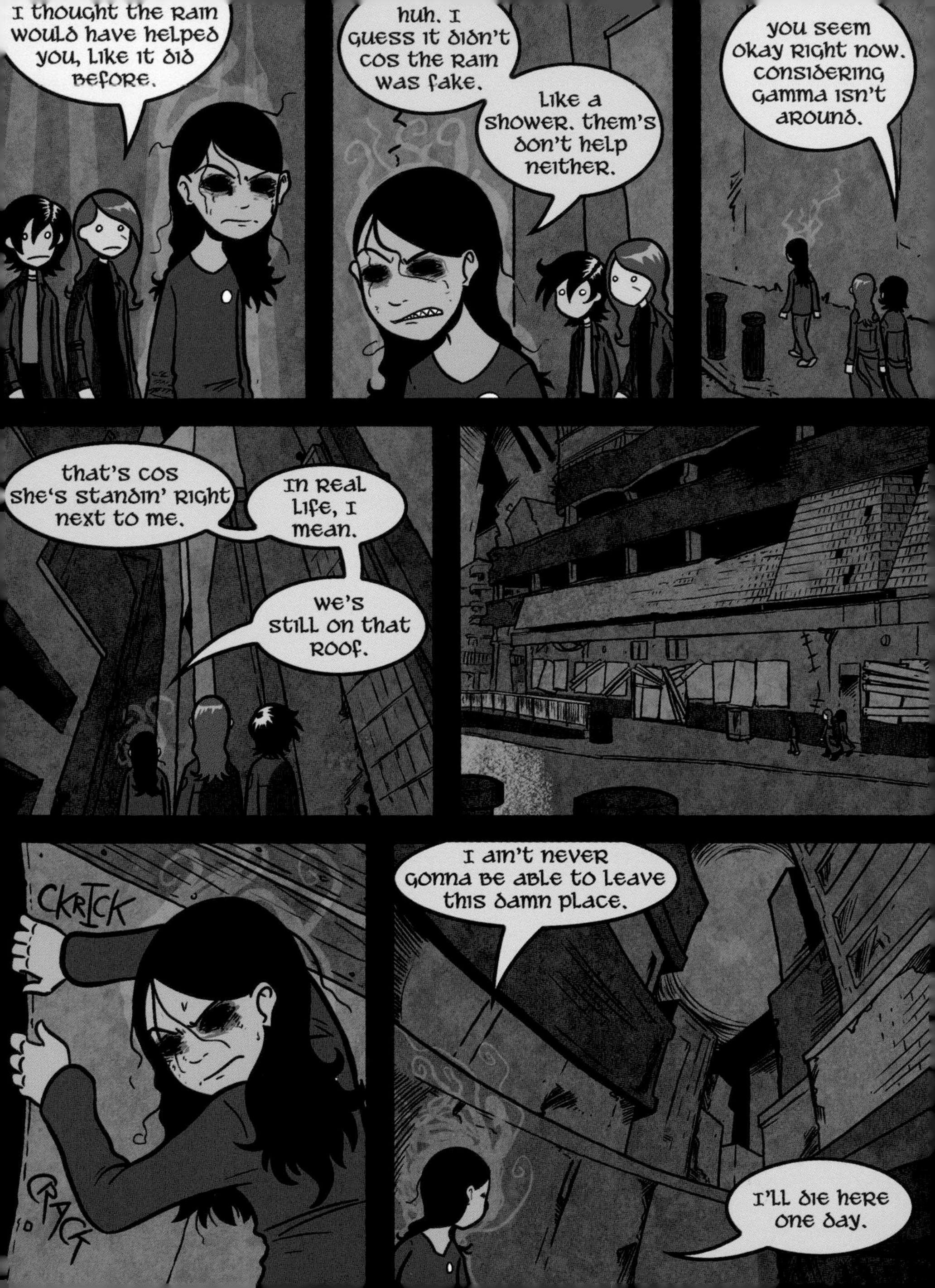
I thought the Rain would have helped you, like it did before.
huh. I guess it didn't cos the Rain was fake.
like a shower. them's don't help neither.
you seem okay right now. considering gamma isn't around.
that's cos she's standin' right next to me.
In real life, I mean.
we's still on that roof.
CKRICK
CRACK
I ain't never gonna be able to leave this damn place.
I'll die here one day.

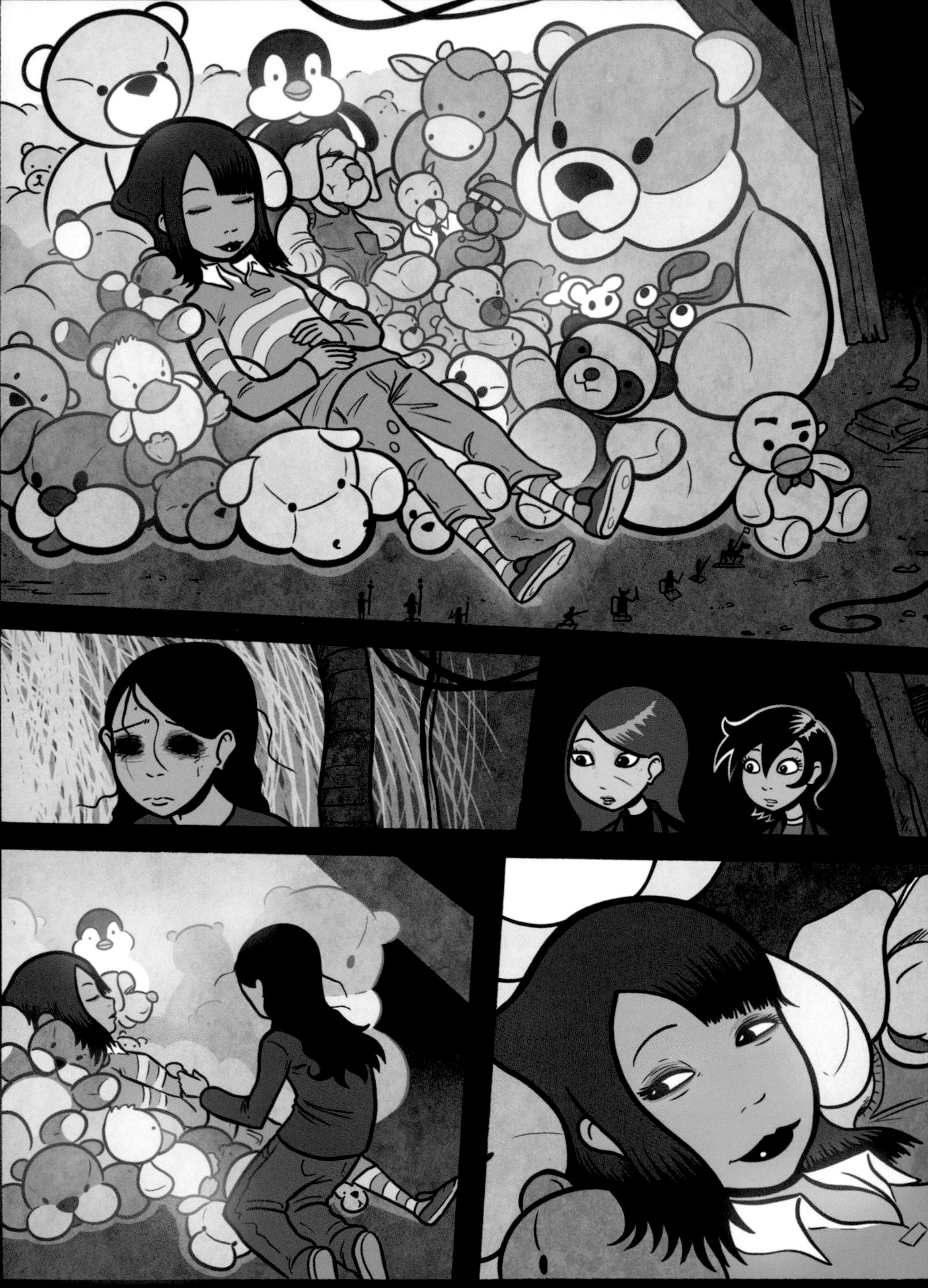

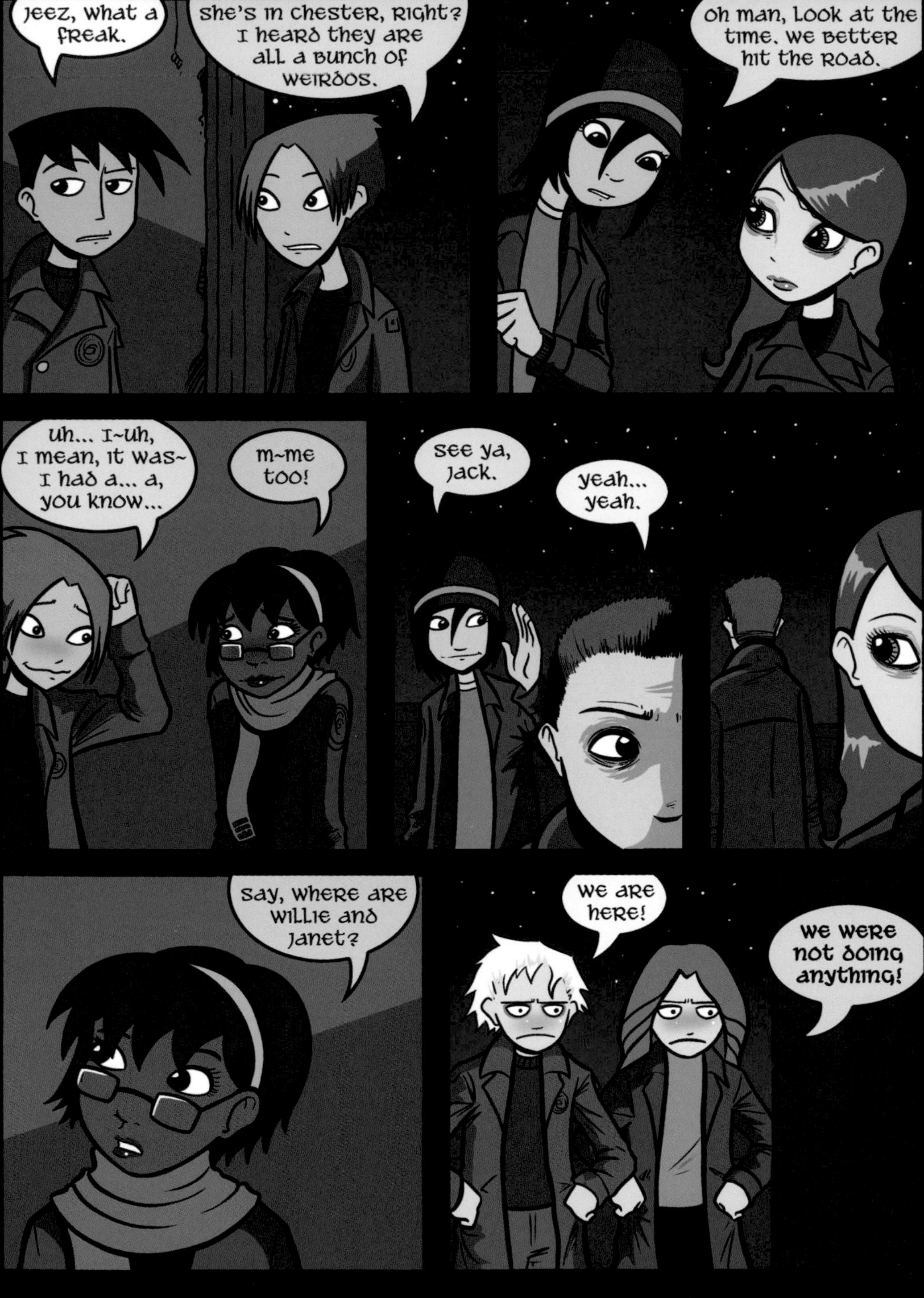
Jeez, what a freak.
She's in Chester, right? I heard they are all a bunch of weirdos.
Oh man, look at the time. We better hit the road.
Uh... I~uh, I mean, it was~ I had a... a, you know...
M~me too!
See ya, Jack.
Yeah... yeah.
Say, where are Willie and Janet?
We are here!
We were not doing anything!

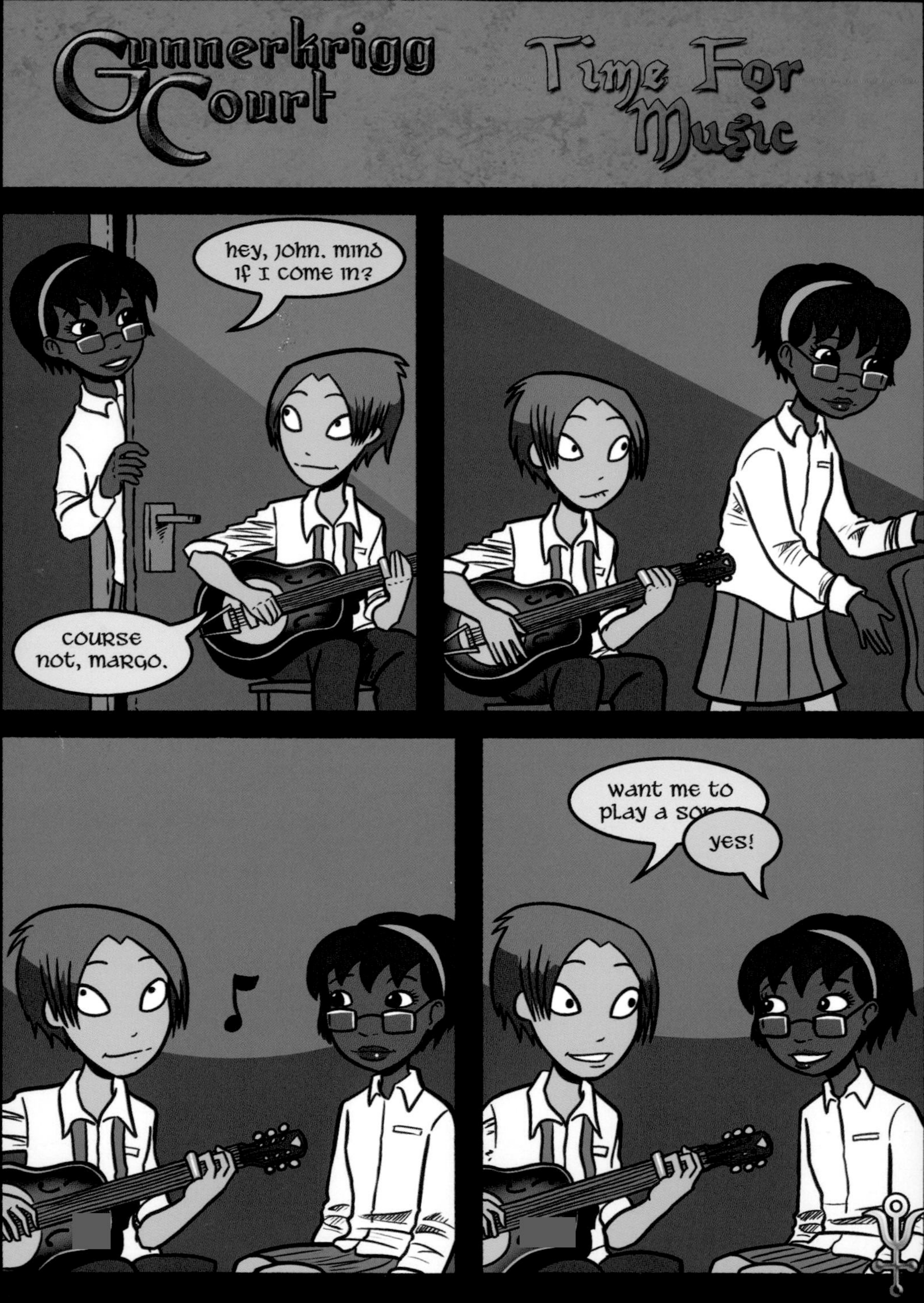
Gunnerkrigg Court
Time For Music
hey, John. mind if I come in?
course not, margo.
want me to play a so
yes!

Gunnerkrigg Court

Chapter 20:

Coyote Stories

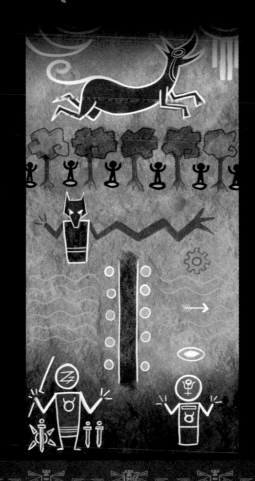

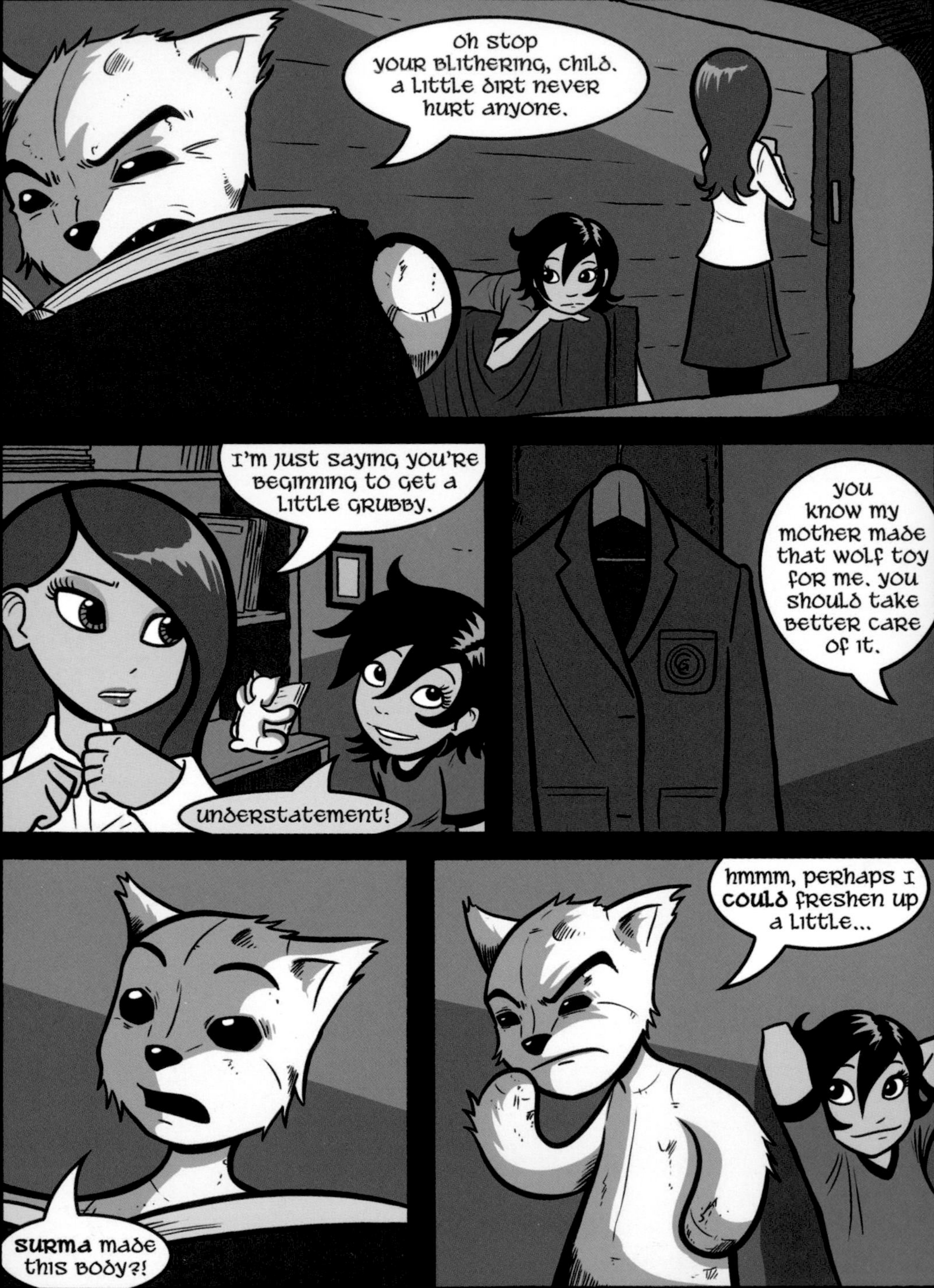
oh stop your blithering, child. a little dirt never hurt anyone.
I'm just saying you're beginning to get a little grubby.
understatement!
you know my mother made that wolf toy for me. you should take better care of it.
surma made this body?!
hmmm, perhaps I could freshen up a little...

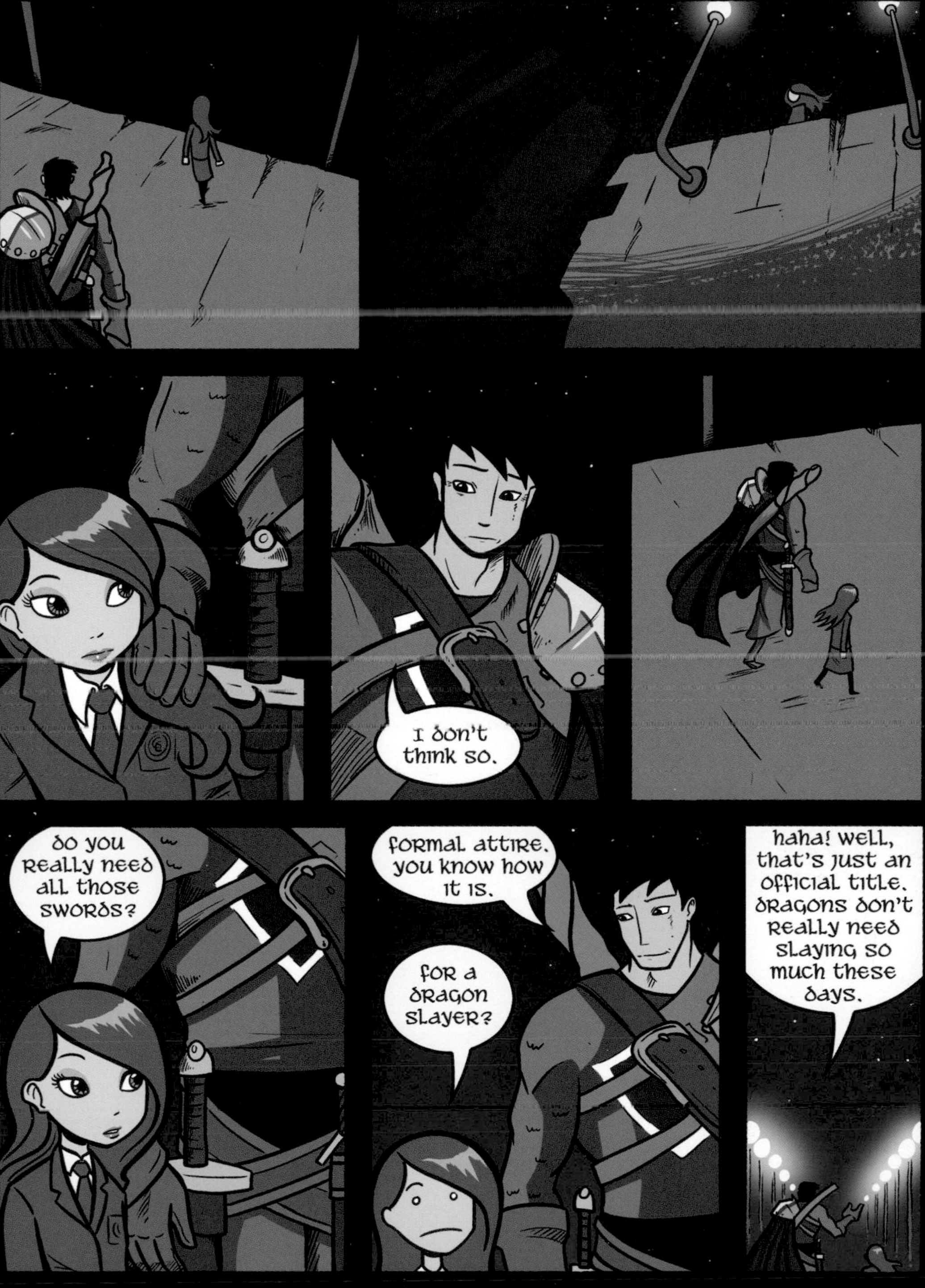
I don't think so.
do you really need all those swords?
formal attire. you know how it is.
for a dragon slayer?
haha! well, that's just an official title. dragons don't really need slaying so much these days.

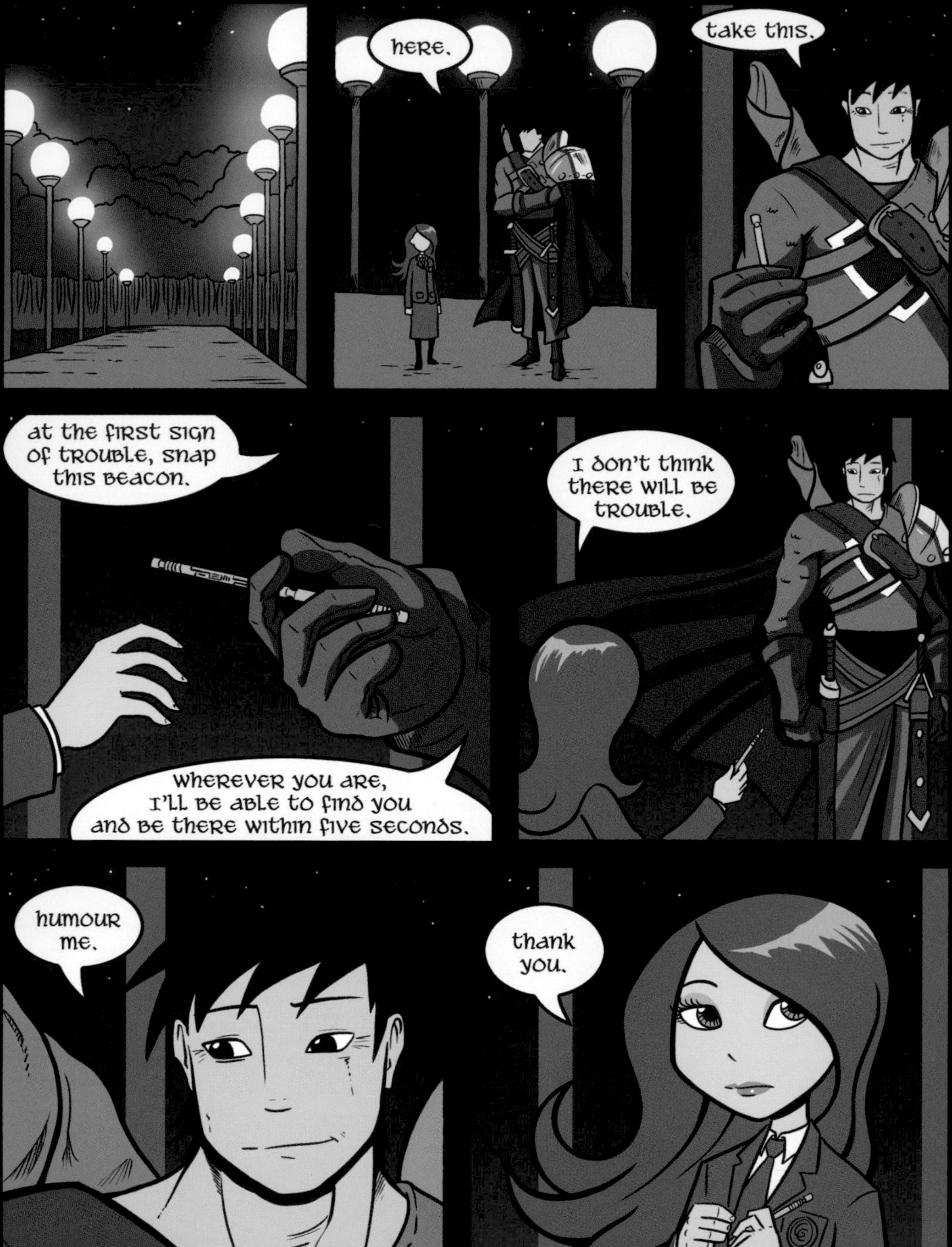

here.
take this.
at the first sign of trouble, snap this beacon.
wherever you are, I'll be able to find you and be there within five seconds.
I don't think there will be trouble.
humour me.
thank you.

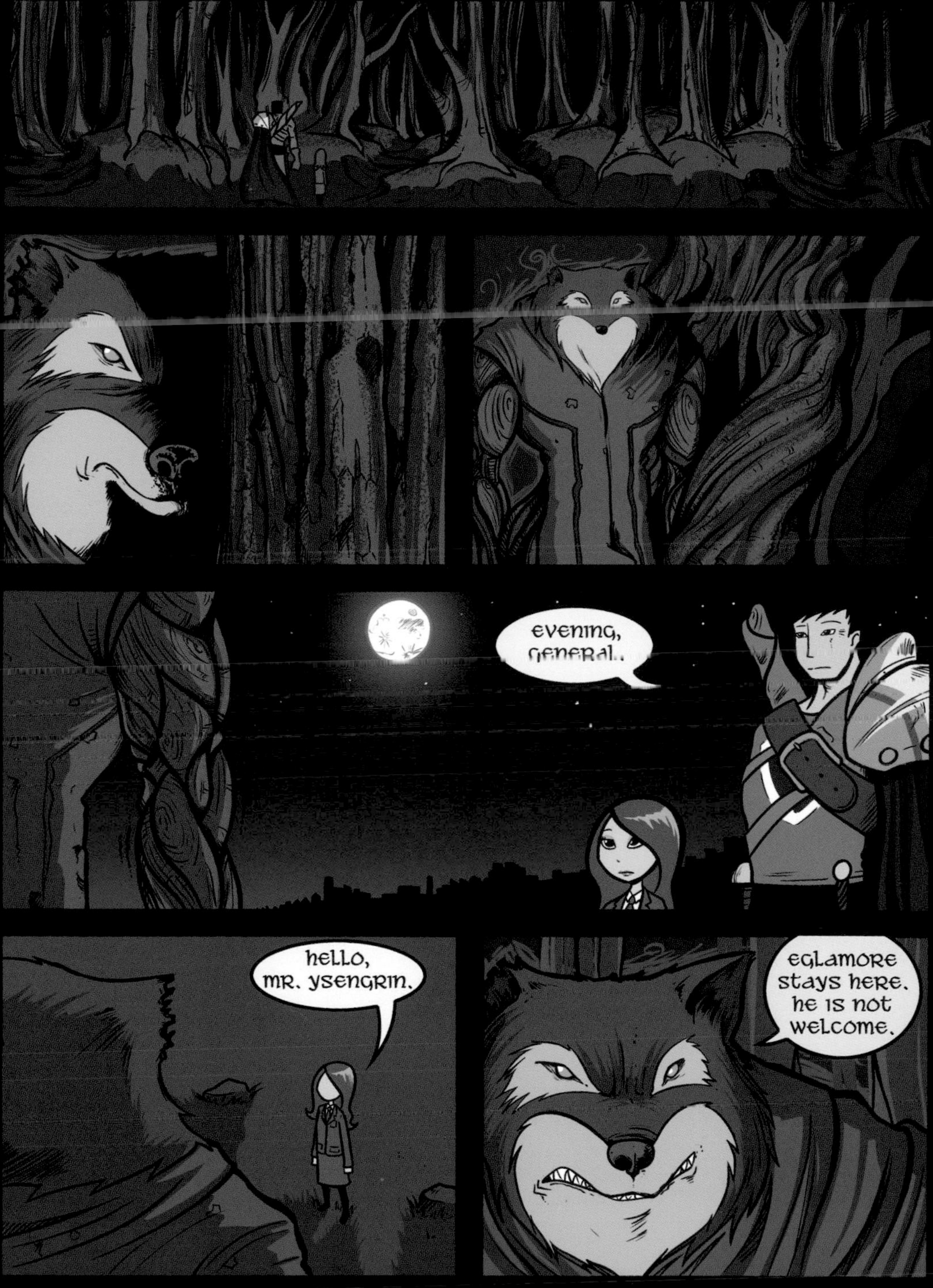
evening, general.
hello, mr. ysengrin.
eglamore stays here. he is not welcome.

CARVER?

that's fine. I doubt I will be very long.

hurff. taking orders from a little girl, SIR EGLAMORE?

you, you will take me to coyote now.

...

Scratch Scratch

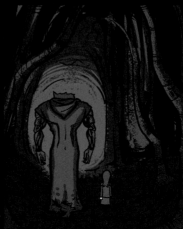

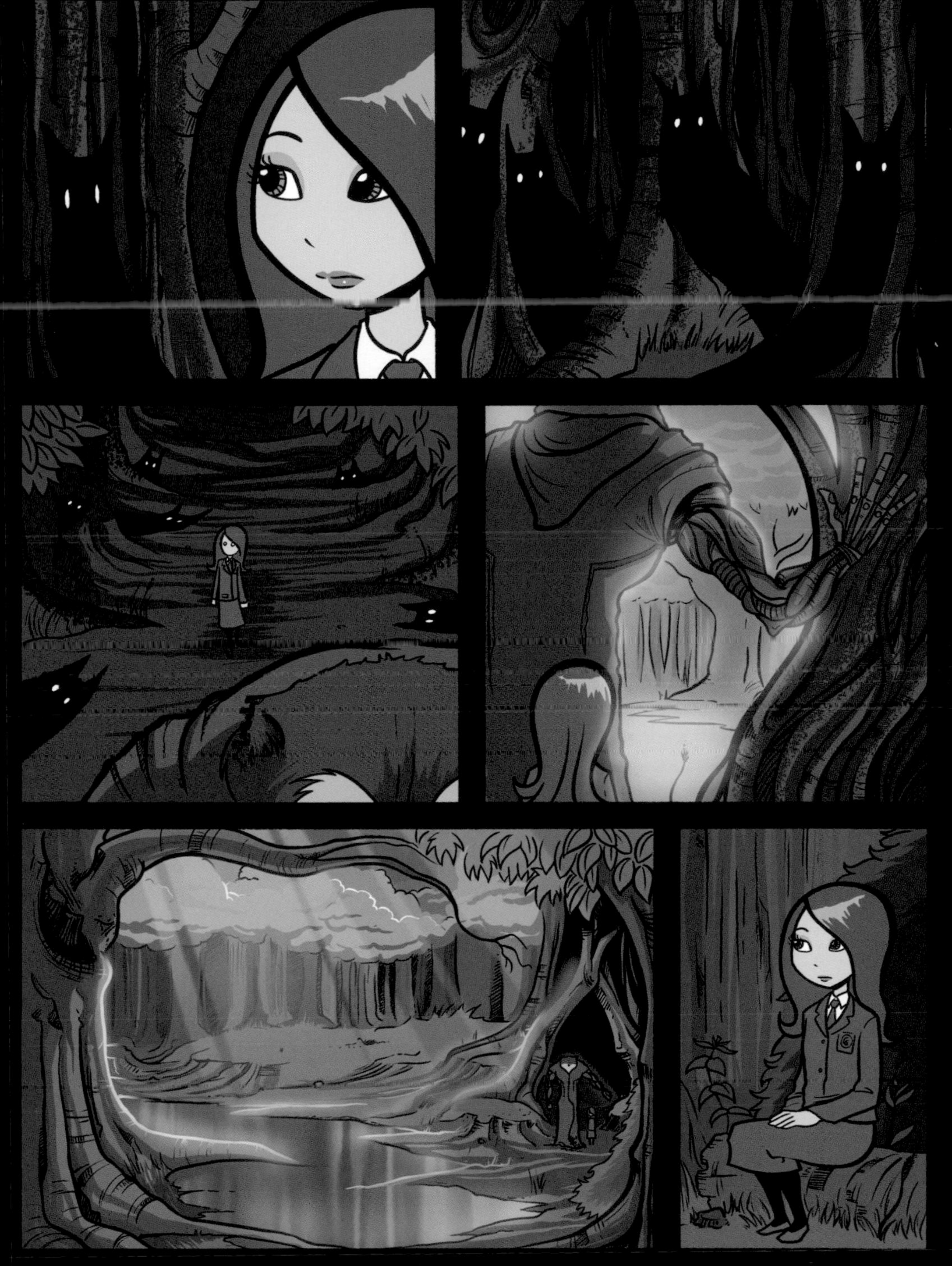

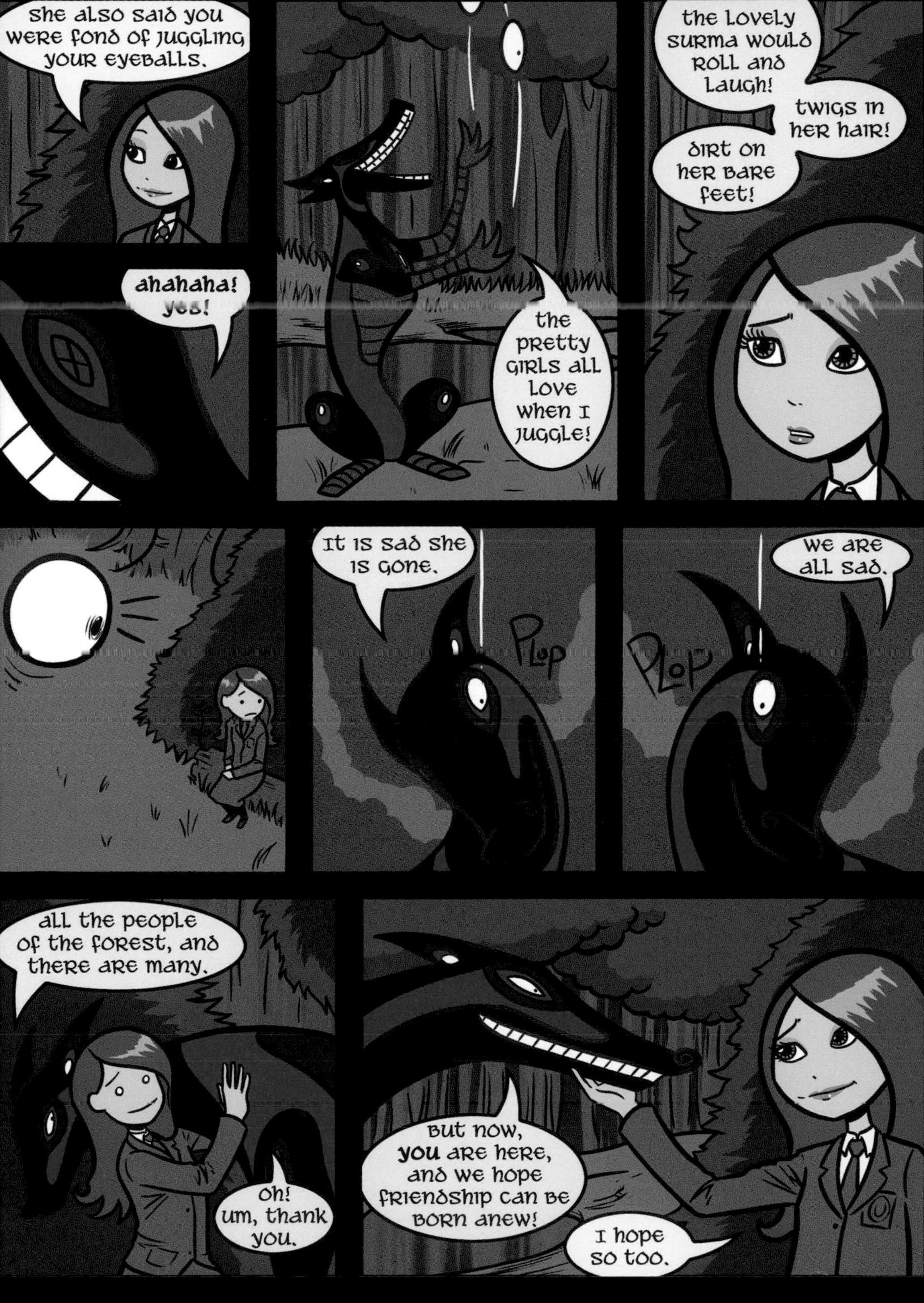
she also said you were fond of juggling your eyeballs.
the lovely surma would roll and laugh!
twigs in her hair!
dirt on her bare feet!
ahahaha! yes!
the pretty girls all love when I juggle!
It is sad she is gone.
PLOP
PLOP
We are all sad.
all the people of the forest, and there are many.
oh! um, thank you.
But now, you are here, and we hope friendship can be born anew!
I hope so too.

IS this the test I've heard about?

THERE IS A TEST, yes.

SOME CREATURES OF THE FOREST WISH TO BE HUMAN, ALSO.

TRAITORS.

haha, IT WAS YSENGRIM'S IDEA TO NO LONGER ALLOW HUMANS INTO THE FOREST.

NOT WITHOUT GIVING UP THEIR BODIES FIRST.

have HUMANS LIVED HERE BEFORE, THEN?

OH yes! WHEN I DIVIDED THE FOREST AND COURT THERE WERE SOME HUMANS AND CREATURES LIVING ON BOTH SIDES.

MANY OF THE CURRENT INHABITANTS ARE DESCENDED FROM THOSE HUMANS.

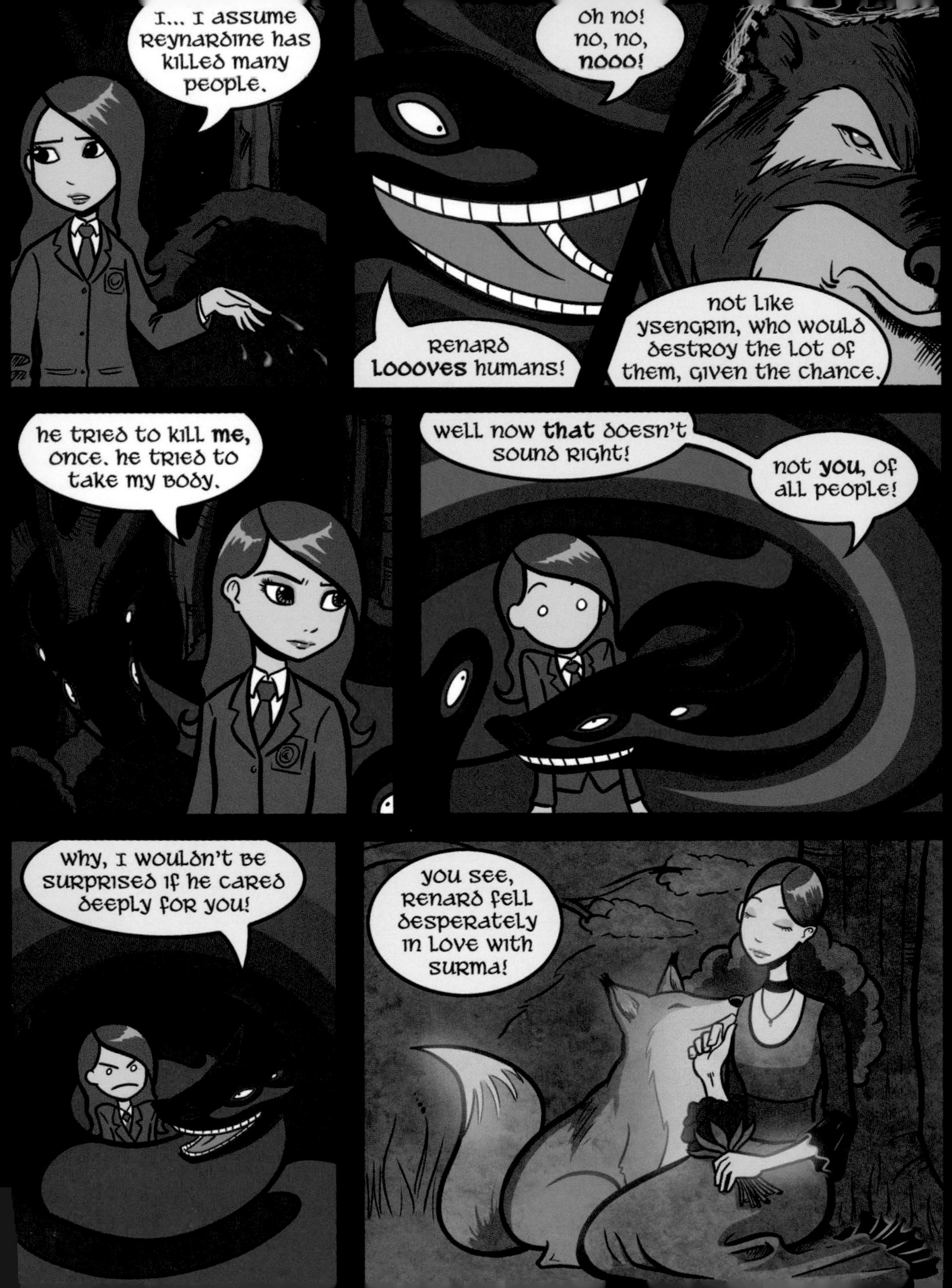
I... I assume Reynardine has killed many people.
Oh no! no, no, nooo!
Renard loooves humans!
not like Ysengrin, who would destroy the lot of them, given the chance.
he tried to kill me, once. he tried to take my body.
well now that doesn't sound right!
not you, of all people!
why, I wouldn't be surprised if he cared deeply for you!
you see, Renard fell desperately in love with Surma!

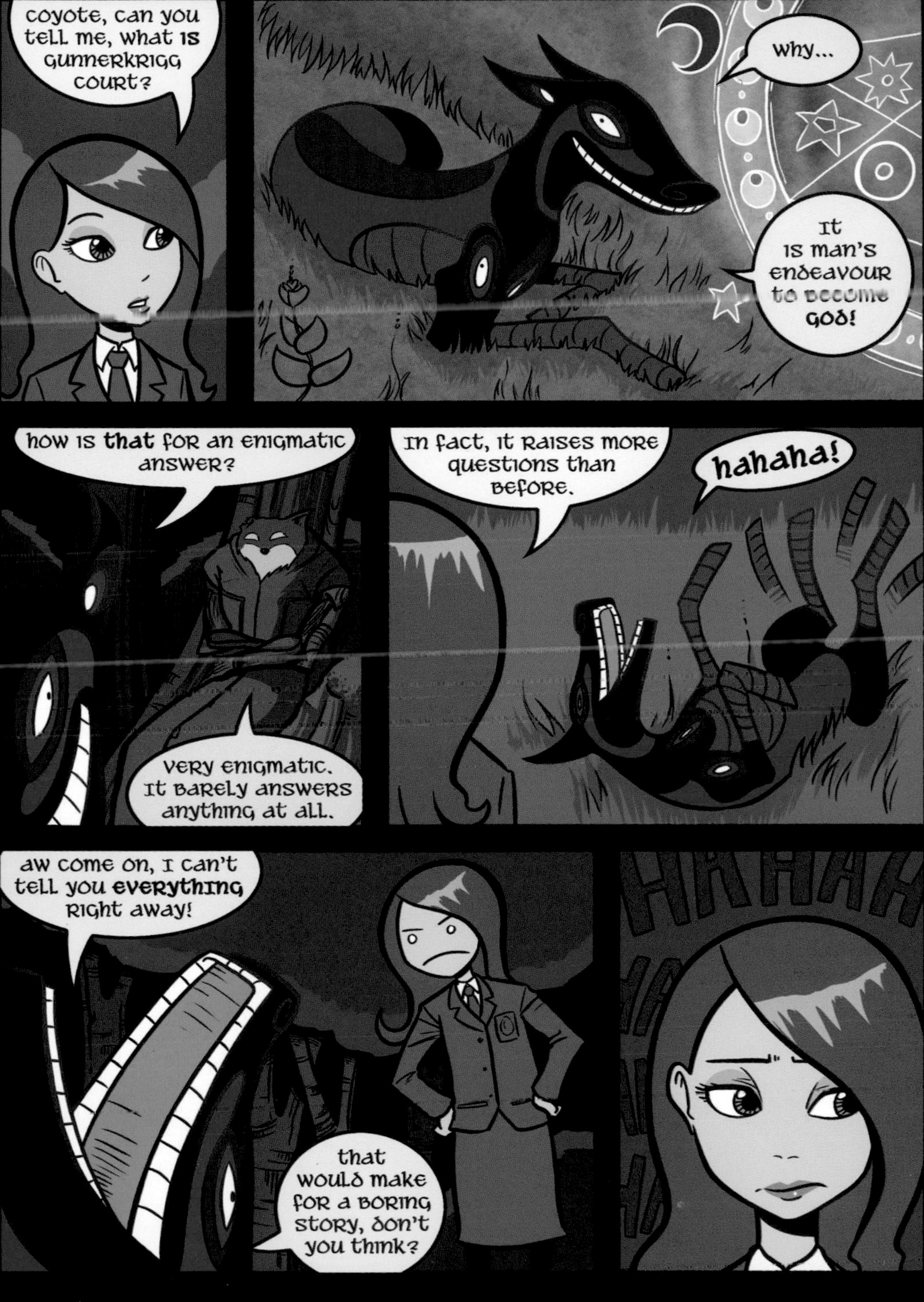
coyote, can you tell me, what IS Gunnerkrigg court?
why...
It is man's endeavour to become god!
how is that for an enigmatic answer?
very enigmatic. It barely answers anything at all.
In fact, it raises more questions than before.
hahaha!
aw come on, I can't tell you everything right away!
that would make for a boring story, don't you think?
HAHAHA
HA HA HA HA

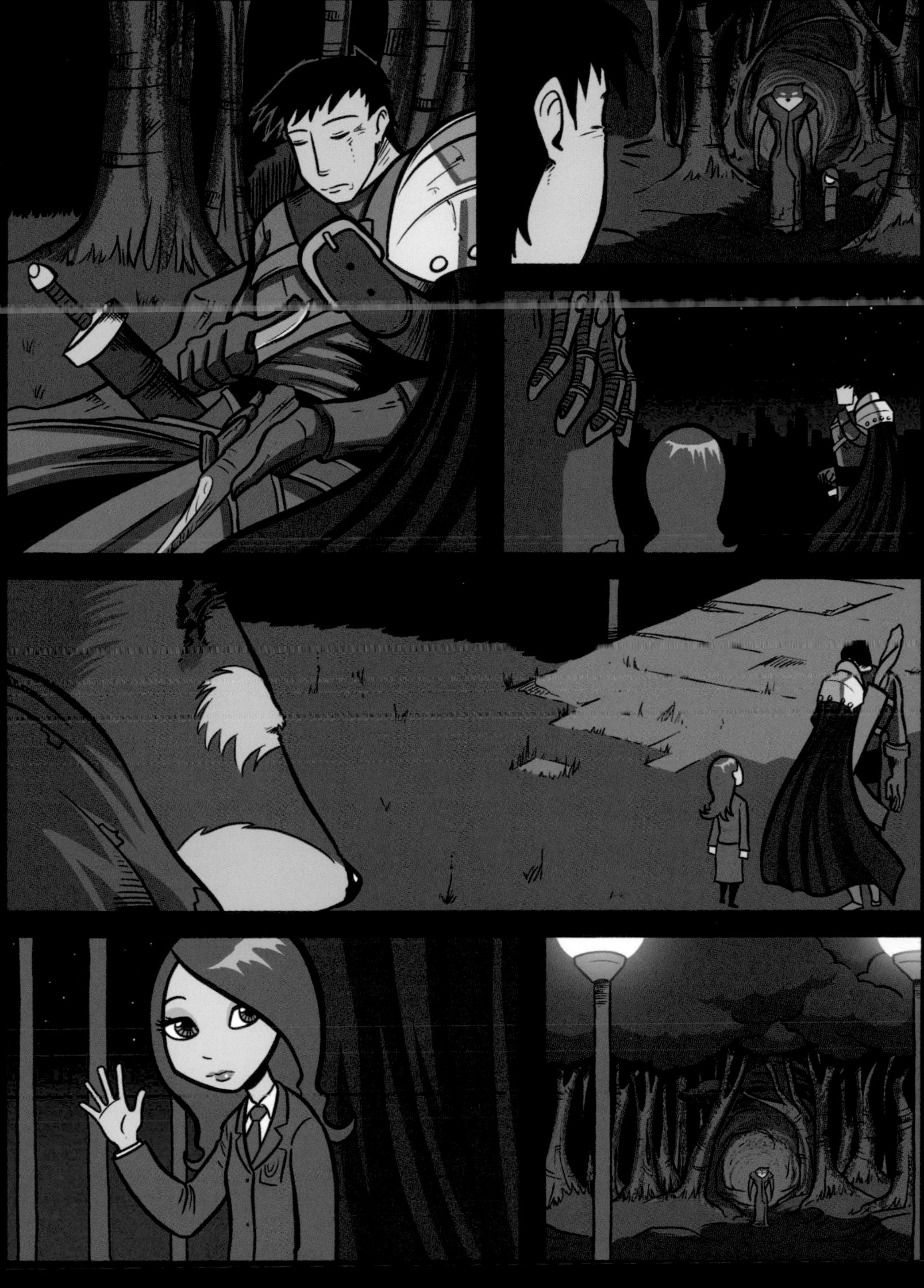

haha, you should see the poor guy. he came out all curly!

he took a hair brush and was all

"leave me beeee!"

hmmm.

welp, I dunno what you were looking for, but there hasn't been any irregular lunar activity recorded over the past few hours.

everything's the same as it always is.

TAP TAP

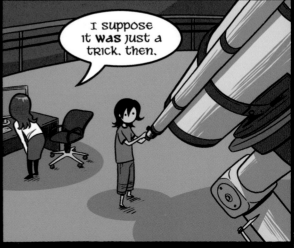

I suppose it **was** just a trick, then.

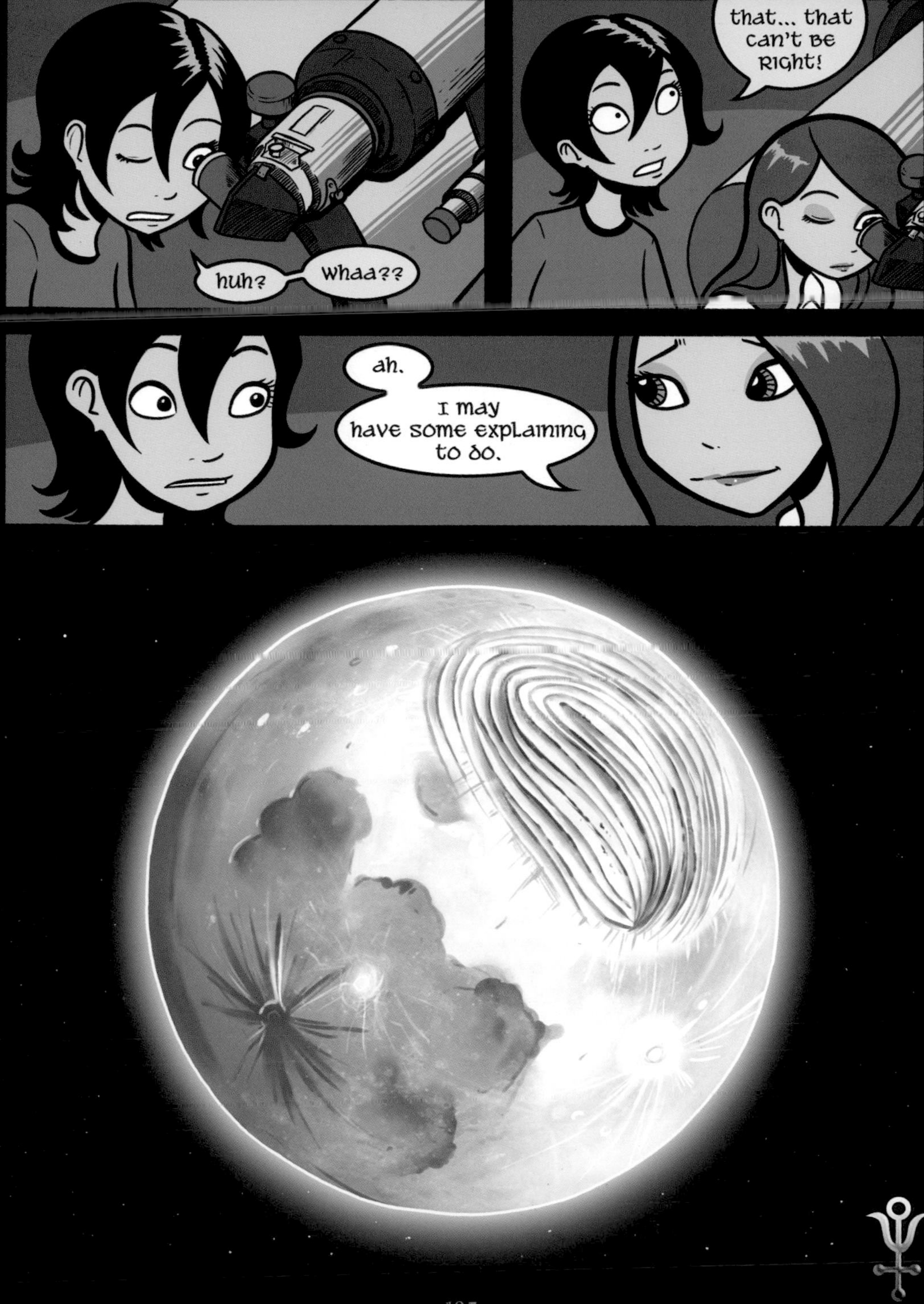
huh?
whaa??
that... that can't be right!
ah.
I may have some explaining to do.

Gunnerkrigg Court

Chapter 21:

Blinking

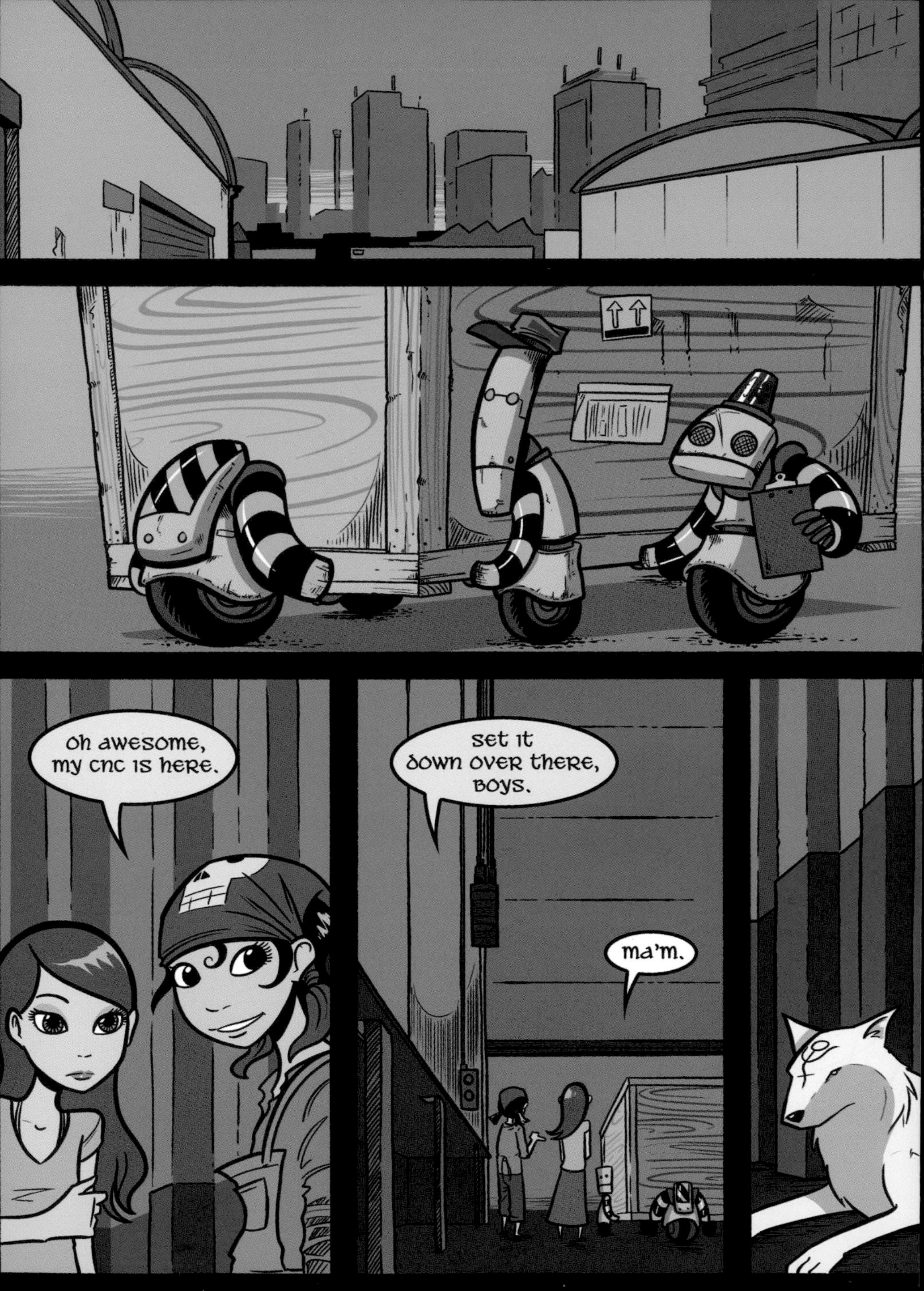
oh awesome, my cnc is here.
set it down over there, boys.
ma'm.

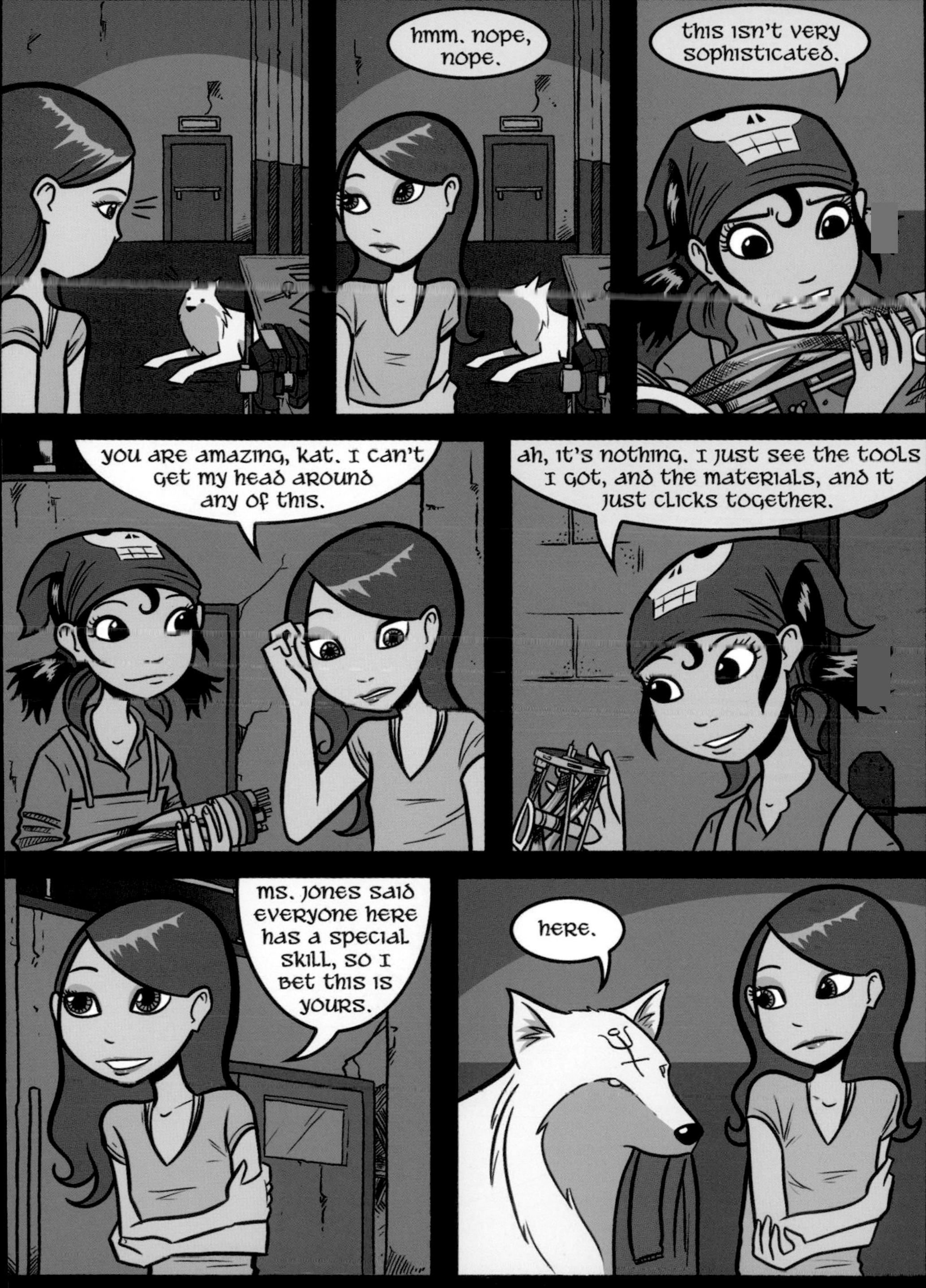
hmm. nope, nope.
this isn't very sophisticated.
you are amazing, kat. I can't get my head around any of this.
ah, it's nothing. I just see the tools I got, and the materials, and it just clicks together.
ms. jones said everyone here has a special skill, so I bet this is yours.
here.

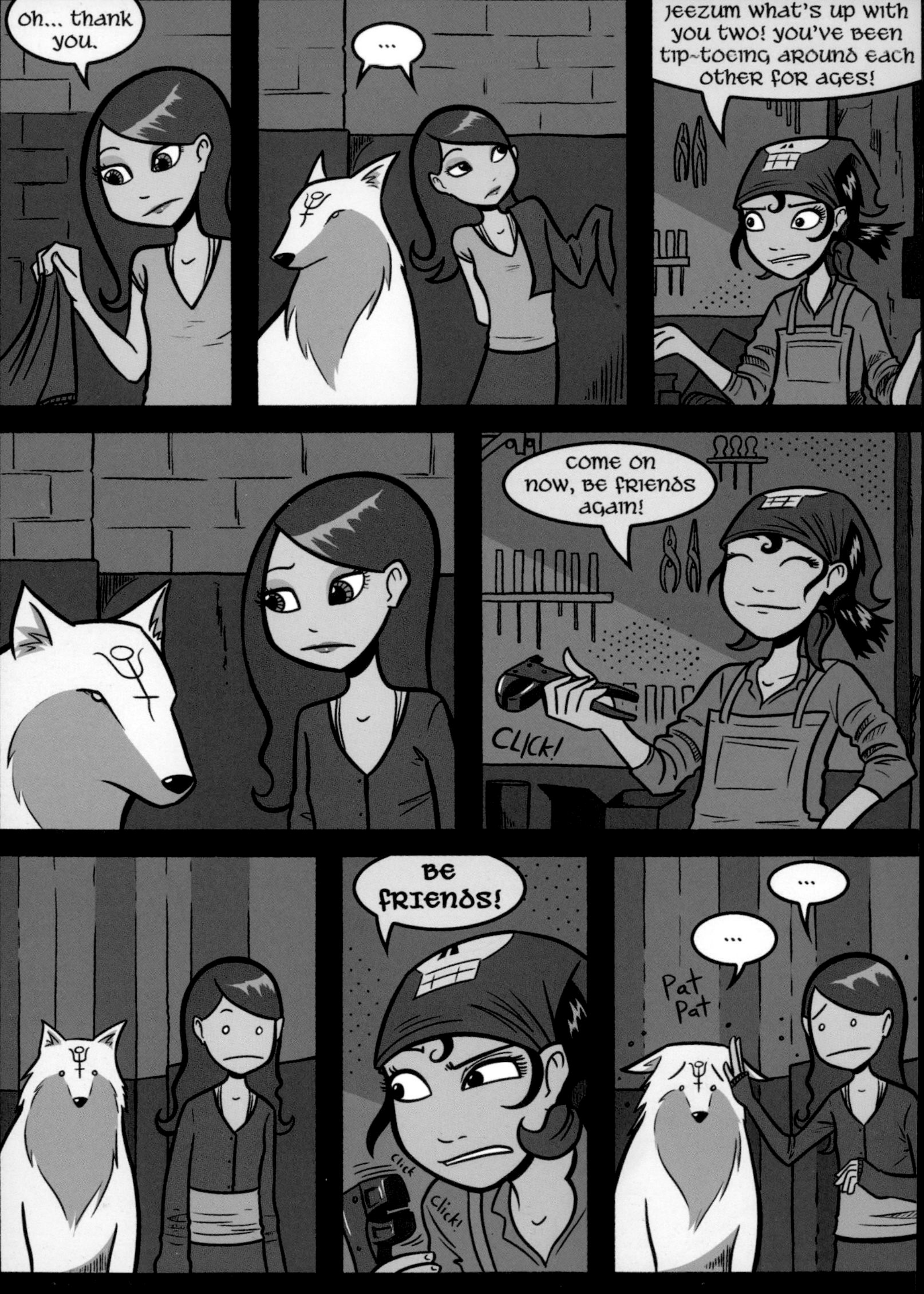
Oh... thank you.
...
Jeezum what's up with you two! You've been tip-toeing around each other for ages!
Come on now, be friends again!
CLICK!
Be friends!
Click
Click!
...
...
Pat Pat

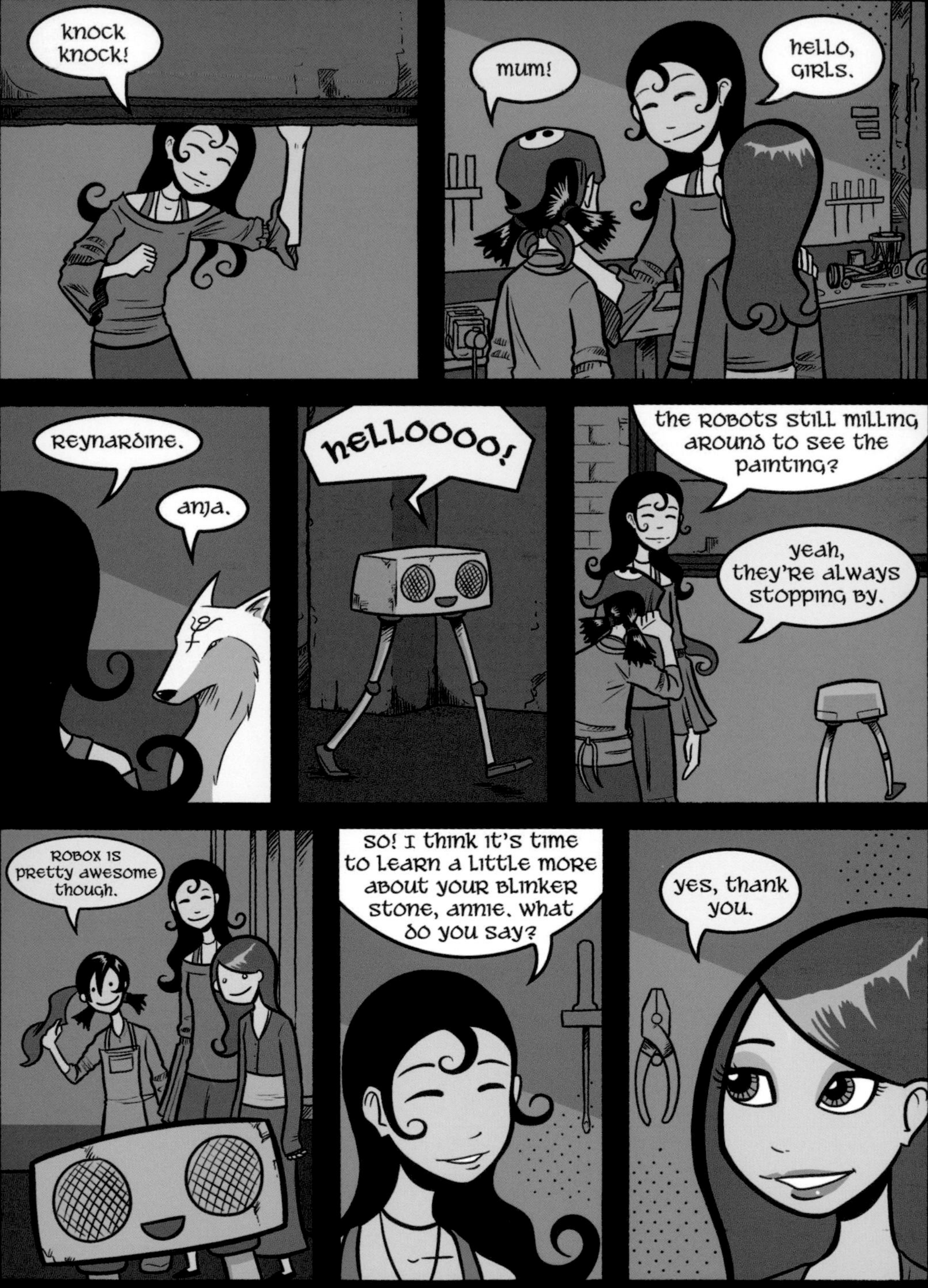
knock knock!
mum!
hello, girls.
reynardine.
anja.
hellOOOO!
the robots still milling around to see the painting?
yeah, they're always stopping by.
robox is pretty awesome though.
so! I think it's time to learn a little more about your blinker stone, annie. what do you say?
yes, thank you.

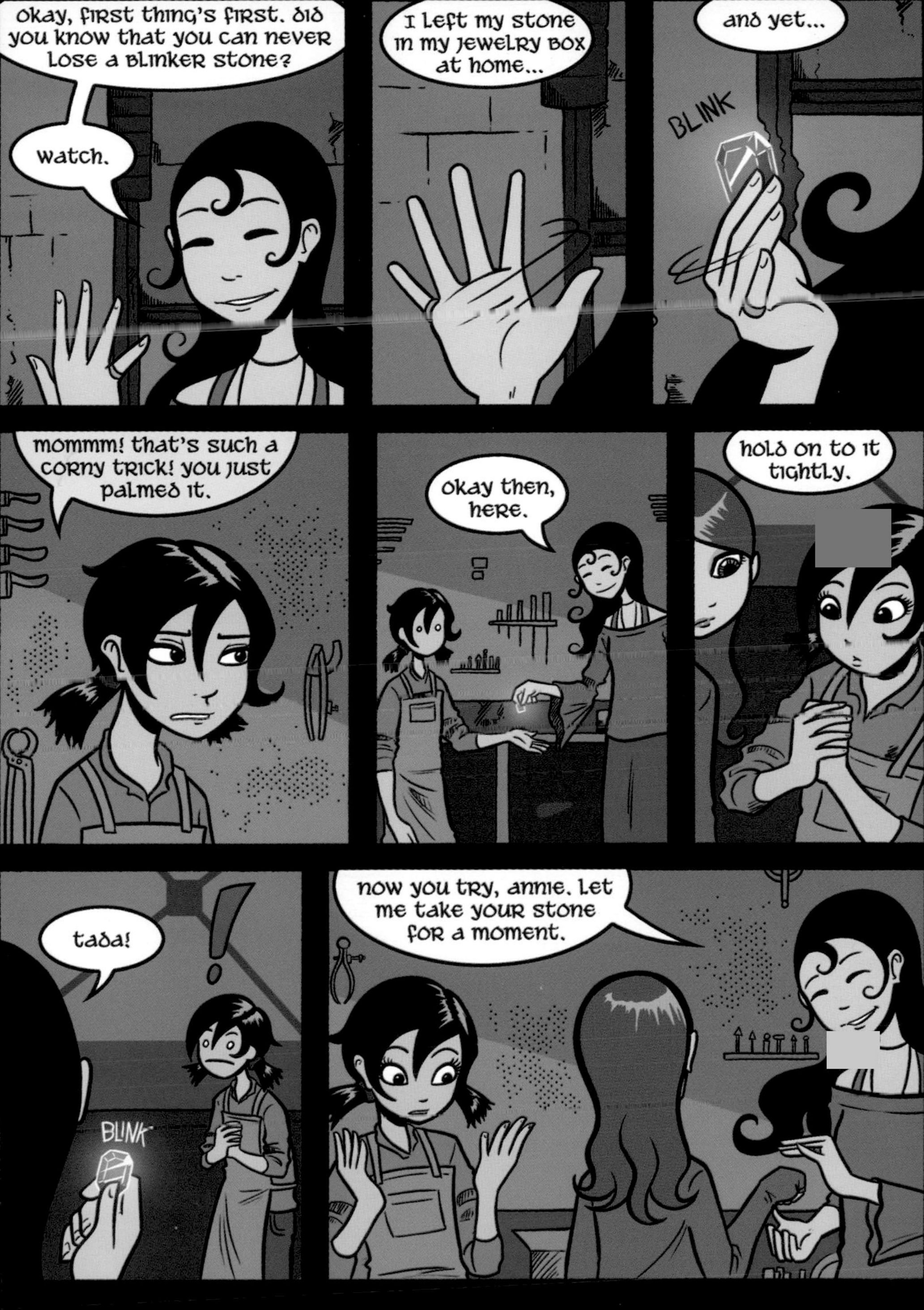
okay, first thing's first. did you know that you can never lose a blinker stone?
watch.
I left my stone in my jewelry box at home...
and yet...
BLINK
mommm! that's such a corny trick! you just palmed it.
okay then, here.
hold on to it tightly.
tada!
!
BLINK
now you try, annie. let me take your stone for a moment.

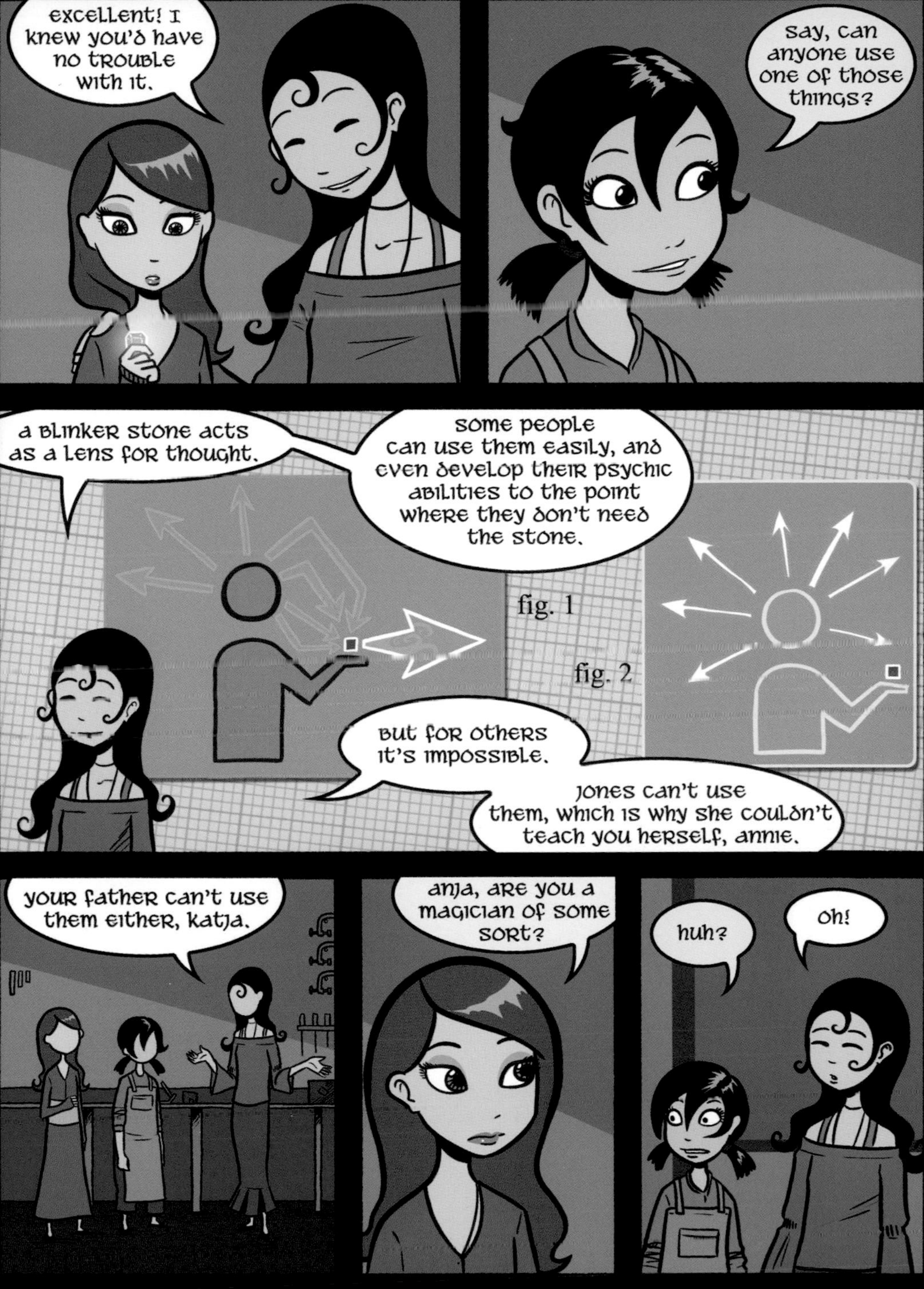
excellent! I knew you'd have no trouble with it.
say, can anyone use one of those things?
a blinker stone acts as a lens for thought.
some people can use them easily, and even develop their psychic abilities to the point where they don't need the stone.
fig. 1
fig. 2
but for others it's impossible.
jones can't use them, which is why she couldn't teach you herself, annie.
your father can't use them either, katja.
anja, are you a magician of some sort?
huh?
oh!

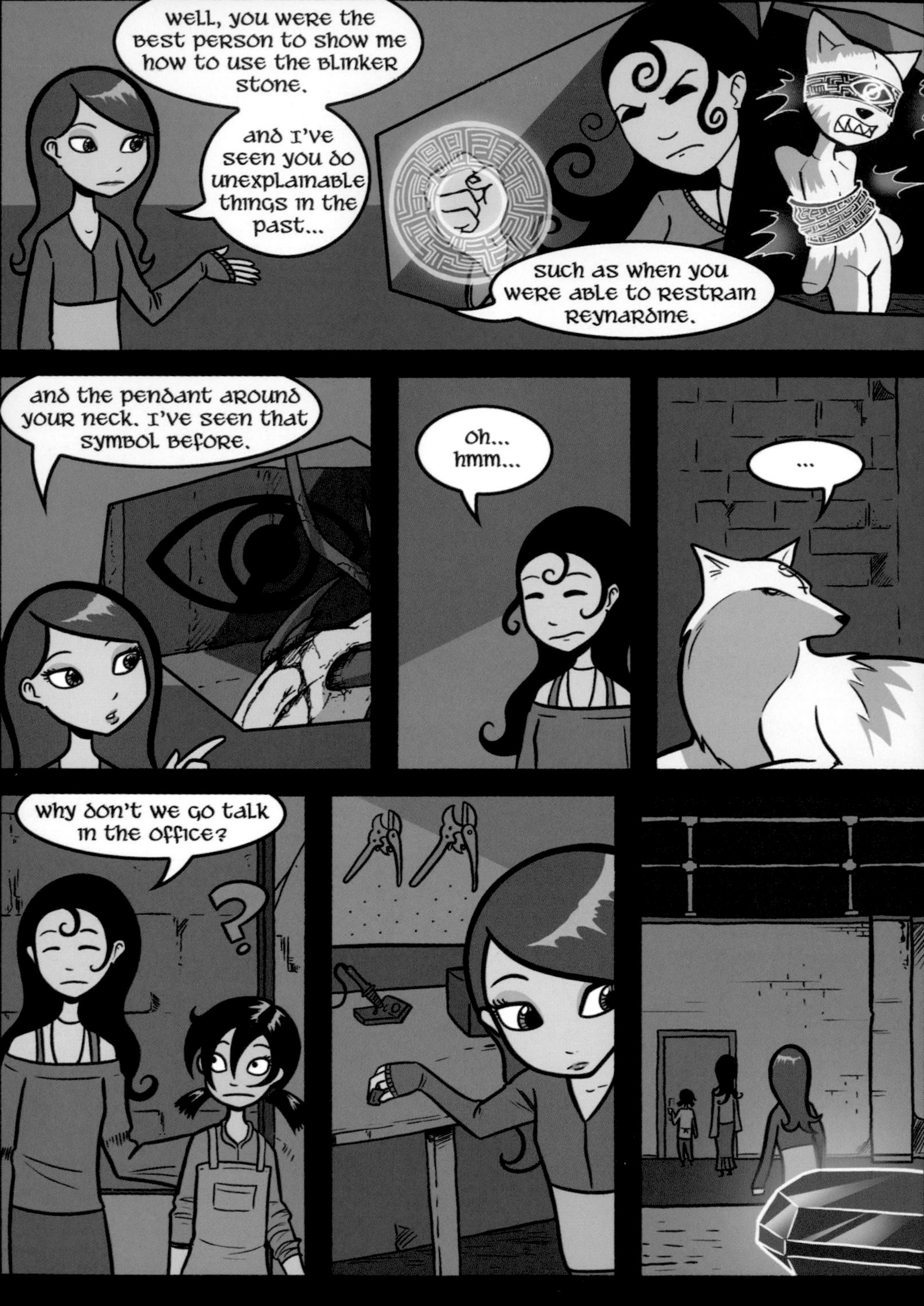
Well, you were the best person to show me how to use the blinker stone.
and I've seen you do unexplainable things in the past...
such as when you were able to restrain Reynardine.
and the pendant around your neck. I've seen that symbol before.
Oh... hmm...
...
why don't we go talk in the office?
?

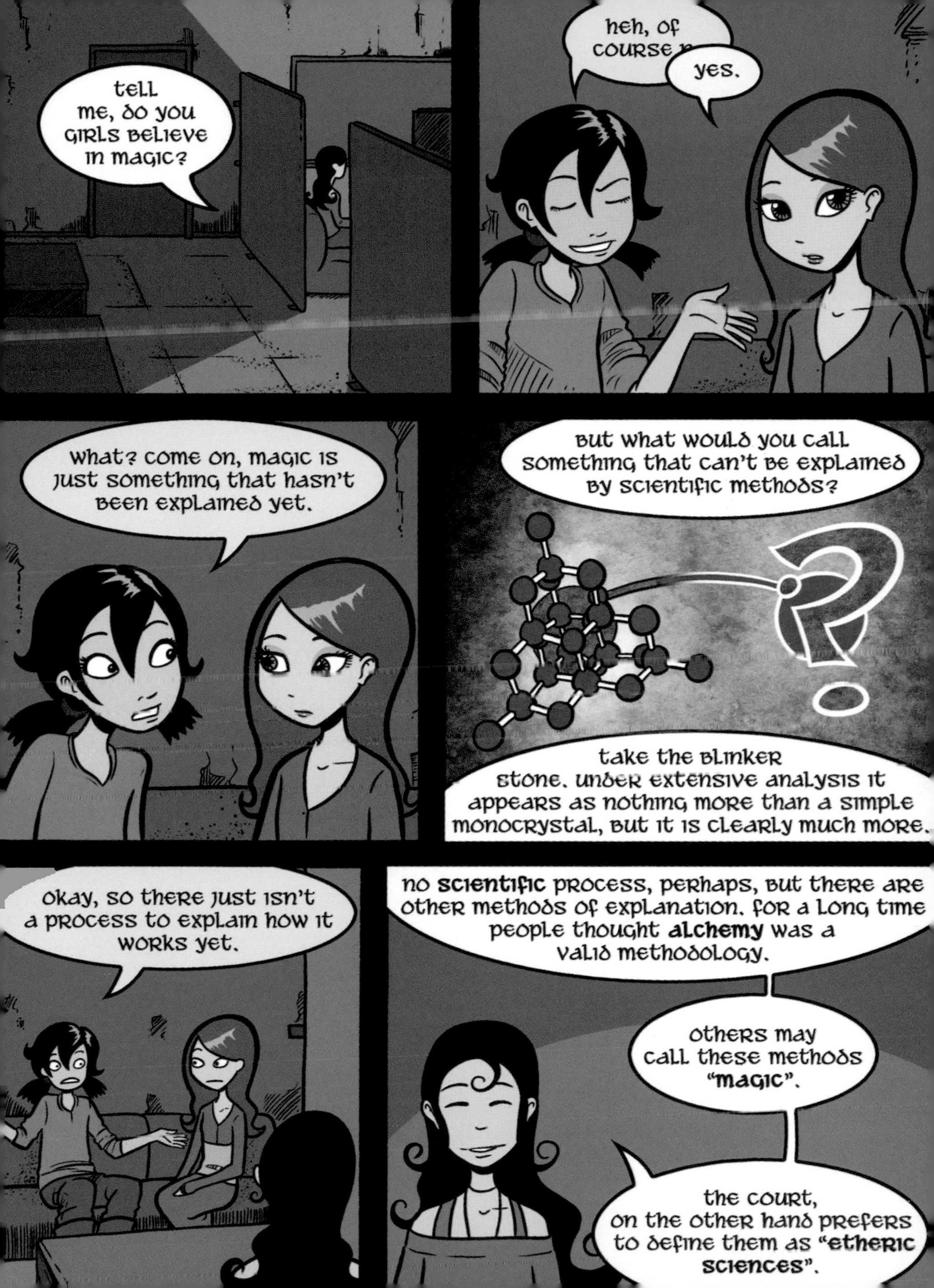
tell me, do you girls believe in magic?
heh, of course n
yes.
what? come on, magic is just something that hasn't been explained yet.
but what would you call something that can't be explained by scientific methods?
take the blinker stone. under extensive analysis it appears as nothing more than a simple monocrystal, but it is clearly much more.
okay, so there just isn't a process to explain how it works yet.
no scientific process, perhaps, but there are other methods of explanation. for a long time people thought alchemy was a valid methodology.
others may call these methods "magic".
the court, on the other hand prefers to define them as "etheric sciences".

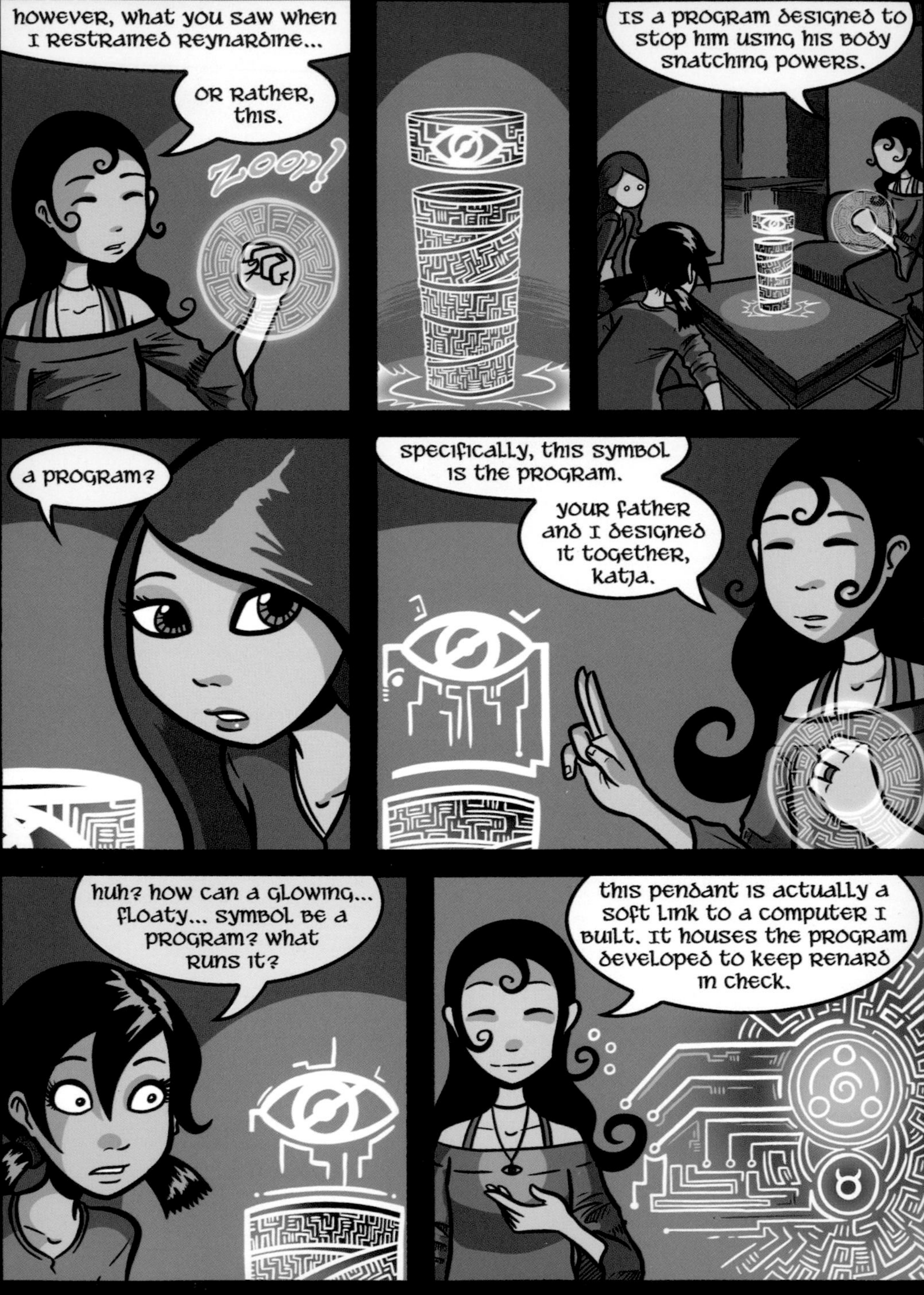
however, what you saw when I restramed reynardine...
or rather, this.
zoop!
is a program designed to stop him using his body snatching powers.
a program?
specifically, this symbol is the program.
your father and I designed it together, katja.
huh? how can a glowing... floaty... symbol be a program? what runs it?
this pendant is actually a soft link to a computer I built. it houses the program developed to keep renard in check.

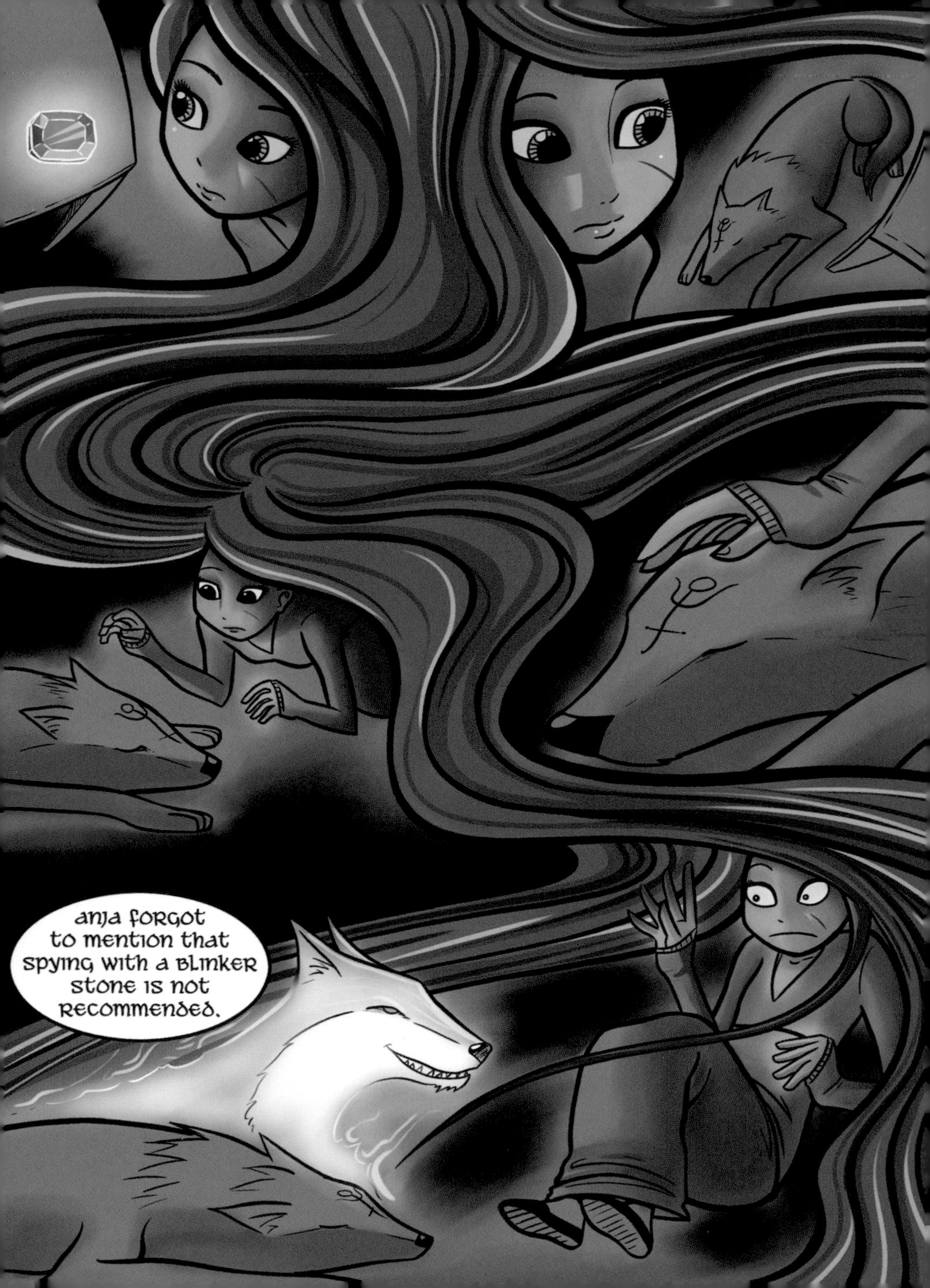
anja forgot to mention that spying with a blinker stone is not recommended.

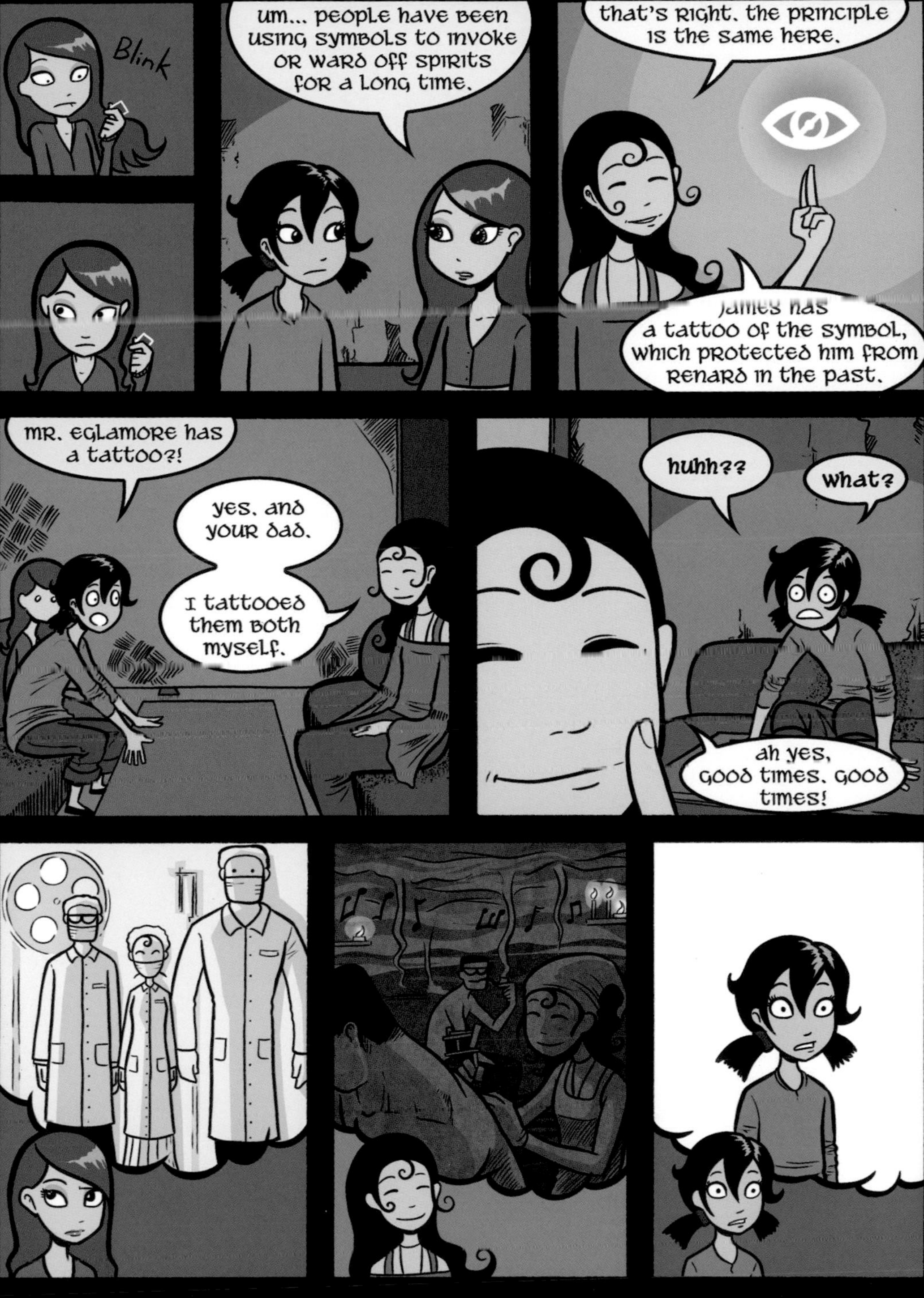
Blink
um... people have been using symbols to invoke or ward off spirits for a long time.
that's right. the principle is the same here.
James has a tattoo of the symbol, which protected him from Renard in the past.
mr. Eglamore has a tattoo?!
yes. and your dad.
I tattooed them both myself.
huhh??
what?
ah yes, good times. good times!

REYNARDINE'S POWER WAS BESTOWED BY COYOTE HIMSELF...

WELL, YES AND NO.

MY COMPUTER IS BASED ON WORK WE DID FINDING A WAY TO CONTROL REYNARDINE.

HOWEVER, JUST LIKE THE BLINKER STONE, THERE IS A LOT ABOUT THE ETHERIC PROCESS WE JUST CAN'T UNDERSTAND.

YET YOU FOUND A WAY TO MANIPULATE IT USING TECHNOLOGY?

BASICALLY, WE CHEATED

THE COMPUTER IS A HYBRID OF COURT TECHNOLOGY AND JUST ENOUGH ETHERIC TECHNOLOGY TO ALLOW IT TO WORK.

BECAUSE OF THIS, THOUGH, THE COURT SEES IT AS A USELESS SYSTEM.

THAT'S NOT FAIR... I MEAN, IT WORKS, RIGHT?

SOME SAY THAT ISN'T GOOD ENOUGH. NOT IF YOU CAN'T FULLY EXPLAIN **HOW** IT WORKS.

SO, ANNIE, I HAVE TO ASK, WHO WAS THE BOY THAT GAVE YOU YOUR STONE?

UM... HIS NAME IS MORT.

BUT HOW DID YOU KNOW IT WAS A BOY?

HAHA! BLINKER STONES ARE TRADITIONALLY GIVEN BETWEEN COUPLES.

DONALD GAVE ME MINE A LONG TIME AGO.

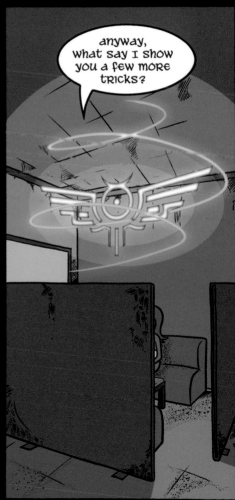

ANYWAY, WHAT SAY I SHOW YOU A FEW MORE TRICKS?

OH MAAANN! I KNEW IT!

I SEE.

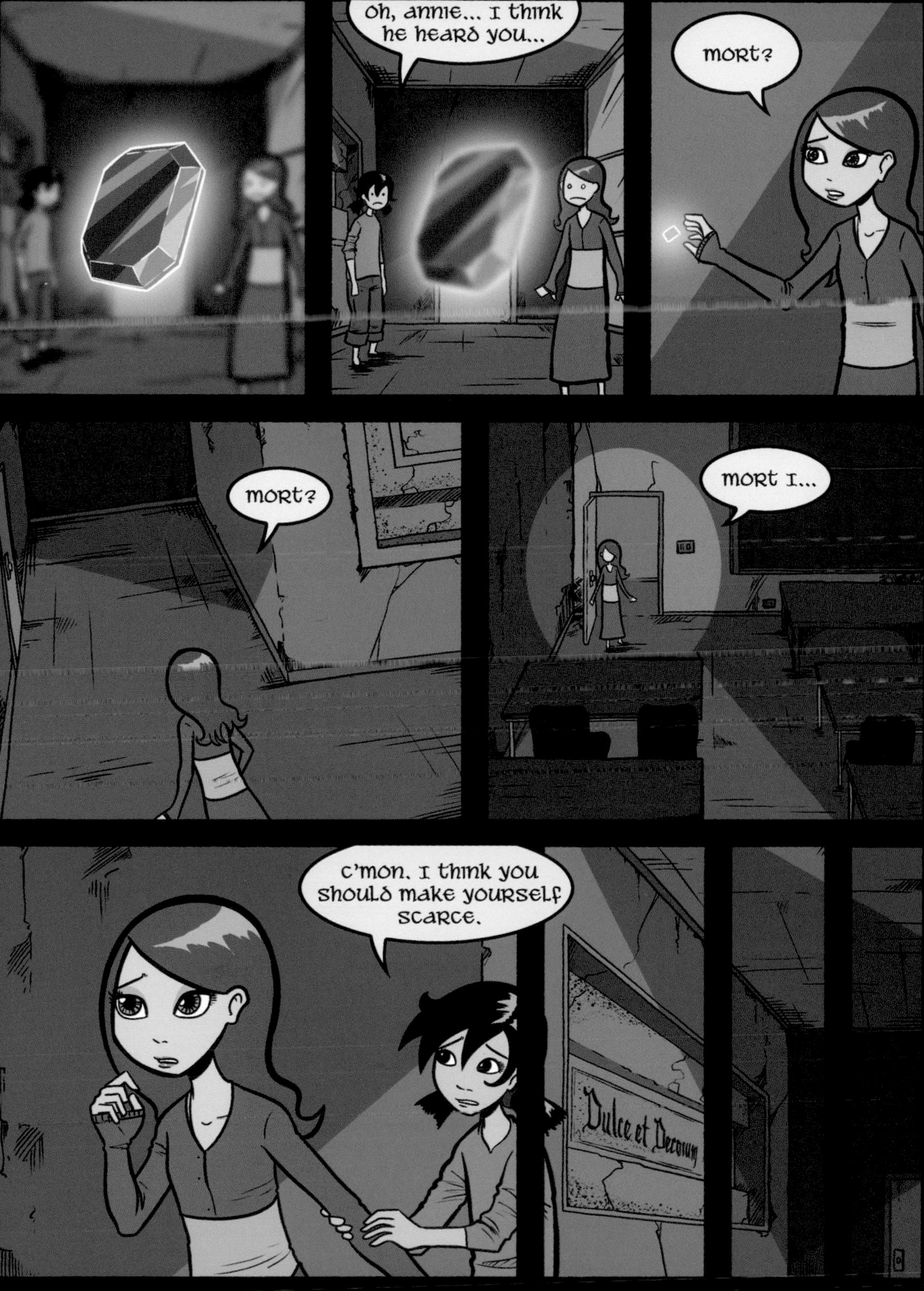
oh, annie... I think he heard you...
mort?
mort?
mort I...
c'mon. I think you should make yourself scarce.
Dulce et Decorum

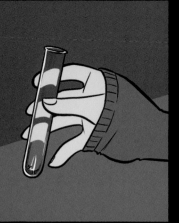

TAP TAP

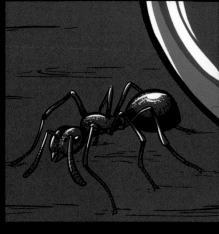

man, it's weird, you know?

I mean, it's just an ant...

But now that I know there is some creepy insect guy that appears when it dies makes this kinda hard to~

oh.

Squish

uh... just make sure I can't see this click~clack guy again.

hello, ketrak.

220

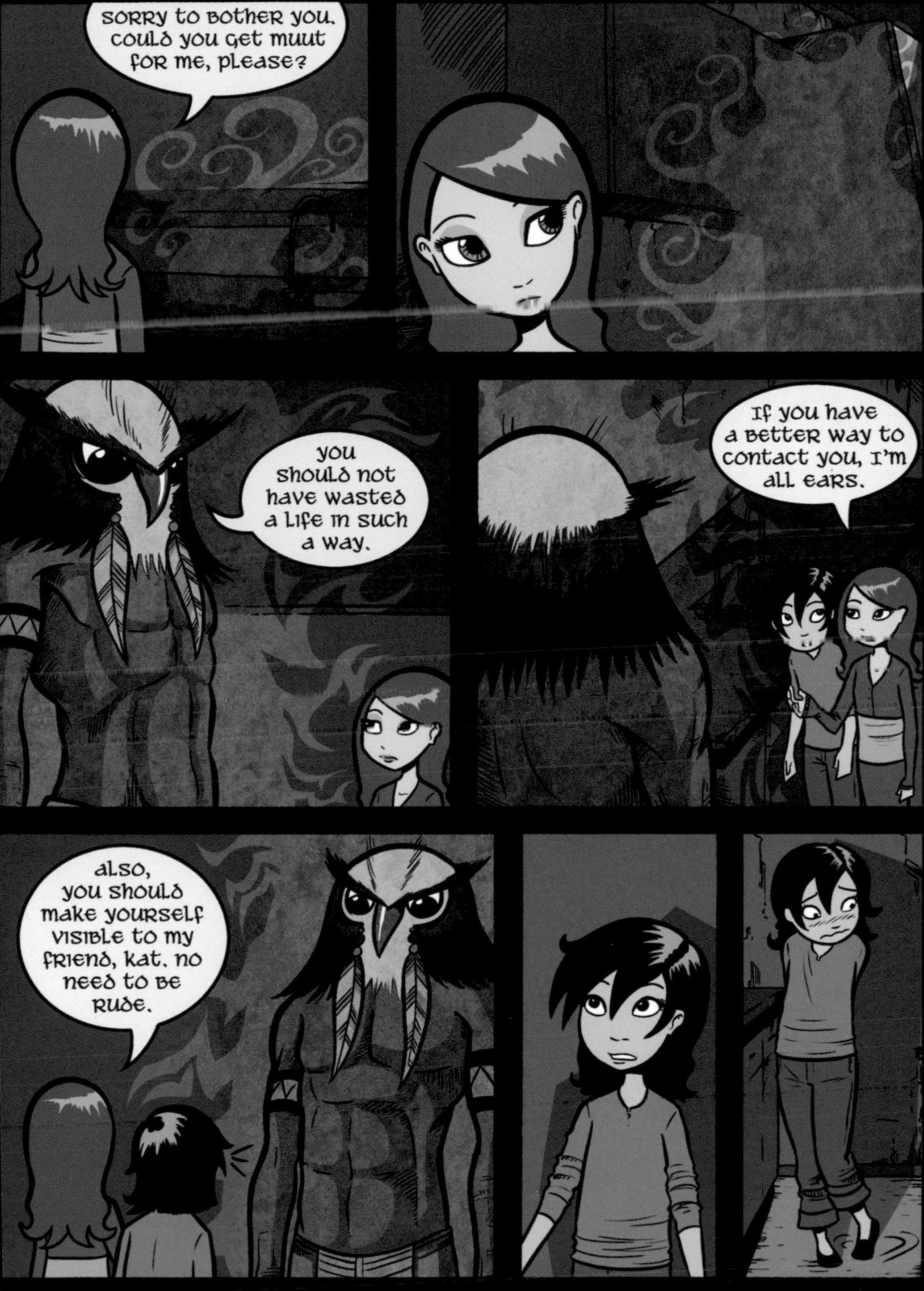
SORRY TO BOTHER YOU. COULD YOU GET MUUT FOR ME, PLEASE?
YOU SHOULD NOT HAVE WASTED A LIFE IN SUCH A WAY.
IF YOU HAVE A BETTER WAY TO CONTACT YOU, I'M ALL EARS.
ALSO, YOU SHOULD MAKE YOURSELF VISIBLE TO MY FRIEND, KAT. NO NEED TO BE RUDE.

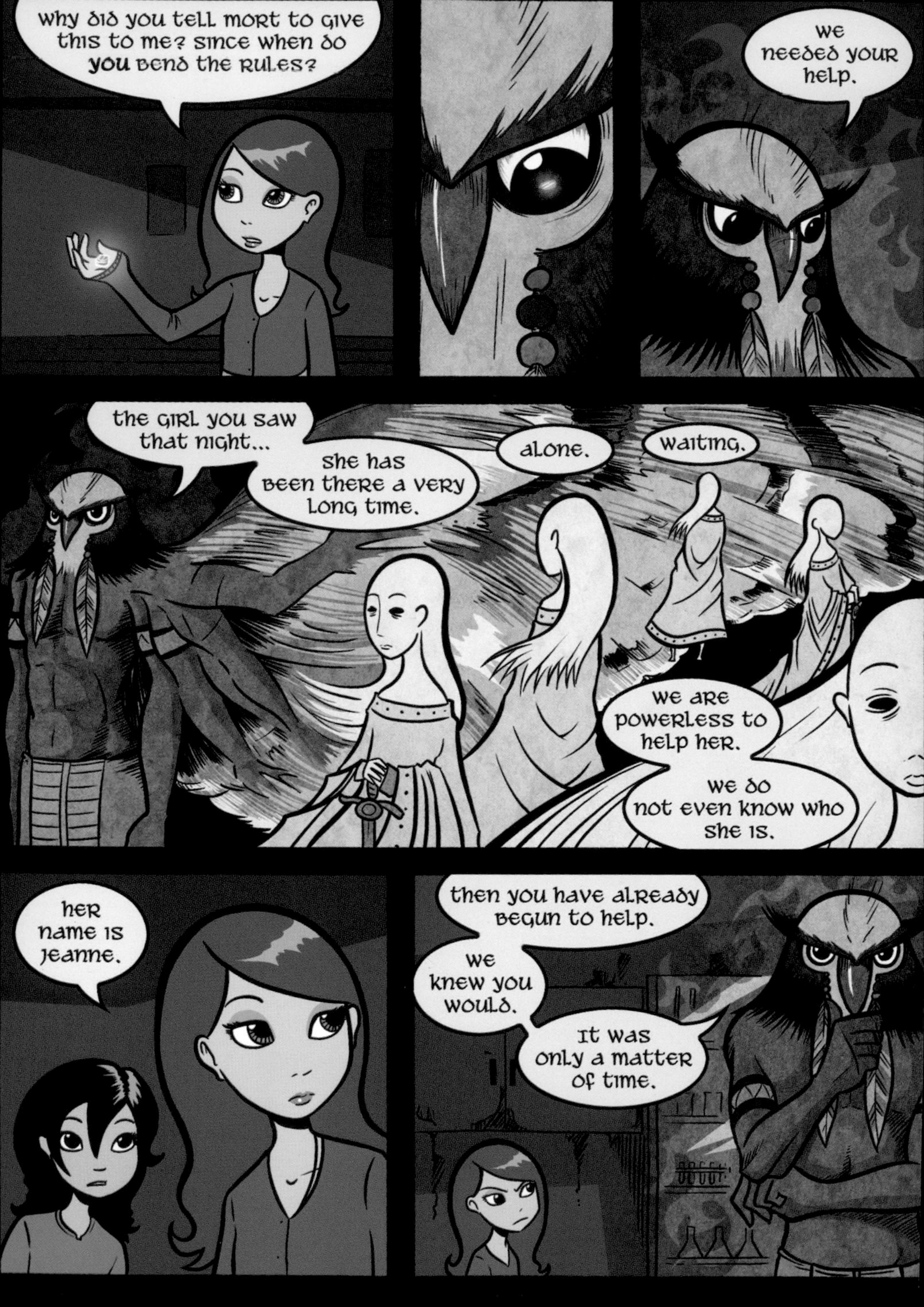
why did you tell mort to give this to me? since when do **you** bend the rules?
we needed your help.
the girl you saw that night...
she has been there a very long time.
alone.
waiting.
we are powerless to help her.
we do not even know who she is.
her name is jeanne.
then you have already begun to help.
we knew you would.
it was only a matter of time.

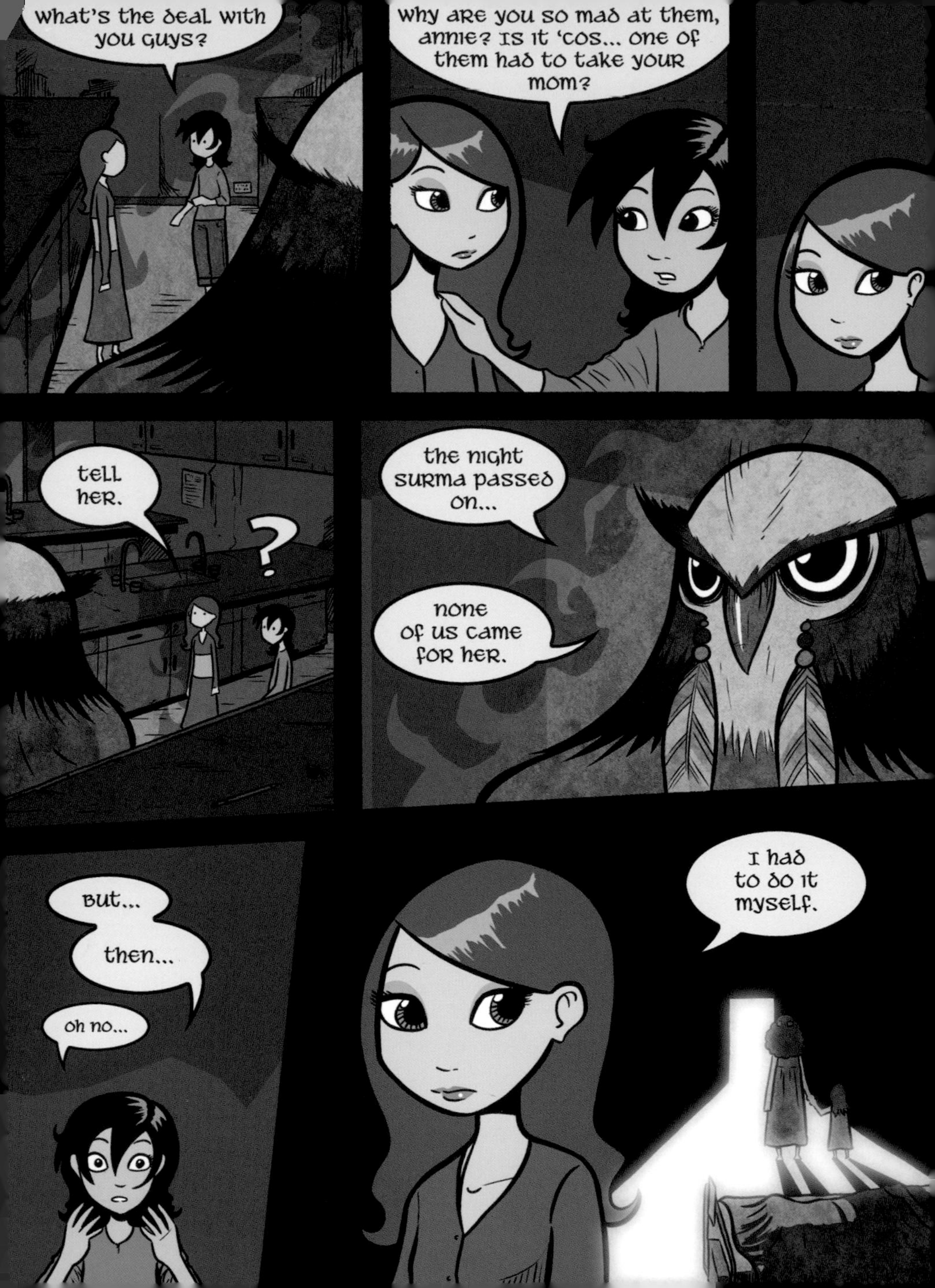
what's the deal with you guys?
why are you so mad at them, annie? is it 'cos... one of them had to take your mom?
tell her.
?
the night surma passed on...
none of us came for her.
but...
then...
oh no...
I had to do it myself.

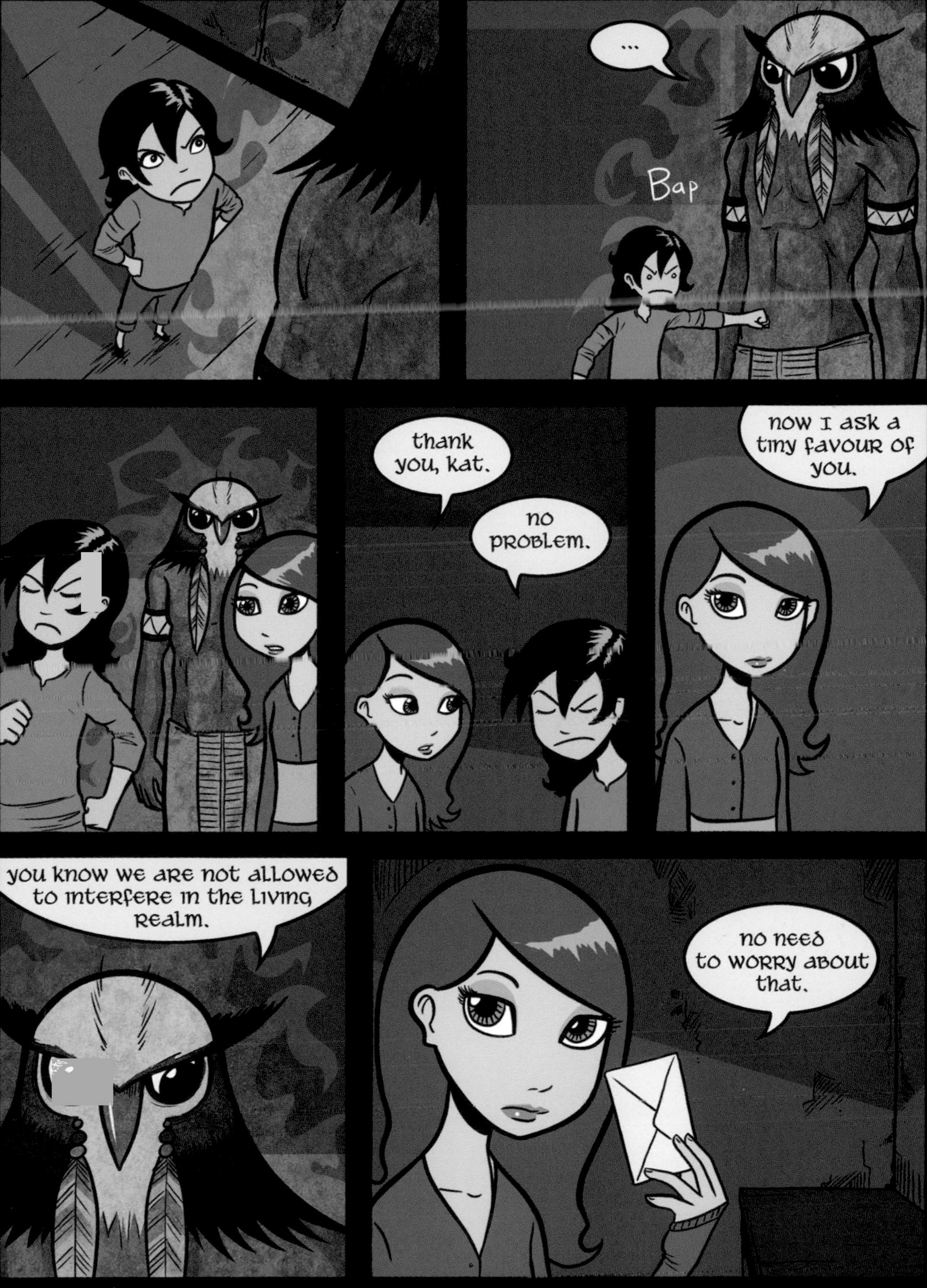
...
Bap
thank you, kat.
no problem.
now I ask a tiny favour of you.
you know we are not allowed to interfere in the living realm.
no need to worry about that.

227

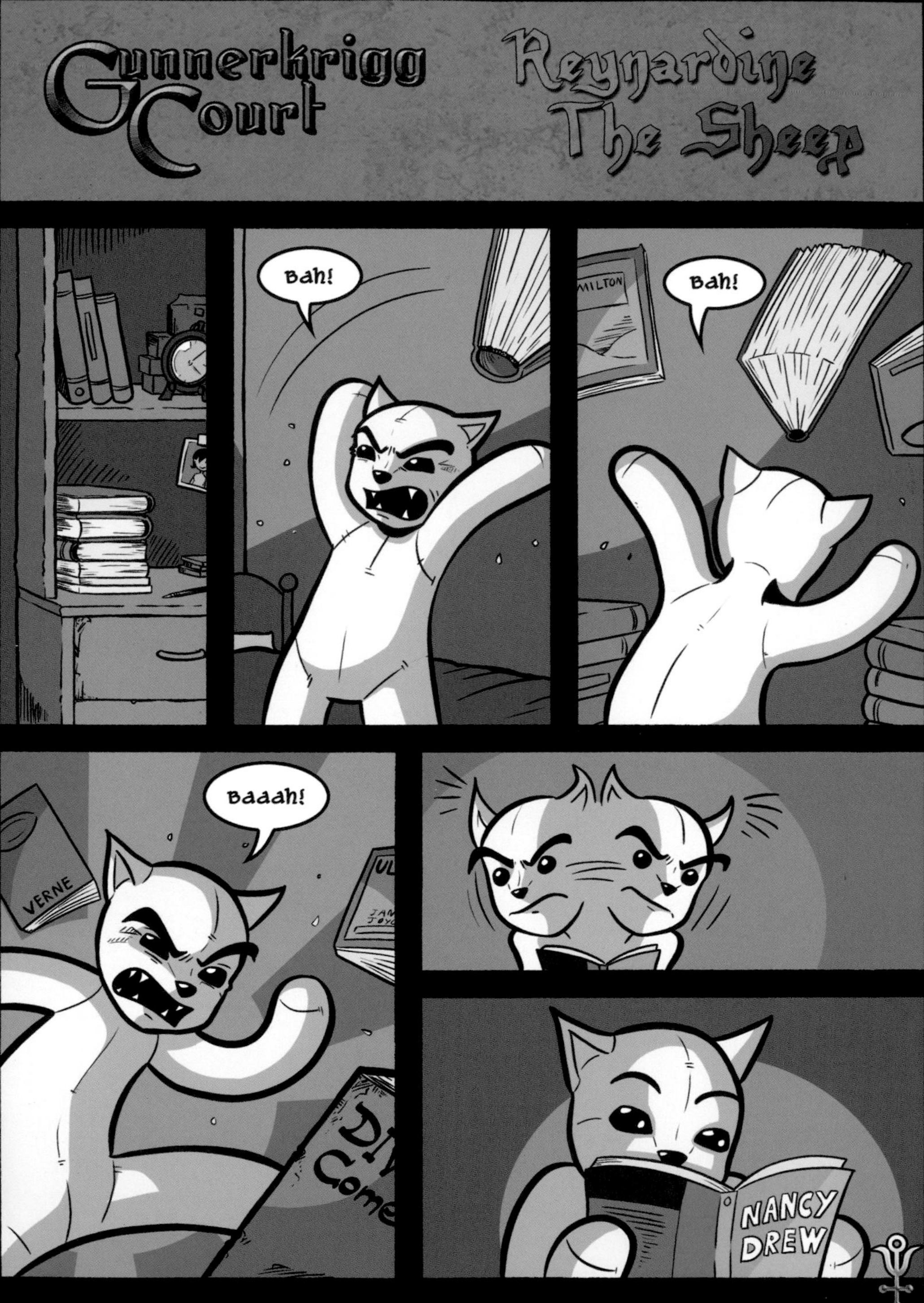

Gunnerkrigg Court
Reynardine The Sheep
Bah!
Bah!
Baaah!
VERNE
NANCY DREW

Gunnerkrigg Court

Chapter 22:

Ties

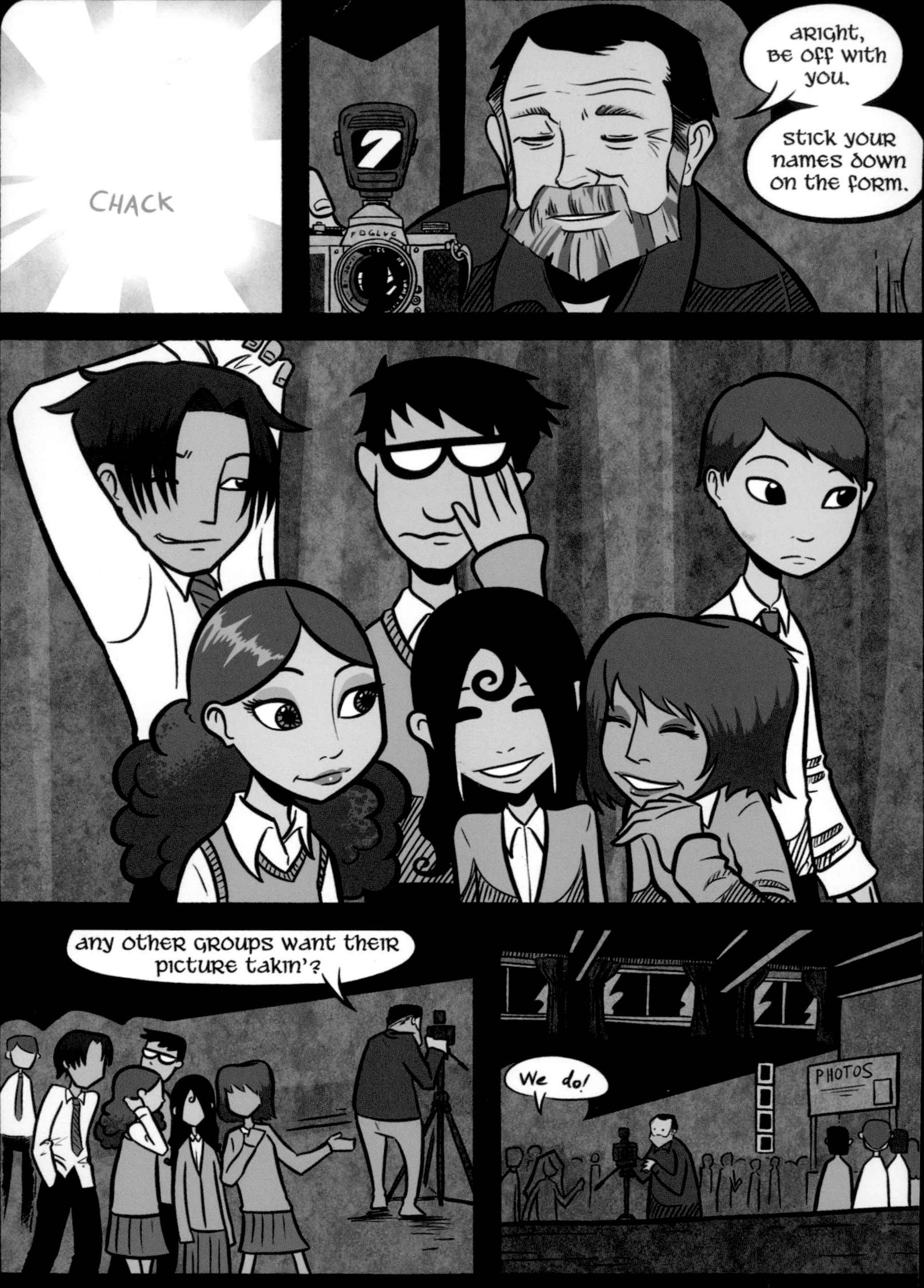
CHACK
aright, be off with you.
stick your names down on the form.
any other groups want their picture takin'?
We do!
PHOTOS

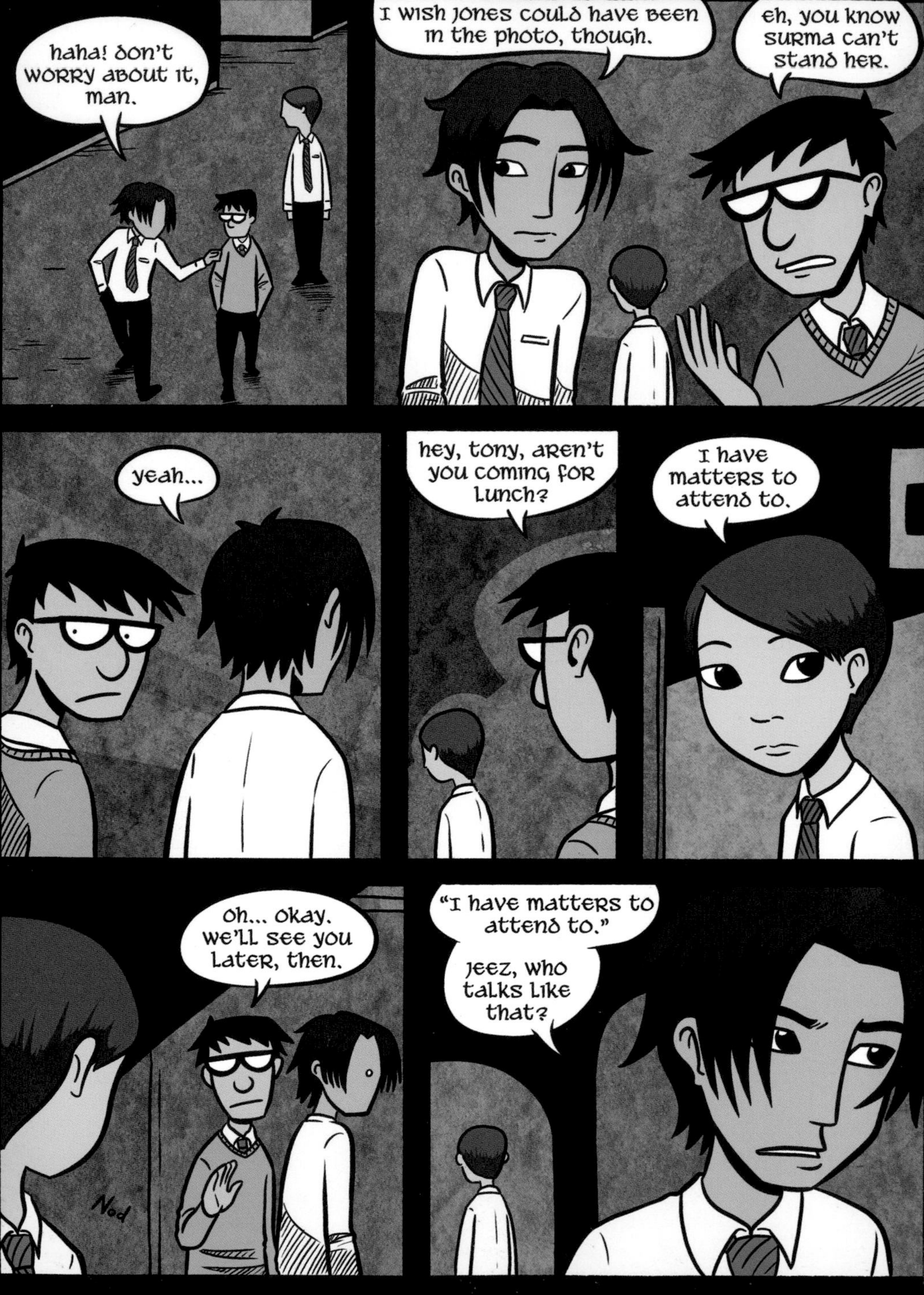
haha! don't worry about it, man.
I wish Jones could have been in the photo, though.
eh, you know Surma can't stand her.
yeah...
hey, Tony, aren't you coming for lunch?
I have matters to attend to.
oh... okay. we'll see you later, then.
Nod
"I have matters to attend to."
jeez, who talks like that?

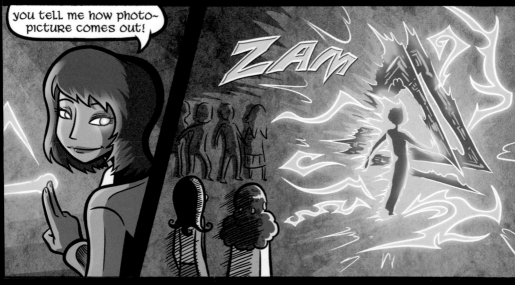

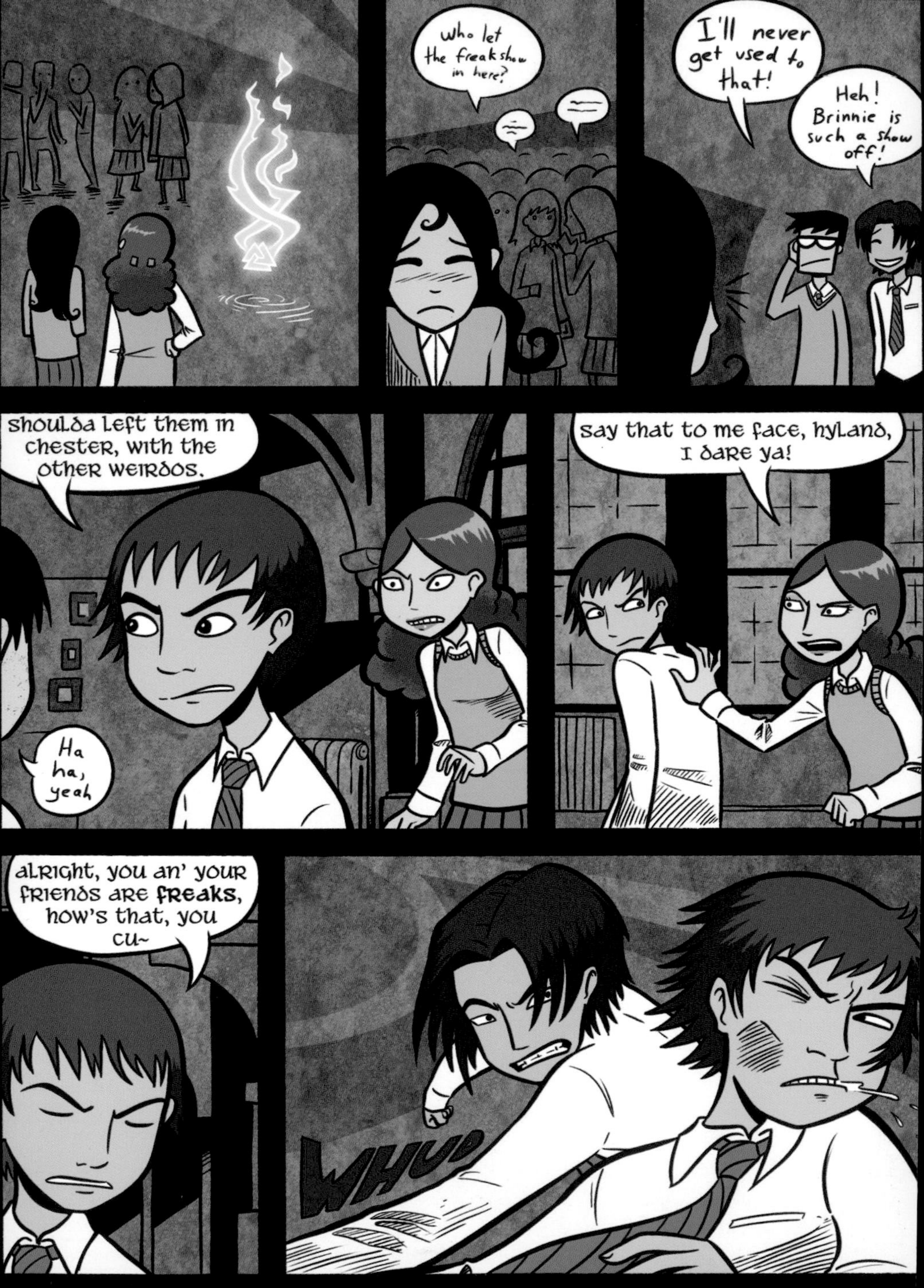

who let the freakshow in here?
I'll never get used to that!
Heh! Brinnie is such a show off!
shoulda left them in chester, with the other weirdos.
Ha ha, yeah
say that to me face, hyland, I dare ya!
alright, you an' your friends are **freaks**, how's that, you cu~
WHUD

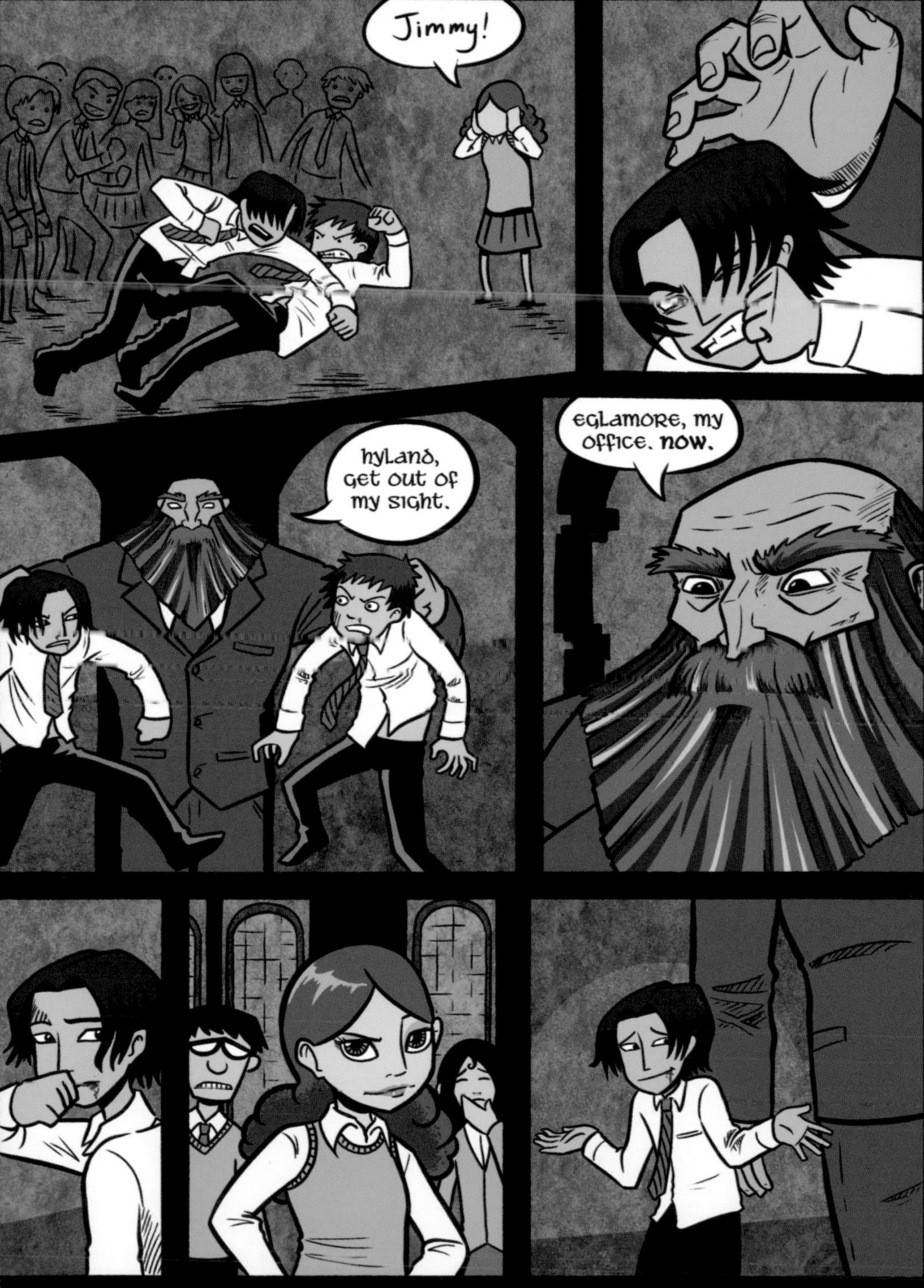
Jimmy!
hyland, get out of my sight.
eglamore, my office. now.

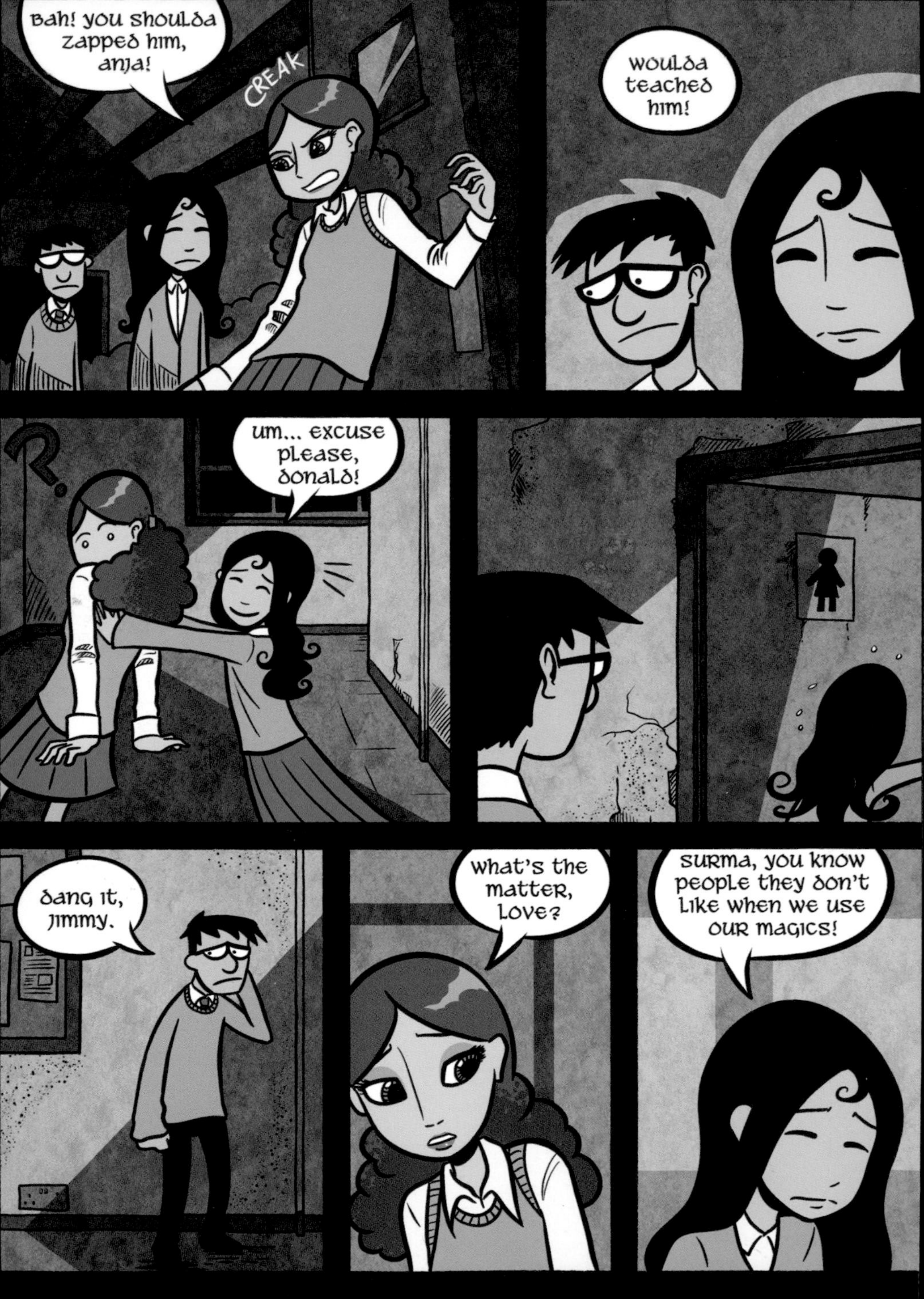
Bah! you shoulda zapped him, anja!
CREAK
woulda teached him!
um... excuse please, donald!
dang it, jimmy.
what's the matter, love?
surma, you know people they don't like when we use our magics!

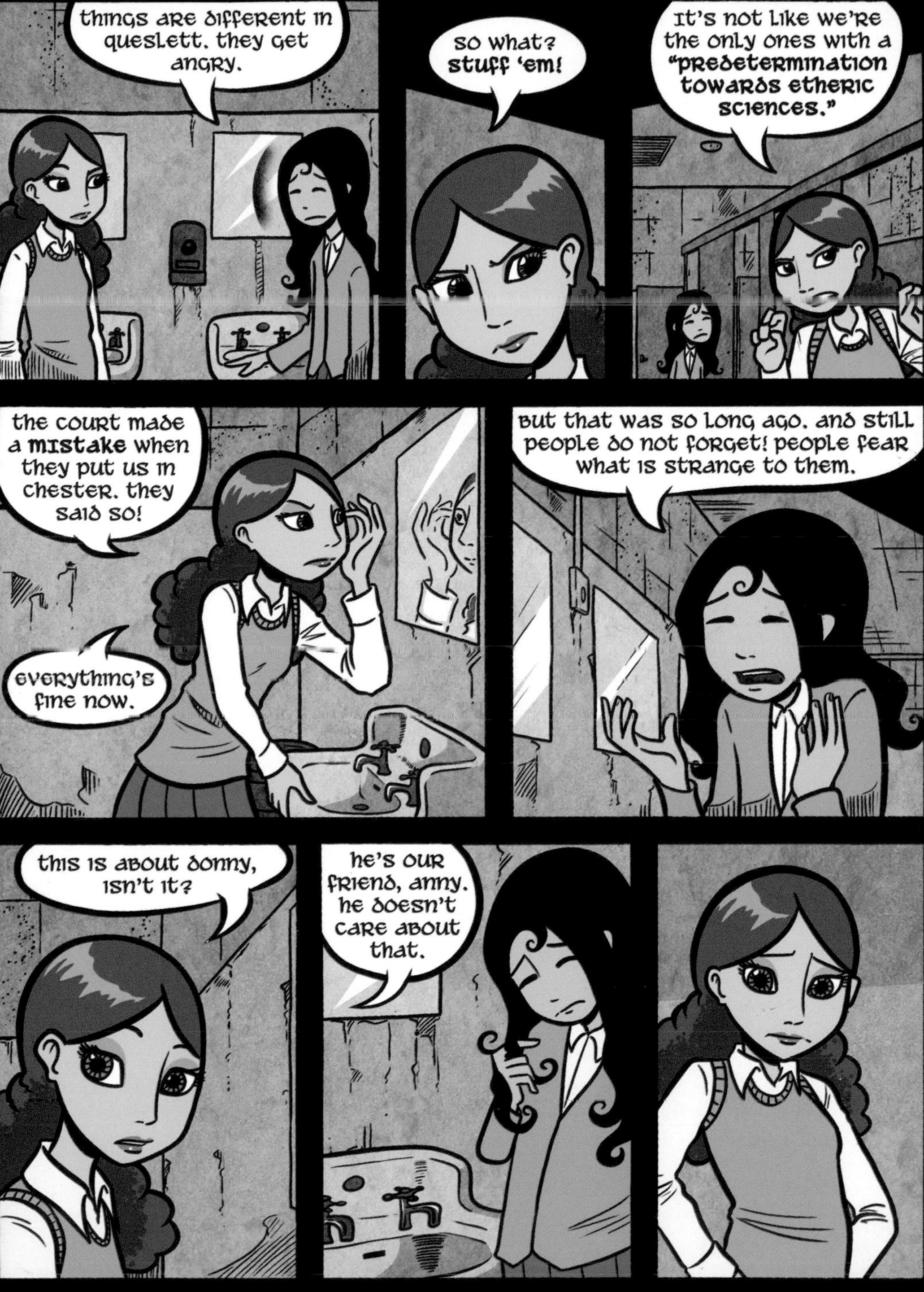
things are different in queslett. they get angry.
so what? stuff 'em!
It's not like we're the only ones with a "predetermination towards etheric sciences."
the court made a mistake when they put us in chester. they said so!
everything's fine now.
but that was so long ago. and still people do not forget! people fear what is strange to them.
this is about donny, isn't it?
he's our friend, anny. he doesn't care about that.

I'M NOT BLIND, OR STUPID.

I KNOW HOW PEOPLE ARE AROUND HERE.

LOOK, SIR, HYLAND STARTED IT! HE'S A JACKASS!

BUT THAT DOESN'T EXCUSE WHAT YOU DID.

HAD ANY OTHER TEACHER BESIDES ME STOPPED YOU, YOU MIGHT BE FACING EXPULSION.

YOU REALISE THAT, RIGHT?

YES SIR...

BUT STILL.

STANDING UP FOR A FRIEND, A NOBLE ACT CANNOT BE DISMISSED.

you fly off the handle too quickly, james.

you need to keep your temper in check.

yes, sir.

you have a future here, and i don't want to see you ruin your chances.

sir?

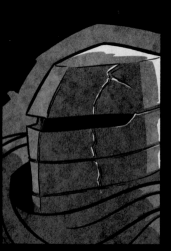

have you ever heard of the rogat orjak?

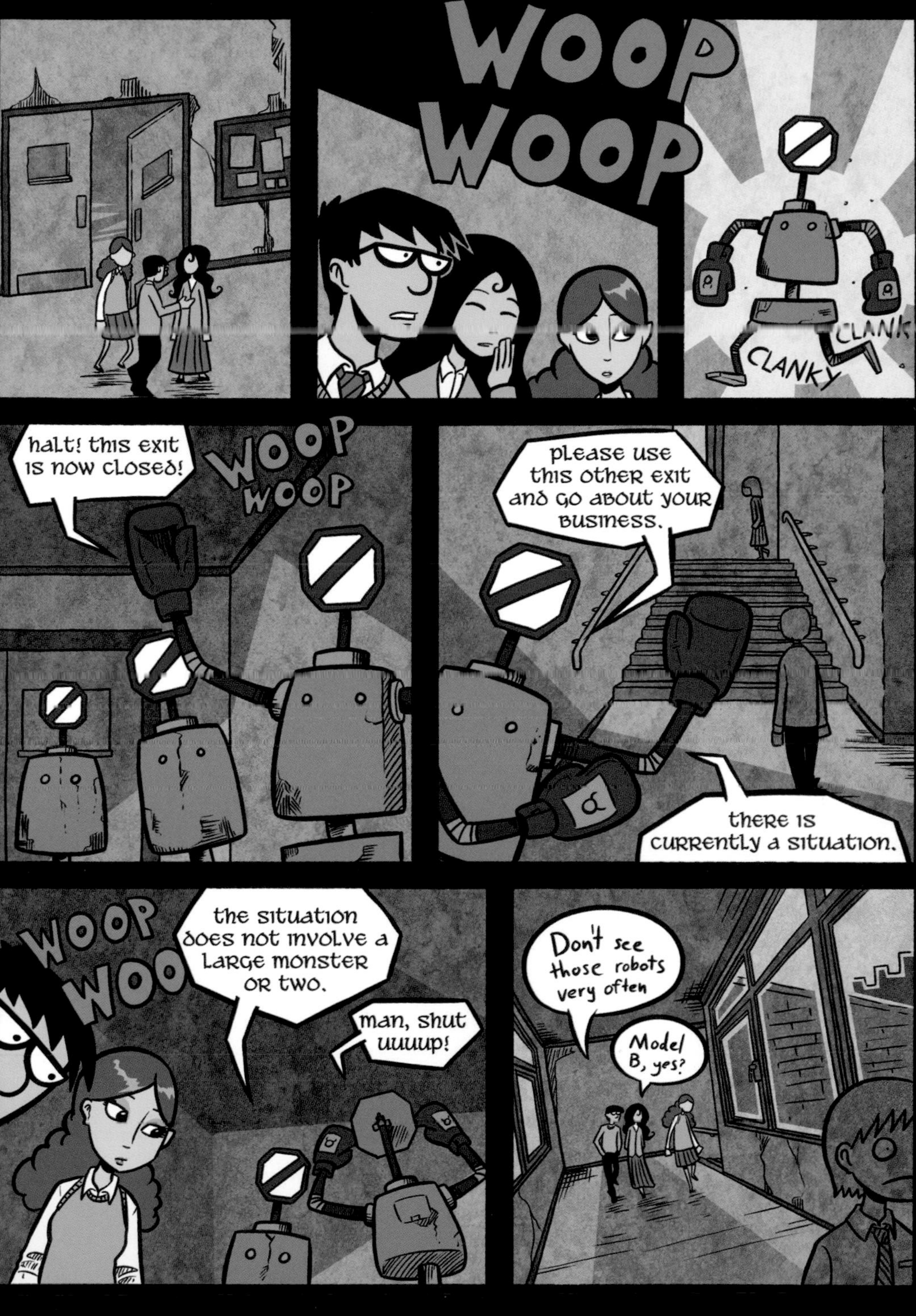
WOOP
WOOP
CLANKY
CLANK
halt! this exit is now closed!
WOOP
WOOP
please use this other exit and go about your business.
there is currently a situation.
WOOP
WOO
the situation does not involve a large monster or two.
man, shut uuuup!
Don't see those robots very often
Model B, yes?

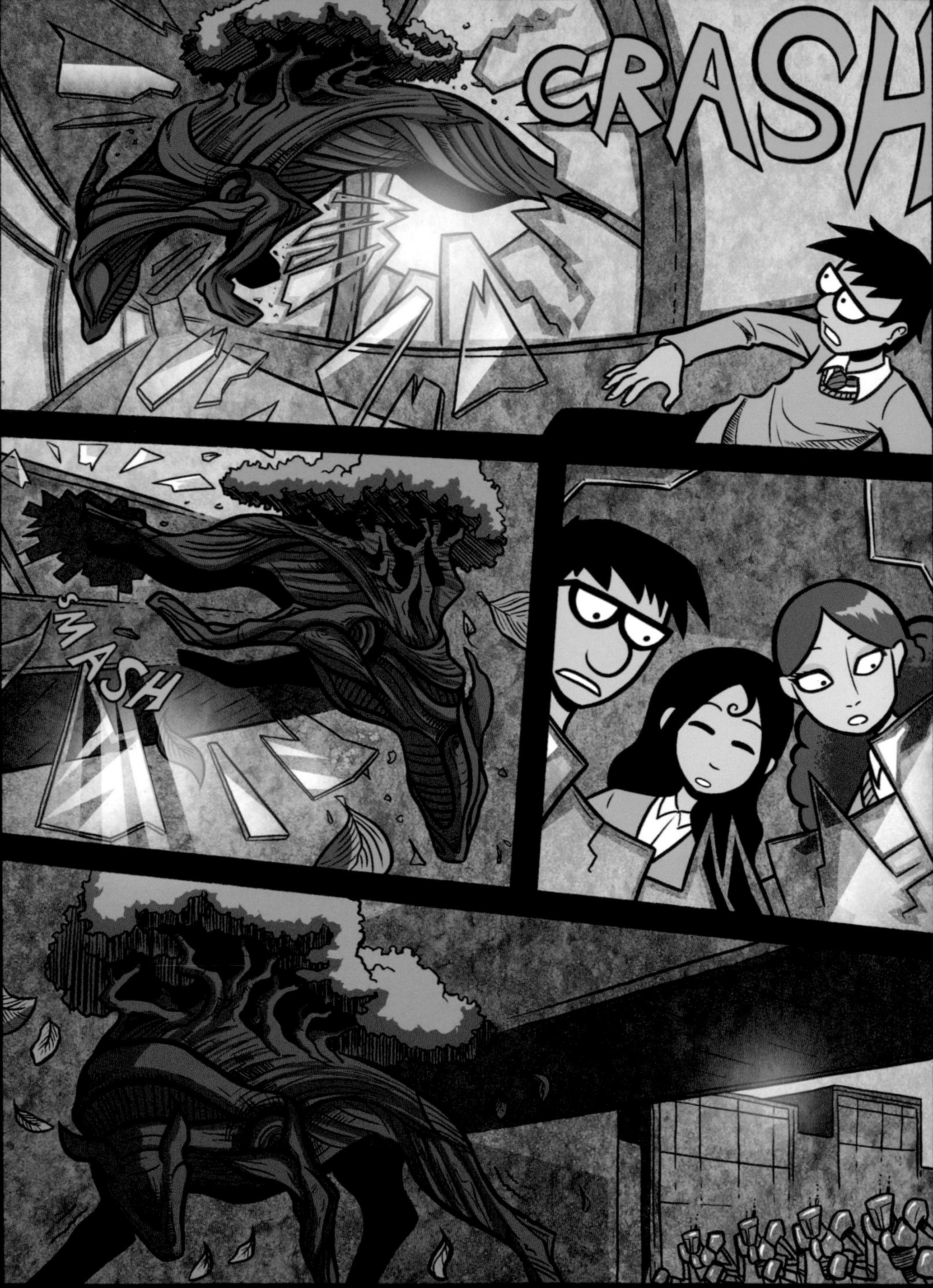
CRASH
SMASH

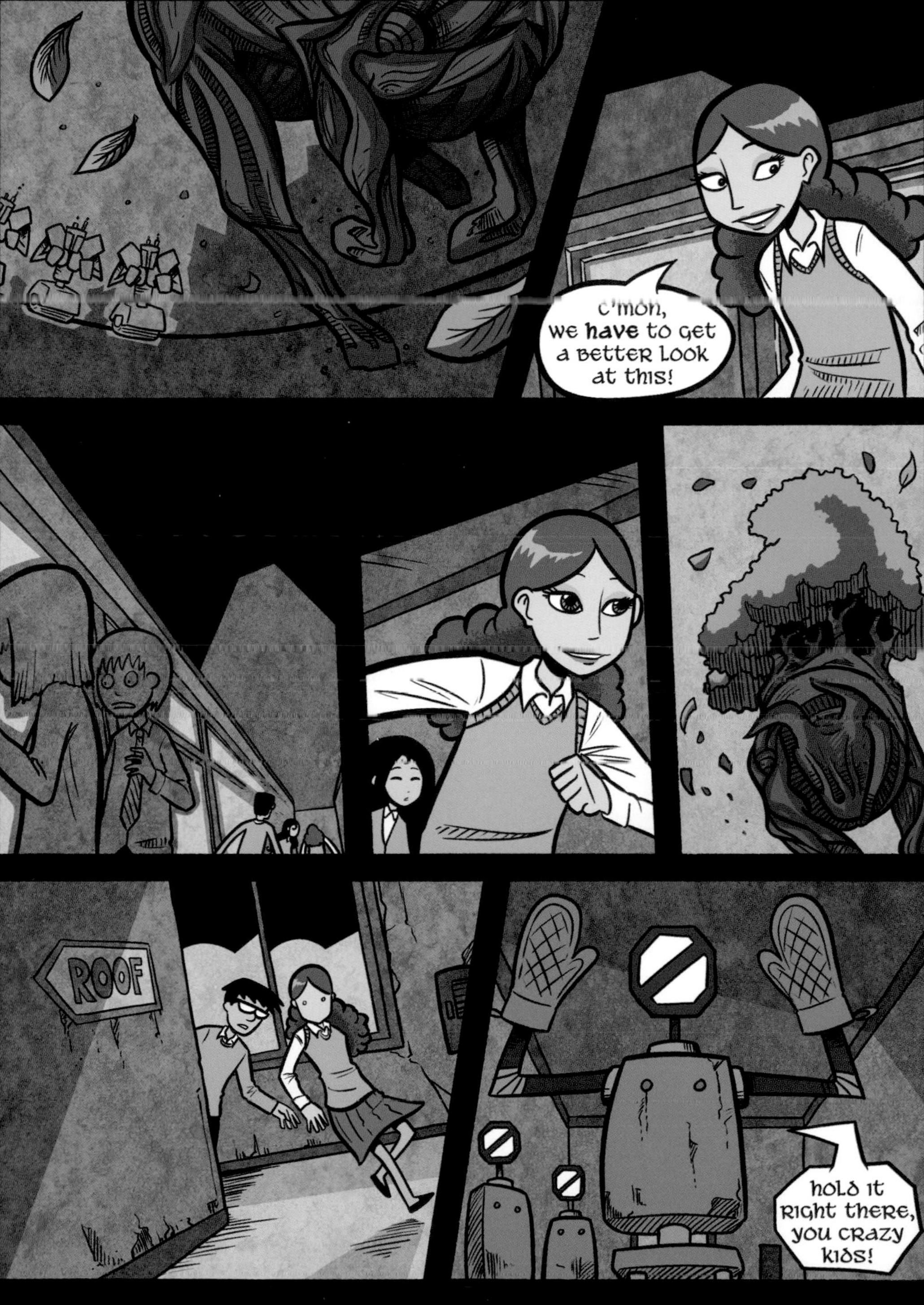
C'MON, WE HAVE TO GET A BETTER LOOK AT THIS!
ROOF
HOLD IT RIGHT THERE, YOU CRAZY KIDS!

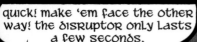

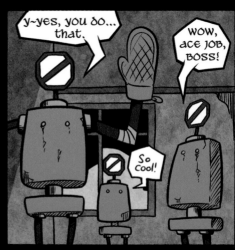

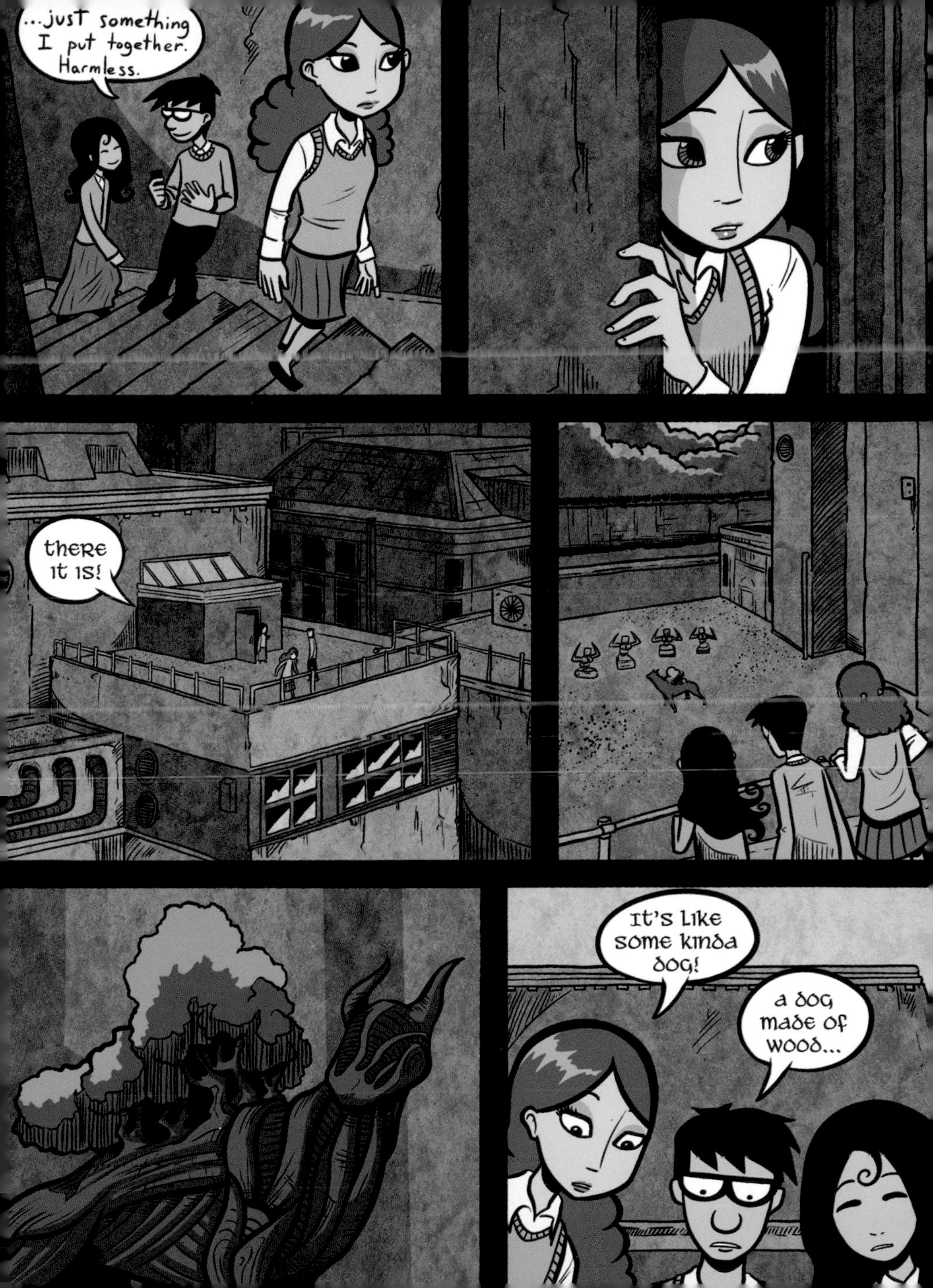
...just something I put together. Harmless.
there it is!
It's like some kinda dog!
a dog made of wood...

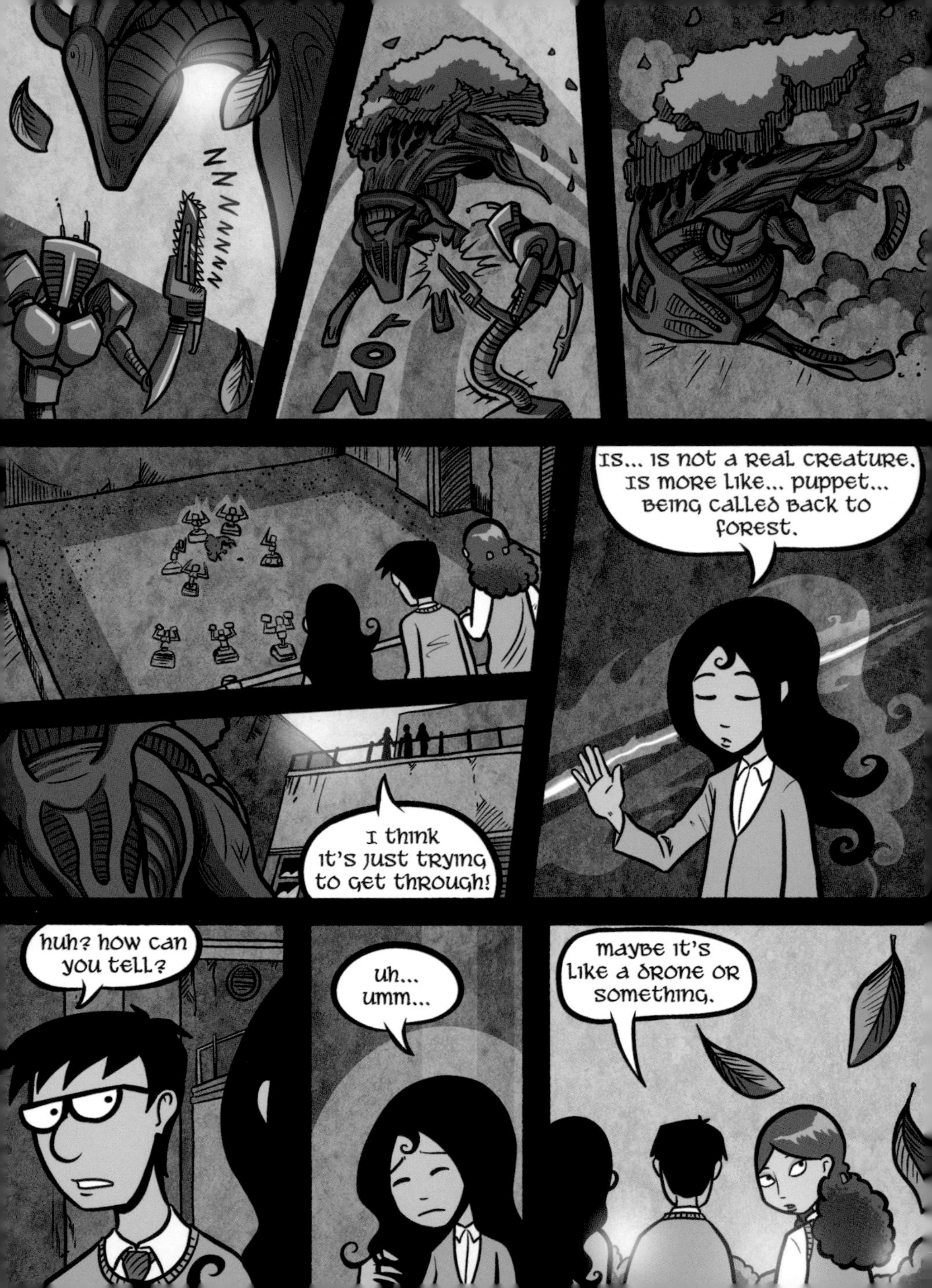
NNNNNNNN
NÓN
IS... IS NOT A REAL CREATURE. IS MORE LIKE... PUPPET... BEING CALLED BACK TO FOREST.
I THINK IT'S JUST TRYING TO GET THROUGH!
HUH? HOW CAN YOU TELL?
UH... UMM...
MAYBE IT'S LIKE A DRONE OR SOMETHING.

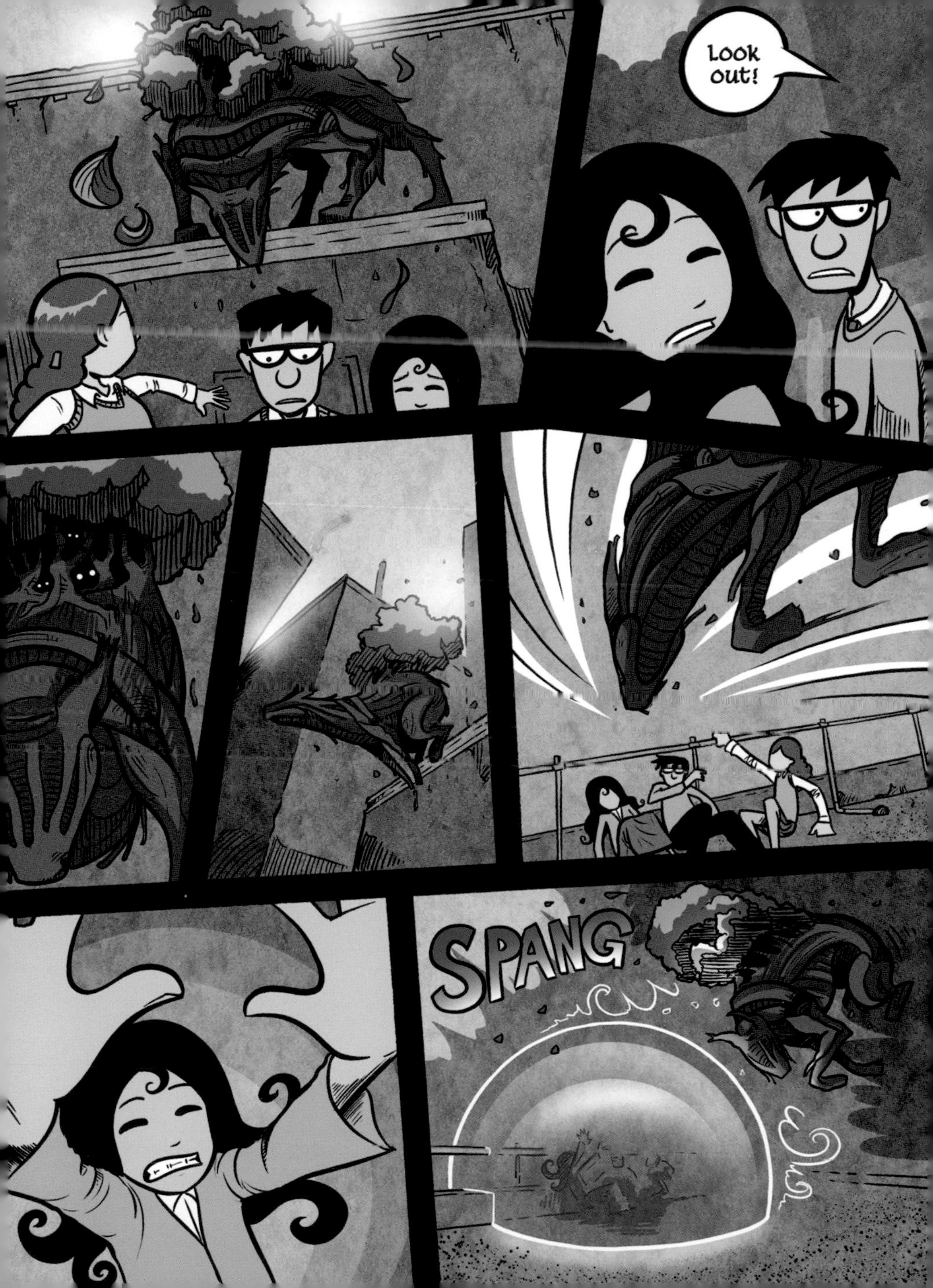
Look out!
SPANG

CHONK

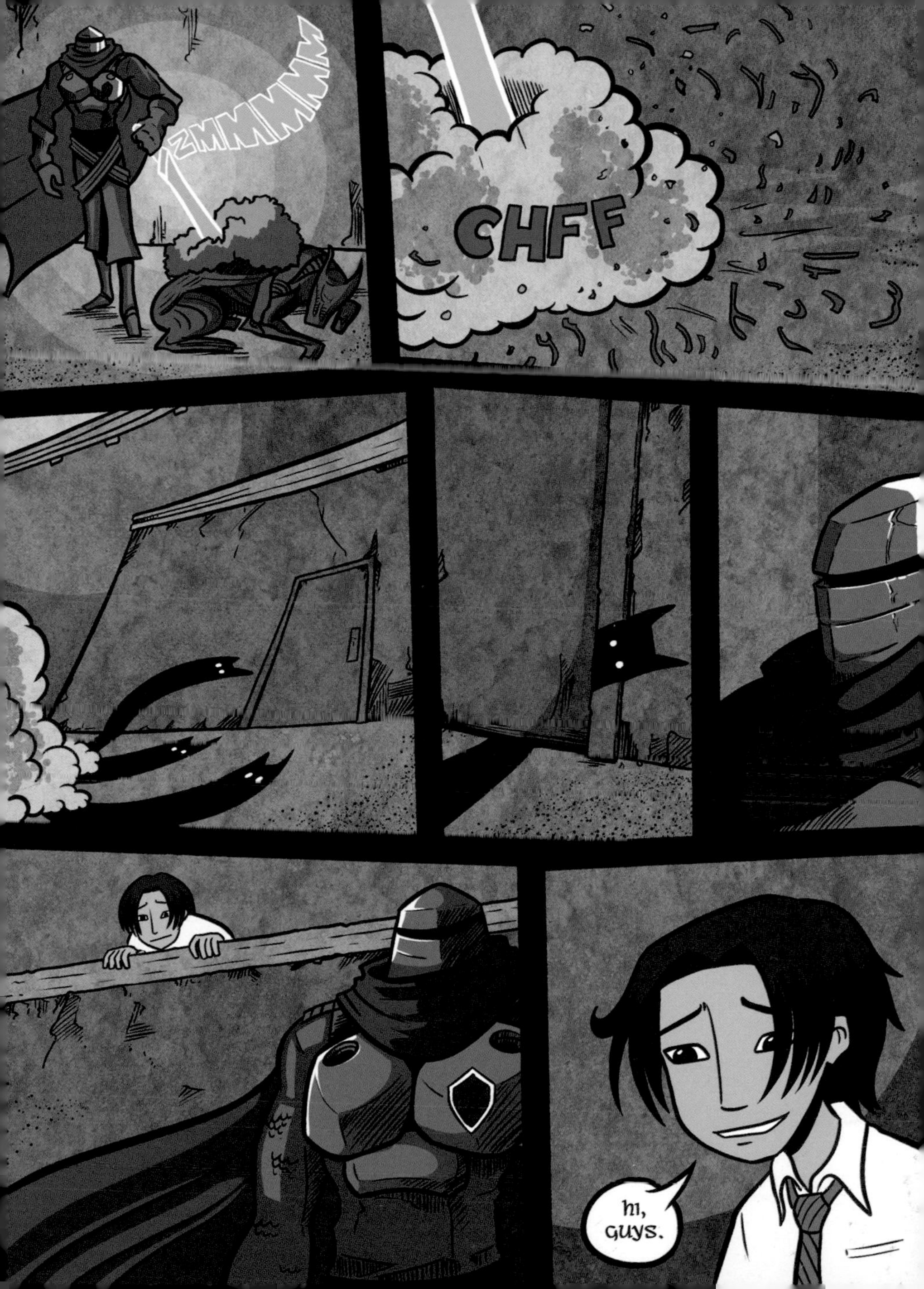
ZMMMMMMM
CHFF
hi, guys.

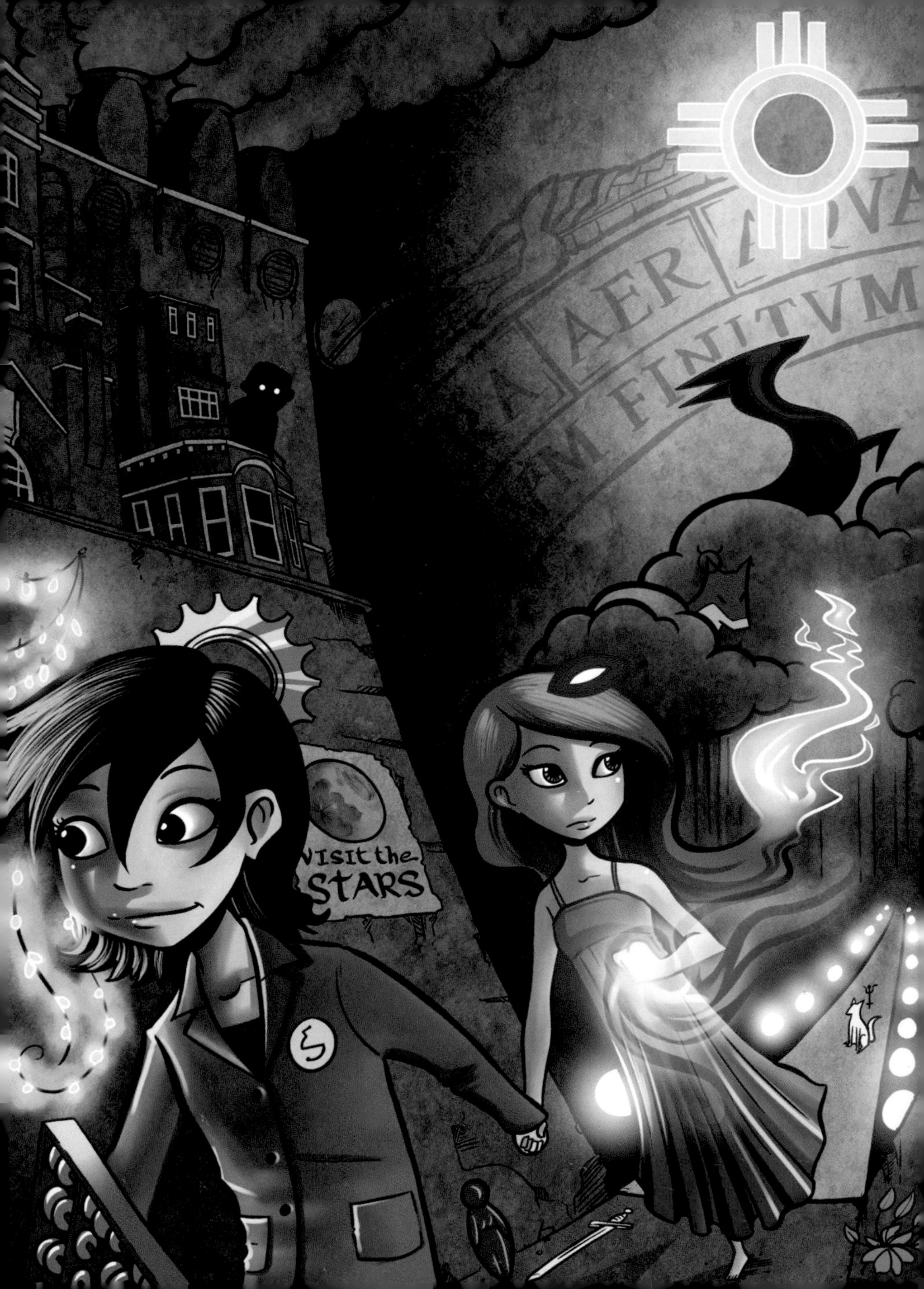
AER
FINITVM
Visit the
STARS

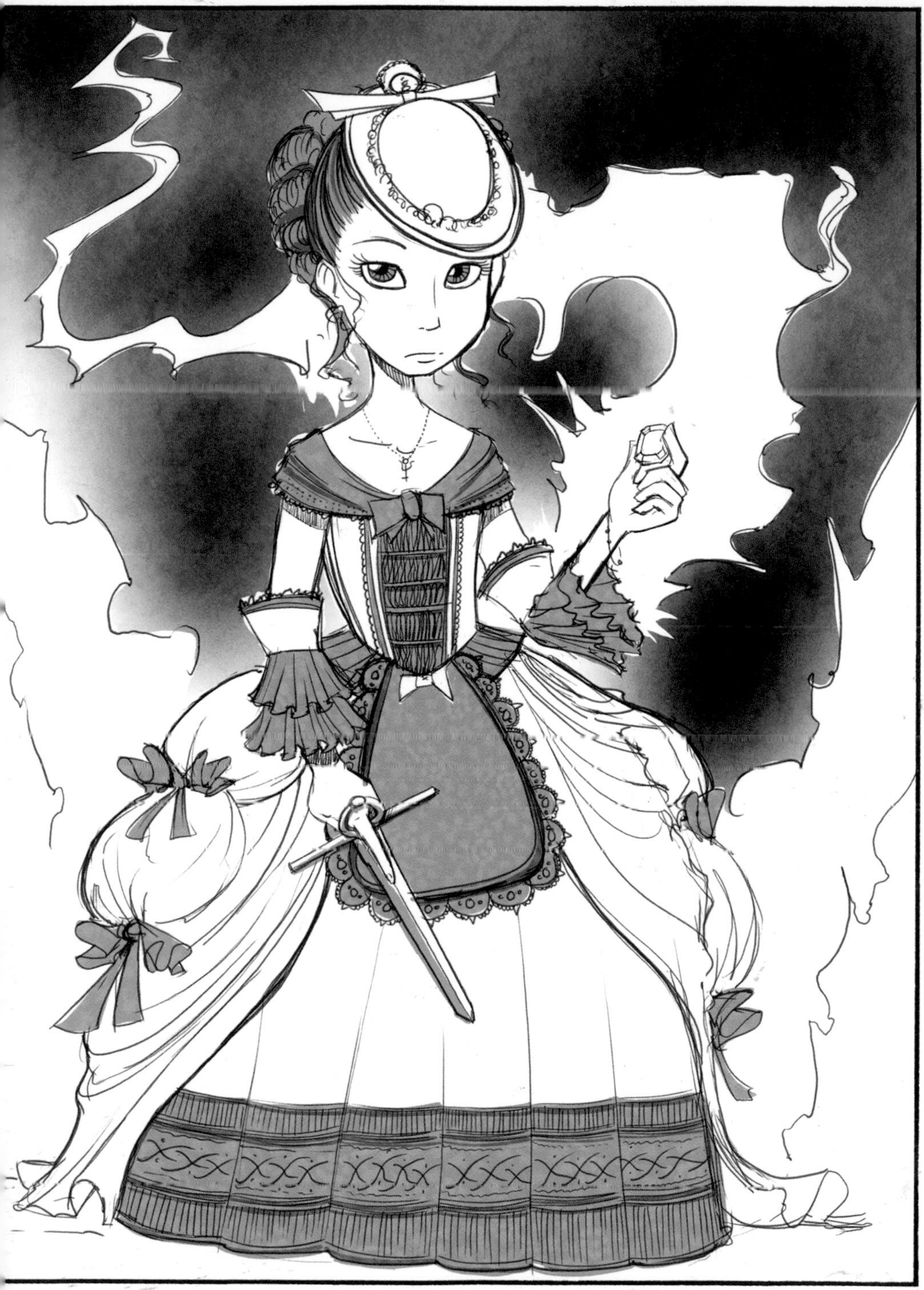

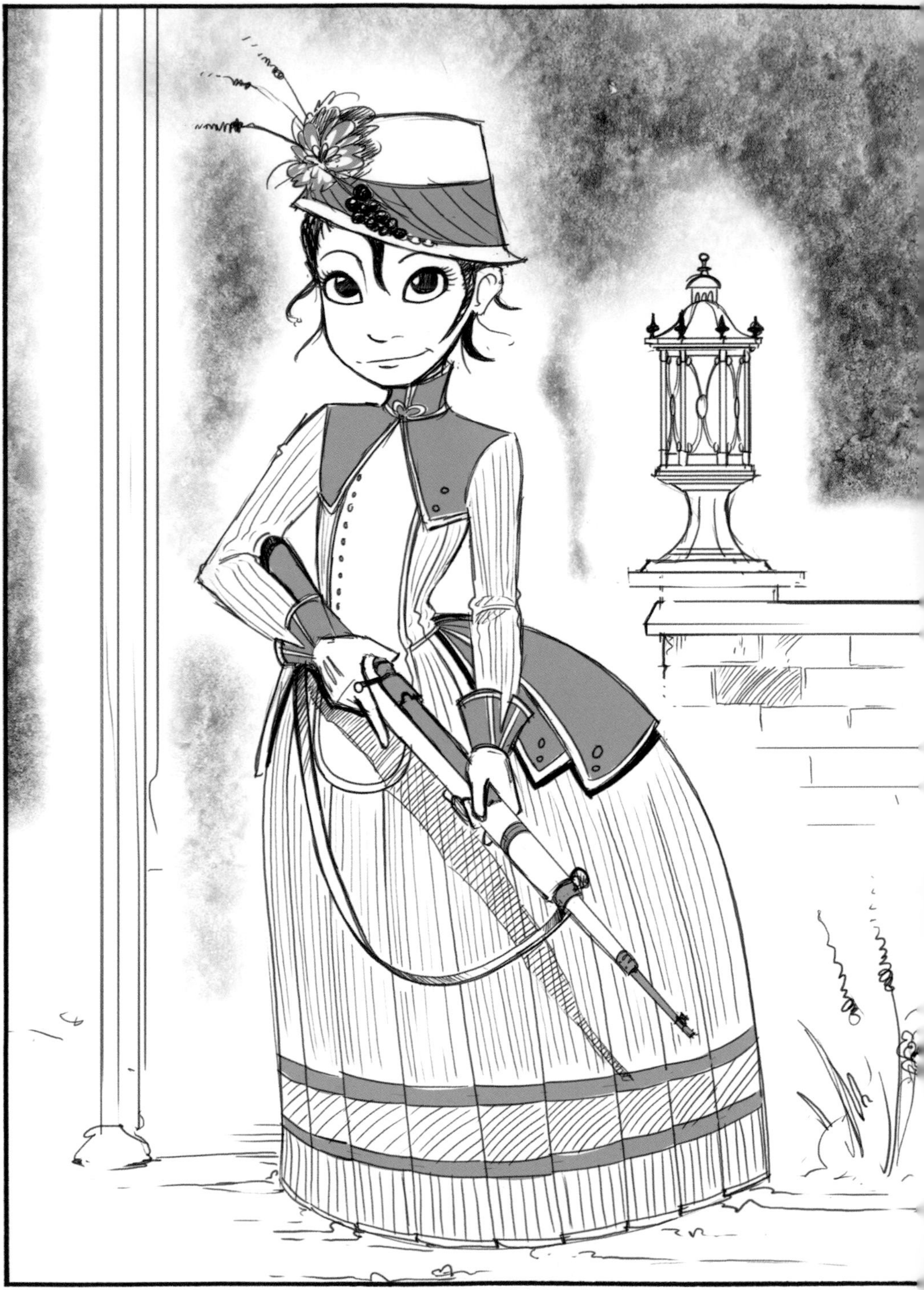

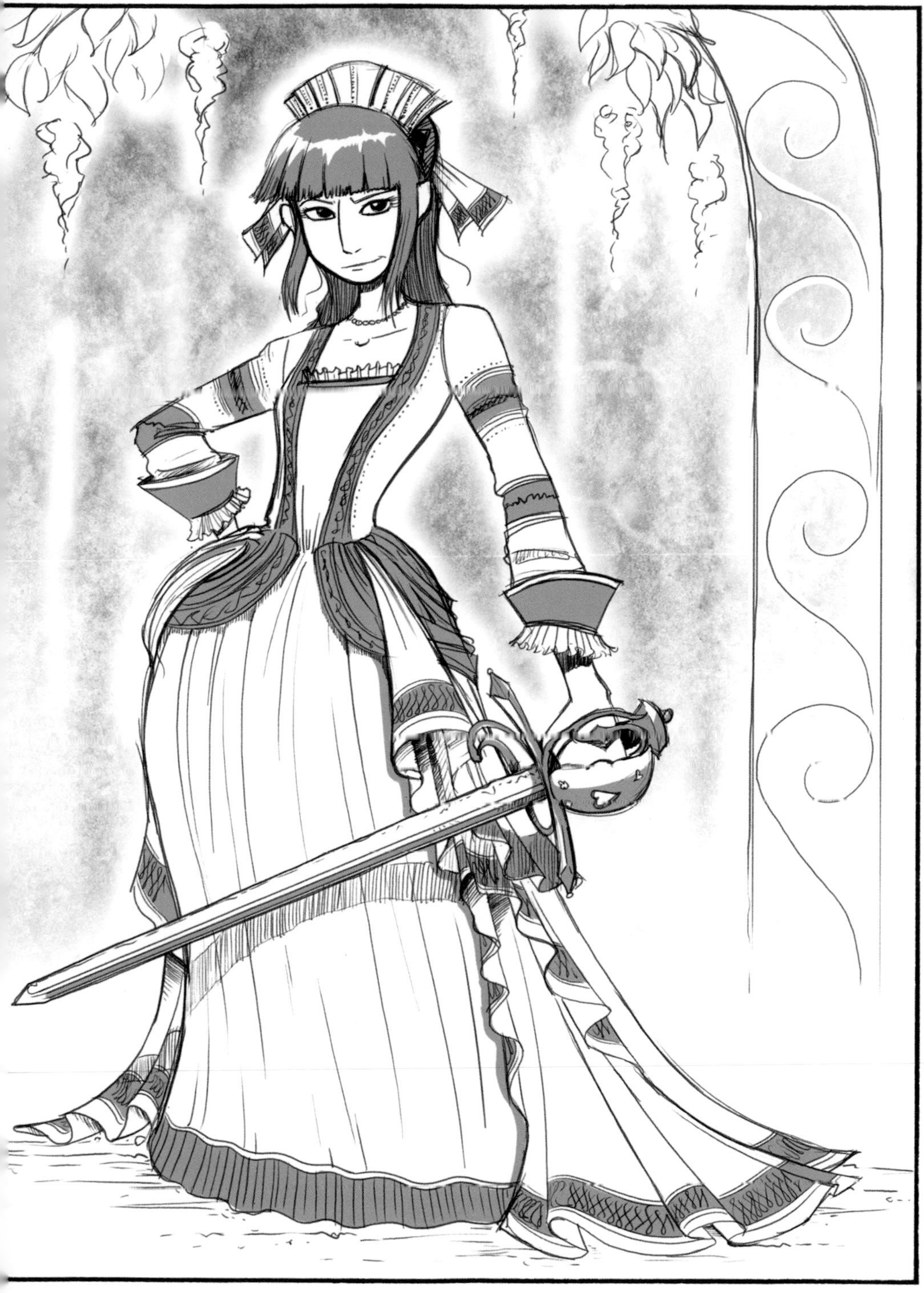

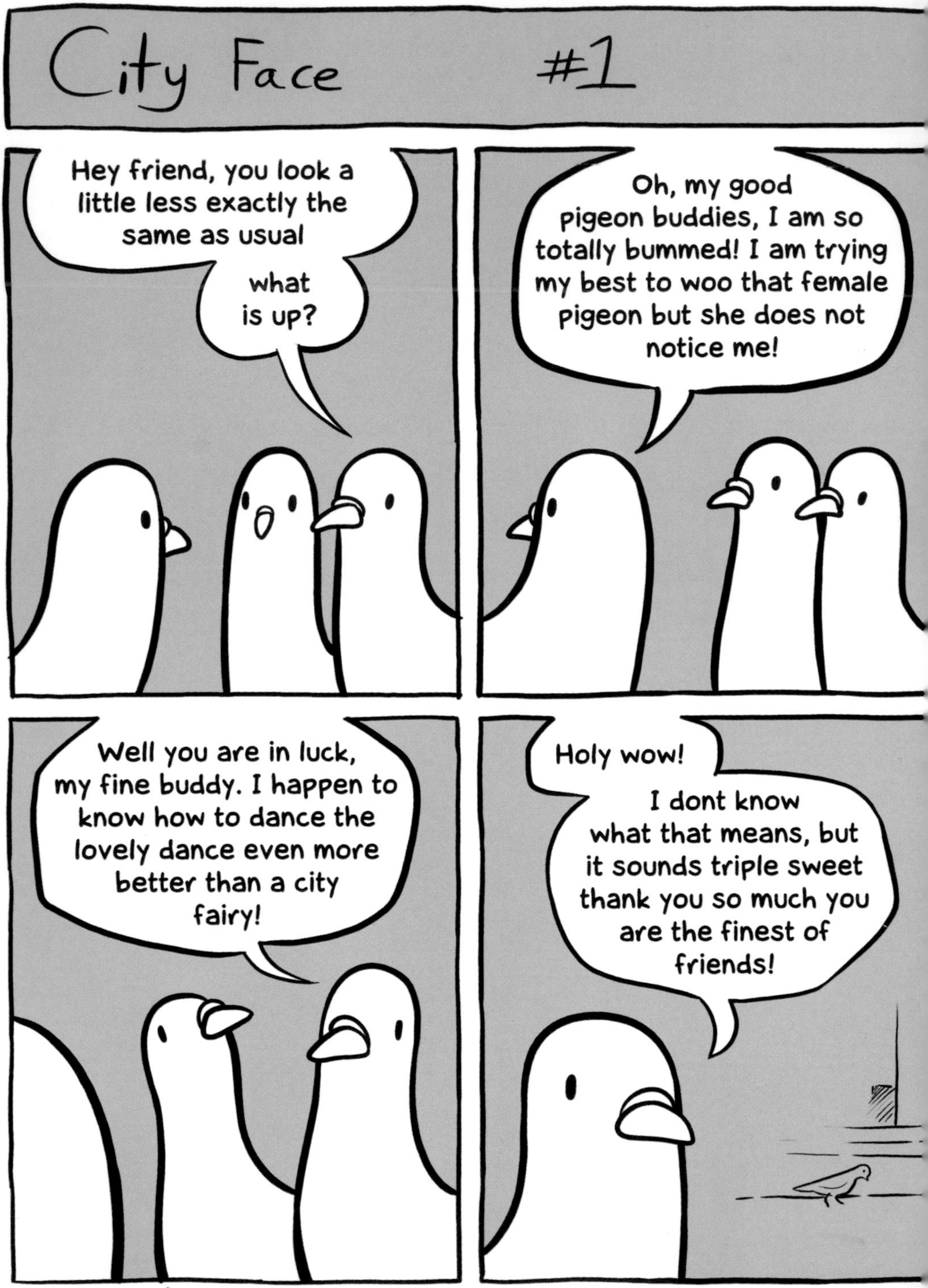
City Face #1
Hey friend, you look a little less exactly the same as usual
what is up?
Oh, my good pigeon buddies, I am so totally bummed! I am trying my best to woo that female pigeon but she does not notice me!
Well you are in luck, my fine buddy. I happen to know how to dance the lovely dance even more better than a city fairy!
Holy wow!
I dont know what that means, but it sounds triple sweet thank you so much you are the finest of friends!
www.gunnerkrigg.com

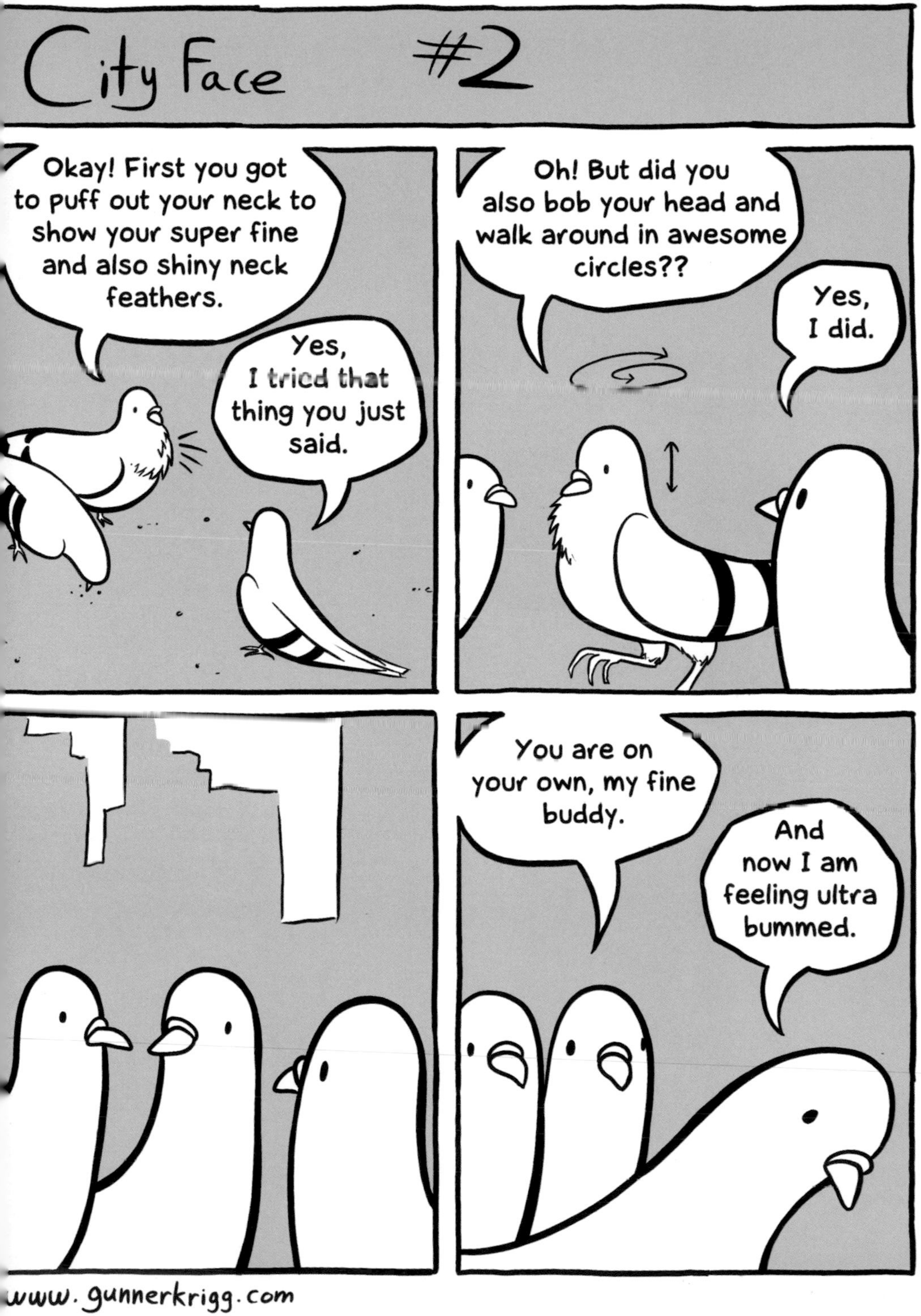
City Face #2
Okay! First you got to puff out your neck to show your super fine and also shiny neck feathers.
Yes, I tried that thing you just said.
Oh! But did you also bob your head and walk around in awesome circles??
Yes, I did.
You are on your own, my fine buddy.
And now I am feeling ultra bummed.
www.gunnerkrigg.com

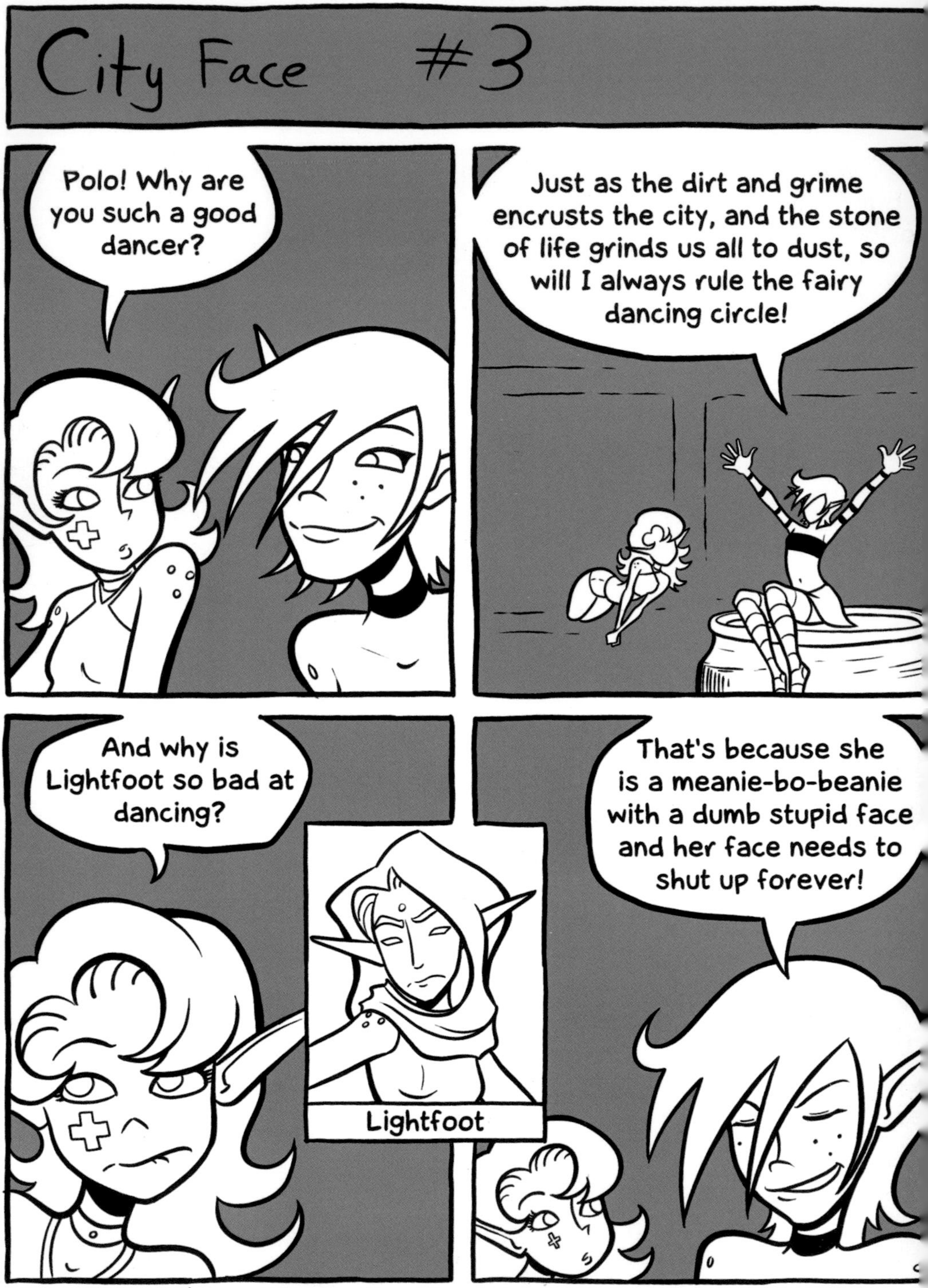
City Face #3
Polo! Why are you such a good dancer?
Just as the dirt and grime encrusts the city, and the stone of life grinds us all to dust, so will I always rule the fairy dancing circle!
And why is Lightfoot so bad at dancing?
Lightfoot
That's because she is a meanie-bo-beanie with a dumb stupid face and her face needs to shut up forever!

www.gunnerkrigg.com

City Face #4

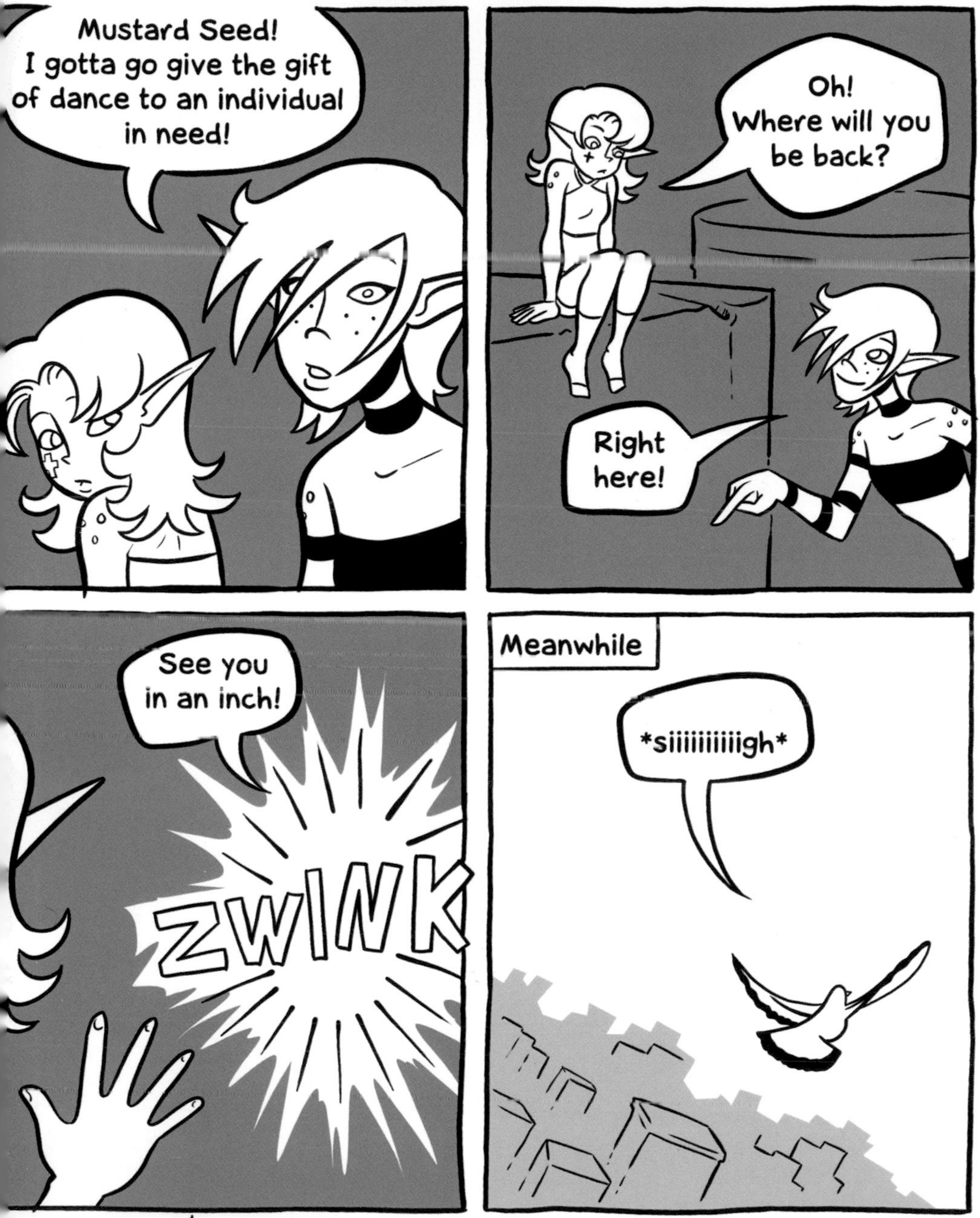
Mustard Seed! I gotta go give the gift of dance to an individual in need!
Oh! Where will you be back?
Right here!
See you in an inch!
ZWINK
Meanwhile
siiiiiiiiiigh

City Face #5

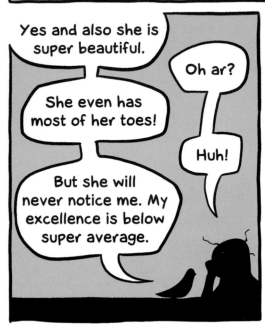

Yes and also she is super beautiful.

Oh ar?

She even has most of her toes!

Huh!

But she will never notice me. My excellence is below super average.

I got the answer to all yerz troubles, fella.

Right here...

In my mouf

Oh wow! You are soo extra kind! Let me take a look. I'll have to put my head in there to see past your ultra fine and also triple sharp teeth!

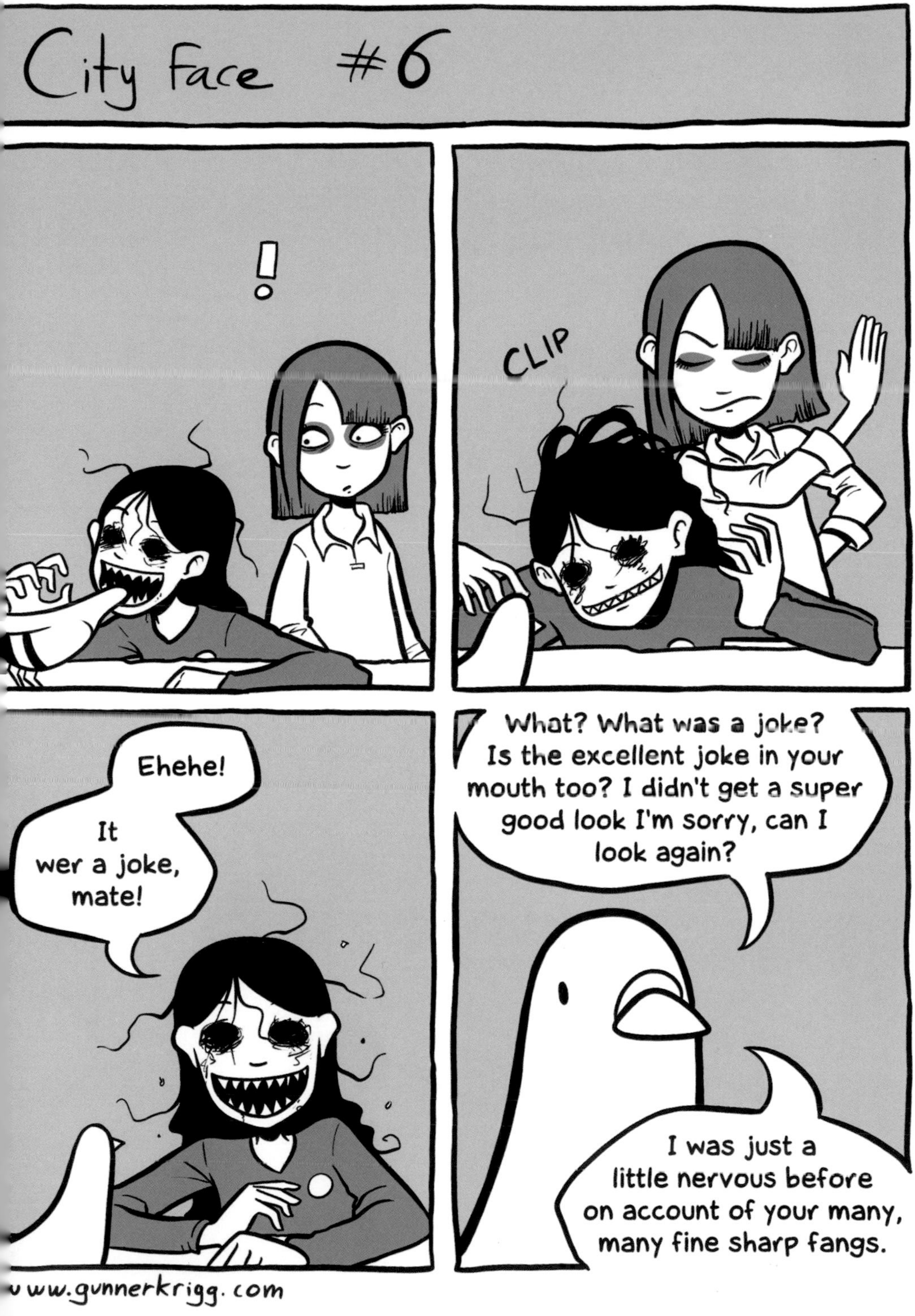
City Face #6
!
CLIP
Ehehe!
It wer a joke, mate!
What? What was a joke? Is the excellent joke in your mouth too? I didn't get a super good look I'm sorry, can I look again?
I was just a little nervous before on account of your many, many fine sharp fangs.
www.gunnerkrigg.com

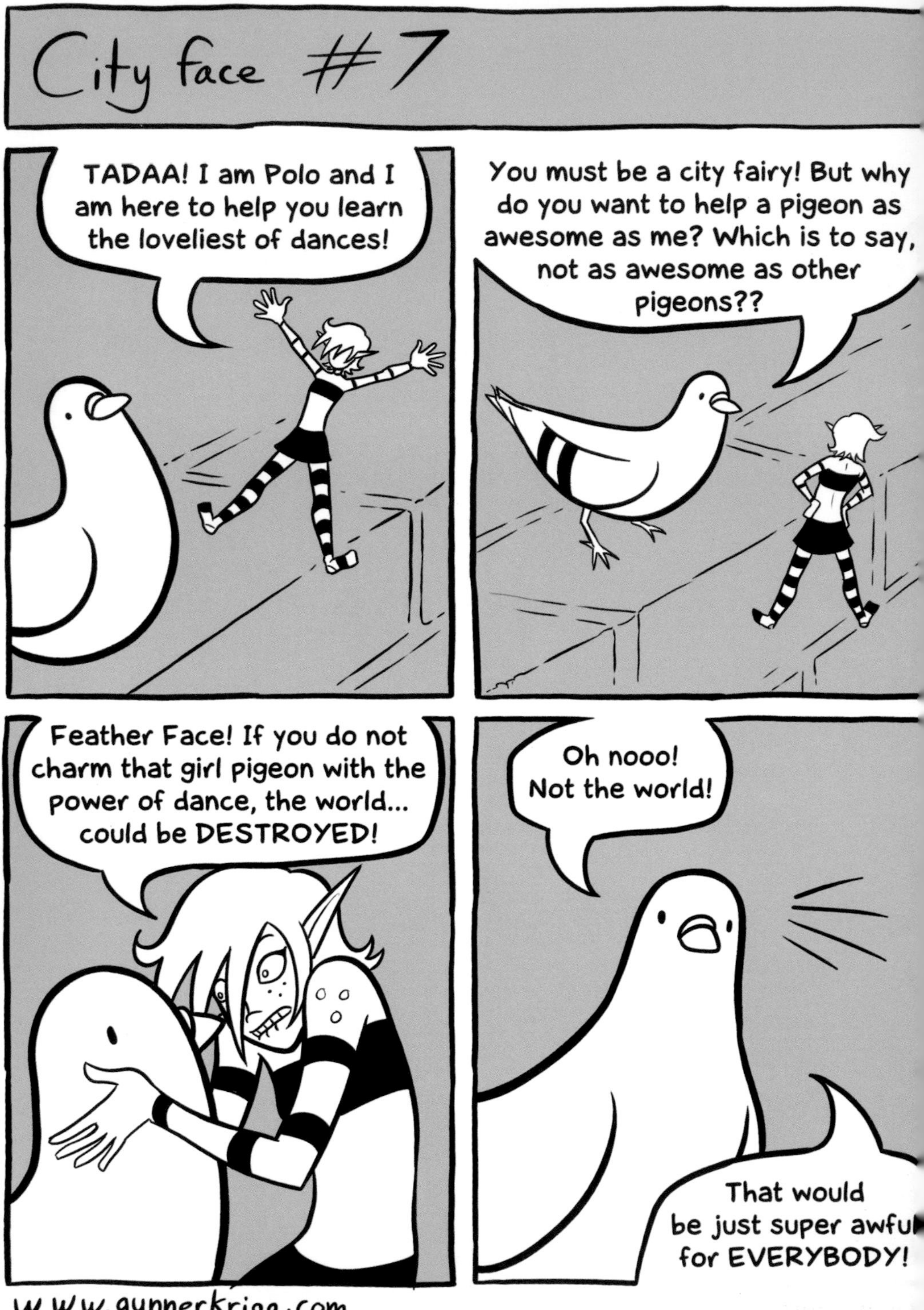
City face #7
TADAA! I am Polo and I am here to help you learn the loveliest of dances!
You must be a city fairy! But why do you want to help a pigeon as awesome as me? Which is to say, not as awesome as other pigeons??
Feather Face! If you do not charm that girl pigeon with the power of dance, the world... could be DESTROYED!
Oh nooo! Not the world!
That would be just super awful for EVERYBODY!

www.gunnerkrigg.com

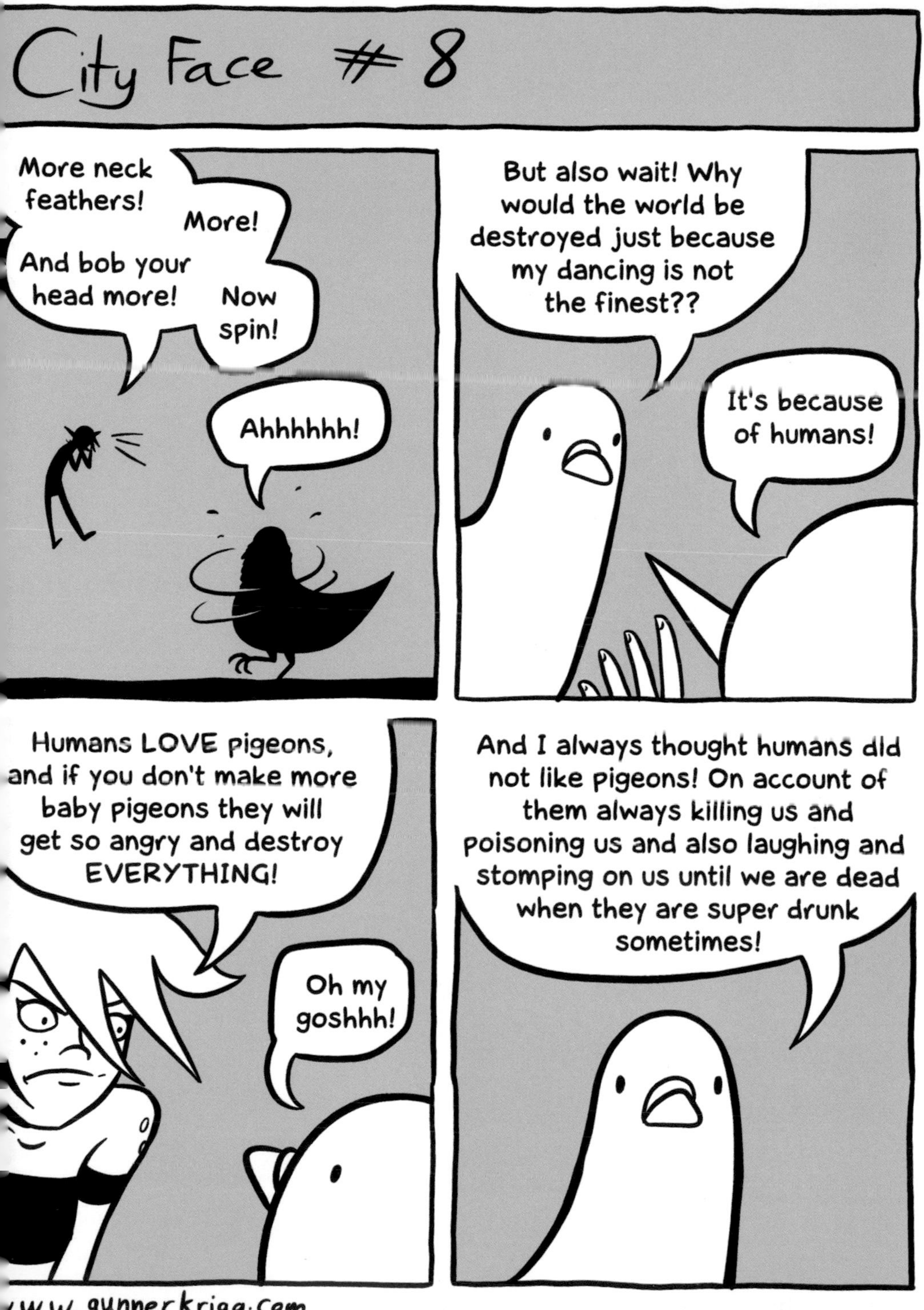
City Face #8
More neck feathers!
More!
And bob your head more!
Now spin!
Ahhhhhh!
But also wait! Why would the world be destroyed just because my dancing is not the finest??
It's because of humans!
Humans LOVE pigeons, and if you don't make more baby pigeons they will get so angry and destroy EVERYTHING!
Oh my goshhh!
And I always thought humans did not like pigeons! On account of them always killing us and poisoning us and also laughing and stomping on us until we are dead when they are super drunk sometimes!
www.gunnerkrigg.com

City Face #9

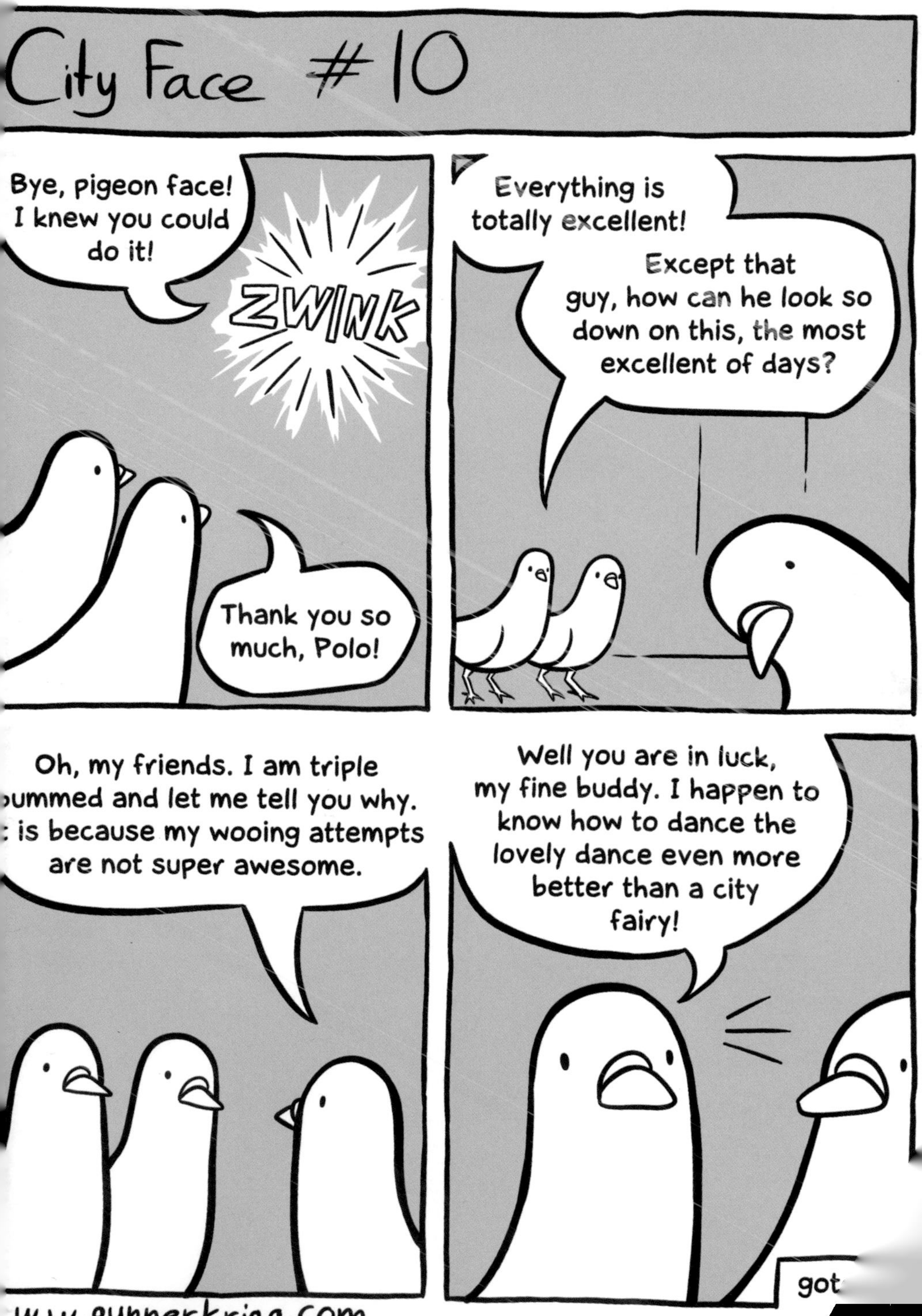
City Face #10
Bye, pigeon face! I knew you could do it!
ZWINK
Thank you so much, Polo!
Everything is totally excellent!
Except that guy, how can he look so down on this, the most excellent of days?
Oh, my friends. I am triple
ummed and let me tell you why.
is because my wooing attempts
are not super awesome.
Well you are in luck, my fine buddy. I happen to know how to dance the lovely dance even more better than a city fairy!
got
w w.gunnerkrigg.com

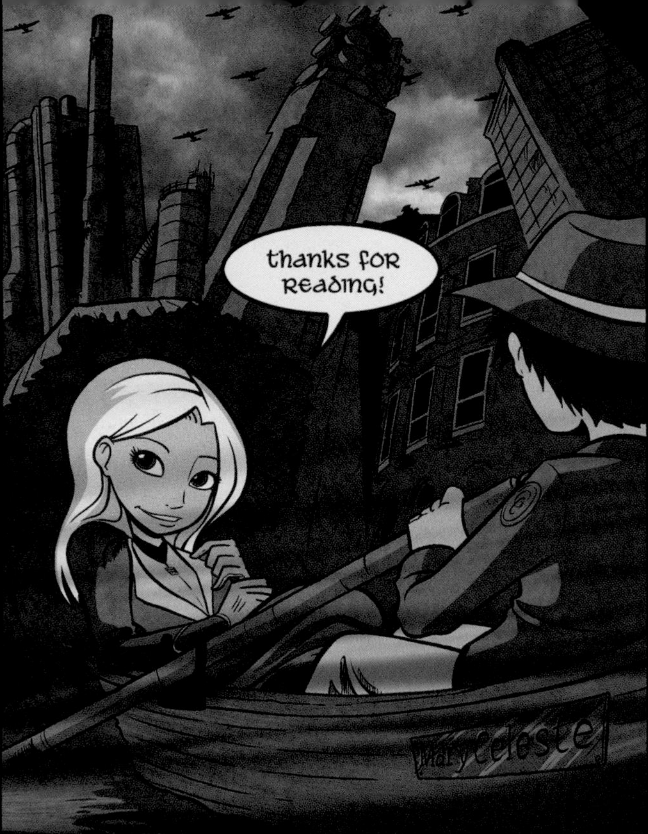
thanks for reading!
Mary Celeste

www.gunnerkrigg.com